INSTITUTIONAL DESIGN IN NEW DEMOCRACIES

Latin America in Global Perspective

The fundamental purpose of this multivolume series is to broaden conceptual perspectives for the study of Latin America. This effort responds to a perception of need. Latin America cannot be understood in isolation from other parts of the world. This has always been so; it is especially true in the contemporary era.

Accordingly, the goal of this series is to demonstrate the desirability and the feasibility of analyzing Latin America in comparative perspective, in conjunction with other regions, and in global perspective, in the context of worldwide processes. A subsidiary purpose is to establish a bridge between Latin American "area studies" and mainstream social science disciplines, to the mutual benefit of both. Ultimately, the intent is to explore and emphasize intellectual challenges posed by dynamic changes within Latin America and in its relation to the international arena.

The present volume, *Institutional Design in New Democracies*, examines the relationship between the challenge of institutional design and the outcomes of the process of economic and political liberalization in Latin America and Eastern Europe. The series thus far includes:

Latin America in Comparative Perspective: New Approaches to Methods and Analysis, edited by Peter H. Smith

EnGENDERing Wealth and Well-Being, edited by Rae Lesser Blumberg, Cathy A. Rakowski, Irene Tinker, and Michael Monteón

Cooperation or Rivalry? Regional Integration in the Americas and in the Pacific Rim, edited by Shoji Nishijima and Peter H. Smith

Latin American Environmental Policy in International Perspective, edited by Gordon J. MacDonald, Daniel L. Nielson, and Marc A. Stern

Civil-Military Relations After the Cold War, edited by David Mares

This series results from a multiyear research program organized by the Center for Iberian and Latin American Studies (CILAS) at the University of California, San Diego. Principal funding has come from the Andrew W. Mellon Foundation.

INSTITUTIONAL DESIGN IN NEW DEMOCRACIES

Eastern Europe and Latin America

edited by

Arend Lijphart
University of California
San Diego

&

Carlos H. Waisman
University of California
San Diego

WestviewPress
A Division of HarperCollins*Publishers*

Latin America in Global Perspective

Copyright © 1996 by Westview Press, A Division of HarperCollins Publishers, Inc.

Published in 1996 in the United States of America by Westview Press, 5500 Central Avenue, Boulder, Colorado 80301-2877, and in the United Kingdom by Westview Press, 12 Hid's Copse Road, Cumnor Hill, Oxford OX2 9JJ

Library of Congress Cataloging-in-Publication Data
Institutional design in new democracies: Eastern Europe and Latin America / edited by Arend Lijphart and Carlos Waisman.
      p.   cm.
Includes bibliographical references and index.
ISBN 0-8133-2108-5 (hbk.).— ISBN 0-8133-2109-3 (pbk.)
   1. Latin America — Politics and government—1980– 2. Latin America—Economic policy. 3. Europe, Central—Politics and government—1989– 4. Europe, Central—Economic policy. 5. Europe, Eastern—Politics and government—1989– 6. Europe, Eastern—Economic policy—1989– 7. Comparative government. I. Lijphart, Arend. II. Waisman, Carlos H.
JL966.I57 1996
324.6'3'09049—dc20   96-6133
                                                                                                        CIP

10   9   8   7   6   5   4   3   2   1

Contents

Tables and Figures

Tables

Figures

Acknowledgments

This volume is the product of a collective endeavor, and we would like to begin by thanking the many scholars who have contributed to it: first, our multinational group of authors (Argentine, Brazilian, Chilean, German, Hungarian, Mexican, Polish, and American) and second, the many other colleagues who participated in the planning of the project and those who commented on earlier versions of the chapters—John M. Carey, Ellen T. Comisso, Wayne A. Cornelius, Paul W. Drake, Carlos Flores, Joseph Grunwald, James Holston, José Luis Manzano, Victor Nee, David Pion-Berlin, Akos Róna-Tas, Matthew S. Shugart, Peter H. Smith, Jadwiga Staniszkis, Kaare Strom, Rein Taagepera, and Jeffrey A. Weldon. We also record with sadness that Carlos Santiago Nino, one of Argentina's most distinguished legal scholars, died before our project was completed; we are fortunate, however, to include his contribution in this volume.

In addition, we wish to express our appreciation to Peter H. Smith, director of the Center for Iberian and Latin American Studies (CILAS) at the University of California, San Diego; Patricia Rosas, CILAS editor, and Deborah Ortiz, CILAS program coordinator, for their continual and enormously valuable support throughout our effort; and to the Andrew W. Mellon Foundation for its financial support.

We close with an expression of gratitude to Barbara Ellington, our editor at Westview Press, whose encouragement has greatly helped to bring this volume to fruition.

Arend Lijphart
Carlos H. Waisman

Acronyms

AFD	Alliance of Free Democrats (Hungary)
BSP	Bulgarian Socialist Party
CFE	Comisión Federal Electoral (Federal Electoral Commission, Mexico)
CP	Communist Party
CPI	consumer price index
DLA	Democratic Left Alliance (Poland)
ENTel	Empresas Nacionales de Teléfonos (National Telephone Company, Argentina)
FPTP	first-past-the-post system
GDP	gross domestic product
HDF	Hungarian Democratic Forum
HSWP	Hungarian Socialist Workers' Party
HUF	Hungarian forint
IMF	International Monetary Fund
ISP	Independent Smallholders' Party (Hungary)
KCS	Czechoslovakian koruny
KPN	Confederation for an Independent Poland
LYD	League of Young Democrats (Hungary)
MOC	Ministry of Ownership Change (Poland)
MP	member of parliament
MSZP	Socialists (Hungary)
NSF	National Salvation Front (Romania)
OKP	Civic Parliamentary Club (Poland)
PAIS	Partido Amplio de Izquierda Socialista (Party of the United Socialist Left, Chile)
PAN	Partido Acción Nacional (National Action Party, Mexico)
PChD	Christian Democratic Party (Poland)
PCHU	Hungarian Communist Party

PDC	Partido Demócrata Cristiano (Christian Democratic Party, Chile)
PDT	Democratic Labor Party (Brazil)
PL	Partido Liberal (Liberal Party, Chile)
PMDB	Brazilian Democratic Movement Party
PN	Partido Nacional (National Party, Chile)
PNR	Partido Nacional Revolucionario (National Revolutionary Party, Mexico)
POC	Center Civic Alliance (Hungary)
PPD	Democratic Party (Partido por la Democracia, Chile)
PR	proportional representation
PRD	Partido de la Revolución Democrática (Democratic Revolutionary Party, Mexico)
PRI	Partido Revolucionario Institucional (Institutional Revolutionary Party, Mexico)
PSBR	public-sector borrowing requirement
PSL	Polish Peasant Party
PT	Workers' Party (Brazil)
PZPR	Polish United Workers' Party
"S"	Autonomous Independent Trade Unions "Solidarity" (Poland)
SD	Democratic Party (Poland)
SdRP	Social-Democracy of the Republic of Poland
II PND	Second Development Plan (Brazil)
SHC	State Holding Company (Hungary)
SLD	Democratic Left Alliance (Poland)
"SP"	Solidarity of Labor (Poland)
SPA	State Property Agency (Hungary)
UD	Democratic Union (Poland)
UDF	Union of Democratic Forces (Bulgaria)
YPF	Yacimientos Petrolíferos Fiscales (National Oil Deposits, Argentina)
ZSL	United Peasant Party (Poland)

INSTITUTIONAL DESIGN IN NEW DEMOCRACIES

———————■———————

CHAPTER ONE

■

Institutional Design and Democratization

Arend Lijphart and Carlos H. Waisman

A WAVE OF ECONOMIC and political liberalization is sweeping the world. Most countries in Latin America and almost all nations in Eastern Europe are undergoing these transitions simultaneously: from a semiclosed to an open economy and from an authoritarian to a liberal democratic polity. These regions are, of course, heterogeneous internally and different from each other; the institutional characteristics of their economies and polities are different, and so are the mechanisms of transition and perhaps even the outcomes of the changes underway. But at the same time, they are involved in processes of economic and political liberalization whose model (not always the intended end point) is a combination that is characteristic of the core capitalist countries: a market economy highly integrated into the international system and a competitive polity. □

TRANSITIONS IN EASTERN EUROPE AND LATIN AMERICA

The pervasive nature of these transitions is indicated by the fact that they appear to be independent of the level of development and, especially in the case of Latin America, also of the type of political regime. This is a remarkable aspect of the South American transition: All of the countries in the area, from relatively underdeveloped Bolivia and Paraguay to relatively industrialized Brazil and Argentina, have been moving from military rule to liberal democracy in the past decade. Regarding economic liberalization, we find it in authoritarian Argentina and also in democratic Argentina, under both Radical and Peronist administrations; in both

1

authoritarian and democratic Chile; in state-corporatist Mexico and in social-democratic Venezuela. Cuba appears to be the remarkable, and most likely temporary, exception to these trends. The same phenomenon is also present in Eastern Europe, where the transformation has encompassed all of the former state-socialist regimes—ranging from the relatively "liberal" ones in Poland and Hungary to the solidly Stalinist former states of East Germany and Czechoslovakia, the personalistic dictatorship in Romania, and even the Stalinist regime in Albania.

A comparison of these processes in Latin America and in Eastern Europe shows important commonalities beyond the structural, institutional, and cultural differences between the regions and among nations. Common aspects exist in the nature of the preexisting economic and political regimes, in the cultural and economic environments in which these polities operate, and in the processes by which the transition itself is taking place.

First, the ancien régime combined, in most cases, statized and closed economies (with "medium" levels of statization and closure with respect to the world capitalist system in the overprotected industrial economies of Latin America and "high" levels in the command economies of Eastern Europe) and authoritarian polities, with varying degrees of political participation (military authoritarianism in the Southern Cone and party authoritarianism in Eastern Europe and, to a lesser extent, in Mexico).

Second, the transition is hampered in most of these countries by cultural factors and in all of them by economic ones. Many of the democratizing societies have weak democratic traditions, and thus the legitimacy of the new political institutions is fragile. In some cases the penetration of capitalist economic culture has only reached segments of the upper and middle strata, and much of society still has a communitarian, anticapitalist mentality. Above all, economic conditions are not very favorable. Most of the economies in transition have little ability to compete in world markets (except for the preexisting export sectors in Latin America). Conversion requires not only institutional changes—such as privatization, flexibilization of labor markets, and the opening of the economy— but also large-scale investment in physical capital. Many of these countries also bear the burden of large foreign debts.

Third, in all cases the transition involves what in classical Marxist terminology would be called similar "tasks": in the polity the design or reestablishment of governmental institutions and electoral systems conducive to the legitimation of the new and fragile democracies; in the economy the establishment (in Eastern Europe) or expansion (in Latin America) of the institutional infrastructure of a market economy, a change that involves privatization, deregulation, and the opening up of the economy.

These complex processes allow for a range of possible outcomes, so that the successful institutionalization of both an open market economy and a competitive polity is only one of the possible end points. Obviously, different outcomes appear more likely in different countries on the basis of their level of development, the degree of competitiveness of their economies, their size (small may be beautiful when it comes to economic convertibility), their geopolitical location, their endowment of human capital, their economic and political culture, and the effectiveness with which political elites carry out the "tasks" mentioned previously. Clearly, Chile and the Czech Republic are stronger candidates for successful institutionalization of the new economic and political structures than is either Peru or Romania.

This volume focuses on the relationship between these tasks of institutional design and the outcomes of the process of economic and political liberalization in Latin America and Eastern Europe. There are many different ways of privatizing a statized or semistatized economy, of deregulating markets, and of lowering tariff barriers; and there are many different ways of institutionalizing competitive politics. In both the East and the South, new constitutions and basic laws with a semiconstitutional status are being discussed and enacted. The authors in this volume look into the causes and consequences, for the process of democratization, of the design of some of these political and economic institutions in different structural and institutional settings. By causes we mean the configuration of structural contexts and the processes of collective action by which political elites are likely to prefer some options rather than others (e.g., parliamentarism rather than presidentialism, gradual rather than drastic economic liberalization, and so forth). By consequences we mean the likely short- and long-term effects of these choices in different settings. In all cases we will look into the ways in which institutional design mediates the relationship between the crisis of the old regime and the consolidation of the new one.

The authors focus on three substantive issues: the design of electoral systems, of executive-legislative relations, and of the institutions of a market economy. In each of these areas, contributors focus on the legacy of the preexisting authoritarian regime, the range of preferences developed by strategic actors (such as the government, other state bureaucracies, the opposition parties, and the important interest groups), the causes of these preferences (i.e., why strategic actors prefer different alternatives), and the consequences of the final choices for the institutionalization of effective market economies and liberal democracies. □

THE LOGIC OF THE COMPARISON

Comparative projects, although considered sensible and useful by many people, sometimes evoke reservations that boil down to the argument that "you cannot compare apples and oranges." The fact that transitions aimed at the same sociopolitical model are taking place at the same time in different regions of the world does not in itself validate a comparative project: The potential value of the enterprise depends on the logic of the comparison.

Three objections to comparative methodologies have been raised in discussions among the contributors to this volume. First, political and economic institutions (the points of departure) are very different. Second, the two regions are at different levels of development: East European societies are industrial, whereas the Latin American ones are underdeveloped or Third World. Finally, many scholars are skeptical of comparisons involving societies whose cultures are very different.

The validity of these objections is questionable for two reasons. There are obvious differences among the regions, but, at a high level of abstraction, there are still commonalities; in any case these arguments are not pertinent in relation to projects based on the "most-different-systems" design.

The validity of the first reservation depends on the level of abstraction of the analysis. Clearly, state socialism was different from the statist and highly protected capitalism that existed in many Latin American countries before the transition, and the types of political authoritarianism were also different from each other (Leninist party authoritarianism in Eastern Europe, military authoritarianism in the Southern Cone, and hegemonic party authoritarianism in Mexico). However, at a higher level of abstraction, similarities are clear: In both cases the ancien régime combined economies that restricted the operation of market mechanisms and integration into the capitalist world economy to different degrees and authoritarian regimes that had variable power to control and mobilize their societies.

The second argument falls before evidence that at the beginning of the transition the most "modern" Latin American societies were industrial (albeit noncompetitive, but so were state-socialist societies) and that several had scores on the Human Development Index that were roughly comparable to those prevailing in Eastern Europe (as Table 1.1 indicates). This does not mean, of course, that no important structural differences existed between the state-socialist societies in Eastern Europe and the most industrialized capitalist economies of Latin America. Most of the former had a larger manufacturing sector, which was based on larger plants and encompassed a larger share of the labor force; a more egalitarian distribution of income; health and educational systems of higher quality; and so forth. But the societies we are comparing were all basically urban and industrial. They were not so different in kind that comparisons among them are meaningless.

Finally, and as far as culture is concerned, we would like to make two points. First, at a high level of abstraction there are, as we have pointed out, significant cultural similarities: In most of these societies, the economic culture of capitalism has not penetrated deeply, and democratic traditions are

TABLE 1.1 Industrialization and Social Development in Selected Countries, 1990

	GDP Per Capita[a] (in U.S. dollars)	Industrial Share of GDP[b] (in percentages)	Human Development Index[c]
Poland	4,000	36	.910
Hungary	4,500	32	.915
Czechoslovakia	7,750	56	.931
Romania	3,000	48	.863
Argentina	4,647	41	.910
Chile	4,862	—	.931
Brazil	4,307	39	.784
Mexico	4,624	30	.876

[a] Real GDP per capita (purchasing power parities), 1987. *Source*: Adapted from United Nations Development Programme, *Human Development Report* (New York: Oxford University Press, 1992), p. 129.

[b] Industrial share of GDP, 1990. *Source*: Adapted from United Nations Development Programme, *World Development Report 1992: Development and the Environment* (New York: Oxford University Press, 1992), p. 223.

[c] The Human Development Index is a composite measure based on three indicators: life expectancy, adult literacy rate, and GDP per capita. *Source*: Adapted from United Nations, Development Programme, *Human Development Report*, p. 129. For a description of the index, see United Nations Development Programme, *Human Development Report*, p. 109.

weak or nonexistent. Second, this argument would also affect the validity of intraregional comparisons. In addition to the manifest cultural differences between the regions, there are substantial intraregional differences. This is obvious in Eastern Europe, where there are major linguistic, religious, and historical cleavages; but it is also significant in the case of Latin America, where cultural homogeneity is often assumed by outsiders. The nations we discuss in this volume share Iberian languages and colonial traditions, as well as Catholicism. But they differ sharply in terms of their ethnic compositions and the degrees of integration among the different components of their societies, and in the twentieth century their economic and political trajectories have shaped very different collective experiences for their populations and have led to different kinds of political cultures.

In conclusion, at a high level of abstraction, there are some significant commonalities between the regions we are comparing. However, the reservations discussed earlier refer exclusively to the feasibility of what has been called the "most-similar-systems" design. This type of comparative design, which is based on John Stuart Mill's "method of difference," matches units of analysis that are as similar as possible, except in relation to variables whose causal effects are being studied. In any case, these objections are irrelevant in connection with the most-different-systems design, whose purpose is to test propositions that are valid across units of analysis. For this reason, the objective of the design is to compare societies that are as different as possible.[1]

Our study fits this latter design. It is, however, exploratory rather than confirmatory. Our purpose is to examine the extent to which common patterns exist in processes of economic and political transition that aim at similar outcomes but that take place in relatively different structural, institutional, and cultural environments. □

THE DESIGN OF ELECTORAL SYSTEMS

Part One of this volume discusses the adoption and operation of electoral systems, with a special emphasis on the origins of the new electoral arrangements and their consequences for party systems and effective government. Chapters 2 and 3 are multicountry comparisons, focusing on Eastern Europe and Latin America. Chapters 4 and 5 focus on individual countries—Poland and Chile—within those two regions.

Barbara Geddes, in Chapter 2, analyzes the adoption of new democratic institutions in four East European countries—Bulgaria, Hungary, Poland, and Romania. Her theoretical point of departure is the rational-choice assumption that constitution makers pursue their own individual interests above all else and that these interests center on furthering their political careers. This political self-interest predisposes them to favor some institutional arrangements and oppose others; for instance, leaders of small or declining parties tend to prefer proportional representation over majoritarian electoral laws. This approach has worked very well in explaining institutional change in Latin America, but it is more difficult to apply to Eastern Europe because of the extreme volatility of the party system in the latter region. However, this problem can be overcome when timing is taken into consideration. In the four East European countries Geddes describes, the design of both the electoral laws and executive-legislative relations was the result of the perceived strength and bargaining power of the Communists and their successors (which gradually declined) on the one hand and of the opposition groups on the other and also of the increasing fragmentation of the opposition parties.

In Chapter 3, Dieter Nohlen's wide-ranging examination of the electoral systems used in Latin America finds a large number of common features: (1) They tend to employ proportional representation (PR); (2) however, most of these PR systems deviate significantly from proportionality, in the direction of discouraging small parties; (3) in most systems votes are aggregated, and seats are distributed at the district level, often in fairly small districts; and (4) most use closed-list systems that do not allow the expression of voters' preferences for individual candidates. The argument that proportional representation, in combination with a presidential system of government, produces deadlock and ungovernability in Latin American democracies is shown to be incorrect: Slightly more than half of the thirty-nine legislative elections in fourteen countries during the 1980s produced lower-house majorities for the president. Electoral reform debates in Latin America have focused on two themes: (1) the issue of proportionality versus government effectiveness, and (2) the related issues of party versus personal votes and of the ties between voters and representatives. Nohlen recommends several incremental reforms—in particular, the possibility of single-member district elections within an overall PR system (inspired by the German model), as in the new Venezuelan electoral system.

In Chapter 4, Stanislaw Gebethner traces the history of the fragmentation of the political party system in post-Communist Poland since 1989. He takes issue with the view that the extreme multipartism in the lower house of the Polish Parliament following the second parliamentary elections in 1991—twenty-nine parties were elected—was caused by the electoral law that prescribed an extreme form of proportional representation. A careful analysis of the election results shows that (1) the PR system was not really an extreme one; (2) it is an exaggeration to say that twenty-nine parties were elected, since many of the so-called parties were in fact the same party operating under different labels or independent candidates; (3) a system with a large number of parties had already developed *before* the election; and (4) the Senate was similarly fragmented, although it was elected by plurality. The true reason for multipartism in Poland is the great diversity of political opinions, which even a plurality system would be unable to convert into a two-party system. The same is true for the other Central and East European countries. Hence, Gebethner argues, PR is the most appropriate electoral system for the entire region.

Chile is a notable exception to the pattern described by Nohlen in Chapter 3. As Peter Siavelis and Arturo Valenzuela show in Chapter 5, the electoral reform dictated by Chile's military regime as it left office entailed majoritarian election rules that encouraged a two-party system (instead of the multiparty system of the pre-1973 democratic regime) and that favored the minority of the political right (by discriminating against the majority of the center and left). Although this system has largely accomplished the second objective, it cannot succeed in transforming Chile's traditional multiparty system. Parties adapt to the new electoral law by creating coalitions to maximize their votes and seats without reconfiguring the party system. Moreover, the new electoral system will encourage instability by leaving key sectors without representation and by introducing significant volatility; for instance, the right, which was the intended beneficiary of the electoral system, could lose virtually its entire representation with only a small shift of the vote. Siavelis and Valenzuela advise Chileans to recognize the strong social forces that underlie their multiparty system and, for this reason, to return to proportional representation. □

THE DESIGN OF
EXECUTIVE-LEGISLATIVE RELATIONS

Part Two focuses on the development of executive-legislative relations in the framework of the contrasting models of parliamentary and presidential forms of government. The four authors discuss the causes and consequences of the constitutional choices that have been made and their interrelationships with party systems and electoral systems. Chapters 6 and 7 deal with two East European countries (Poland and Hungary), and Chapters 8 and 9 analyze two Latin American countries (Mexico and Argentina).

In Chapter 6, Jerzy J. Wiatr discusses the instability and fragmentation of the new democratic regime in Poland—in particular, the frequent shifts between presidential and parliamentary dominance—and he compares it with the more stable Hungarian outcome. The cause of this difference does not lie in the two countries' political cultures or socioeconomic structures—which can be viewed as roughly similar—but in the modalities of their transitions: the timing of constitutional reform during the negotiated revolution, the relative strength and behavior of the main political actors (the former government and the opposition) during the process, and the legal framework chosen in the first stage of the new regime. First, in Poland the new political institutions were developed after the transition, whereas, in Hungary they were negotiated at the beginning of the process; second, in Poland the ruling party was more deeply divided and the opposition was stronger than was the case in Hungary; and finally, institutional changes were introduced in Poland in a situation of high uncertainty, and therefore they were less carefully planned and coordinated than those in Hungary.

György Szoboszlai's chapter on the development of parliamentarism in Hungary also emphasizes the unique timing of that country's democratic transition: In contrast to other European countries, Hungarian economic transformation and constitutional transformation preceded the actual transition to democracy. The mixed electoral system, with both majoritarian and proportional elements, produced a moderate multiparty system in the 1990 parliamentary elections. Two of the large parties emerging from the election concluded a pact that gave Hungary a parliamentary system with a dominant prime minister—too dominant, according to Szoboszlai. He argues that this system is insufficiently consensual and that it resembles a multiparty presidential system. Hence, he recommends strengthening various separation-of-powers devices, the constitutional court, and the system of local government.

Juan Molinar Horcasitas analyzes how the hegemonic party in Mexico (the Partido Revolucionario Institucional [PRI] and its predecessors), which has been in permanent control of the powerful presidency, has manipulated the electoral system since 1929. The PRI has been guided by two objectives: to control internal party factionalism and to maintain a weak political opposition in the legislative branch. Recent reforms in the electoral system for legislative elections and in the system for settling disputed election results have been driven by two opposite forces: political liberalization and the introduction of consensual features on the one hand and the strengthening of authoritarian control and pure majoritarianism on the other. This mixed pattern is in part the result of the government's tendency to react to short-term pressures by the opposition and in part reflects the internal division of the Mexican political elite regarding issues of political reform; moreover, in the late 1980s the PRI lost the two-thirds congressional majority necessary for amending the constitution. Molinar concludes that the hegemonic Mexican system and its authoritarian presidentialism are in retreat but are far from being defeated.

In his chapter, Carlos Santiago Nino focuses on the need for constitutional reform in Argentina. He argues that the extreme concentration of power in the hands of the president—creating what he calls a "hyperpresident"—should be reduced but, more important, that the entire system of presidential government should be changed. In 1987 the advisory Council for the Consolidation of Democracy proposed a mixed semipresidential system with both a strong and popularly elected president and a prime minister responsible to the legislature. Nino argues that none of the three main "packages" of executive-legislative relations—parliamentary, presidential, and semipresidential systems—is adequate. However, he shows that these packages can be "unsealed" and that individual elements can be reassembled into an optimally democratic and effective system. His innovative proposal entails the direct popular election of the head of government rather than the head of state. Nino wrote this chapter shortly before his untimely death in 1993. Our editors' postscript summarizes the 1994 constitutional reform, which introduced some of the changes favored by Nino. □

THE DESIGN OF MARKET ECONOMIES

Part Three deals with the dissolution of statized economies. In the three chapters, the authors discuss the ways in which the transition is shaped by preexisting institutions, and they focus in particular on the process of privatization. In Chapter 10 Éva Voszka examines the former Czechoslovakia, Hungary, and Poland. Discussion turns to economic reform in Latin America in Chapters 11 and 12, where Juarez Brandão

Lopes presents the case of Brazil and Roberto Frenkel and Guillermo Rosenwurcel examine Argentina.

Voszka compares the different privatization strategies followed by the former Czechoslovakia, Hungary, and Poland and looks into the causes of their relative success. Her central hypothesis is that the more the preexisting system of planning has been eroded prior to the political turnover, the less successful the government effort to design the privatization process will be. In Poland, the least successful of her three cases, government attempts to recentralize decisions and reclaim ownership rights lost to firms as a consequence of the disintegration of the Communist regime have faced strong opposition from enterprise managers and workers' organizations. Of the three cases, privatization has been the most successful in Czechoslovakia. The reason, in Voszka's view, is that in this country control of the process was always in the hands of the state, and privatization through vouchers was implemented according to the government's design. Hungary, finally, is an intermediate case. Its government was more successful at recentralizing and renationalizing firms than was the government in Poland, but privatization emphasized nonmarket methods of allocation (distribution to local governments, pension funds, previous owners, and the like), and the outcome has been a dispersed ownership structure. This is less effective than the situation in Czechoslovakia, where the voucher process/policy has led to a system of strong corporate governance.

Lopes discusses the obstacles to economic liberalization in Brazil, focusing on the failure of several stabilization and liberalization plans since the reestablishment of democracy in that country. Obstacles to reform have arisen from political and institutional factors. First, presidents elected under constitutional rule have had weak legitimacy (in spite of the fact that the presidency as an institution is strong). Other factors include the amorphous nature of the parties and the fragmentation of the party system; the overrepresentation of the less developed states in the Congress (coupled with the fact that deputies are strongly influenced by the governments of the states they represent); the fragmentation of the executive bureaucracy, which is heavily penetrated by interest groups; and the continuing uncertainty about basic institutional norms. The comparison with Argentina, a country that has embarked on a more radical and systematic course of privatization and opening up of the economy, allows Lopes to highlight additional causes of the failure of economic reform in Brazil. Unlike Argentina, Brazil had experienced high rates of economic growth under autarkic and statized capitalism, and it had been spared the revolutionary situation and the hyperinflation that rocked Argentina in the recent past. As a consequence, unlike their Argentine counterparts, Brazilian elites have failed to reach the conclusion that the existing economic institutions are not viable. However, elite attitudes are also changing in Brazil, and a consensus on the desirability of economic reform is finally taking root.

Finally, Frenkel and Rozenwurcel evaluate the process of privatization in Argentina. They argue that the massive privatization drive in that country did serve short-term political and macroeconomic purposes: In its inception, it enabled the Menem administration to maintain its credibility vis-à-vis the business community during a period of hyperinflation, and later it provided resources with which to close the fiscal gap and reduce the public debt. It is still an open question whether, in the long run, privatization will enhance the productivity of the existing resources and the efficiency of investment decisions, an outcome that will depend on the level of increase in the domestic savings rate and improvements in the competitiveness of the tradable sectors of the economy. The authors are skeptical. So far, privatizations have not been financed by private savings but by a combination of greater private foreign indebtedness and the return of flight capital. Also, most privatized firms are in the nontradables sector, so the positive effects of privatization on international competitiveness are not yet evident. Nevertheless, the contributors point out that privatization has already had an apparently irreversible structural effect: It has strengthened private monopolies and weakened the public sector that is supposed to regulate those monopolies. □

NOTES

1. See David Collier, "The Comparative Method: Two Decades of Change," in Dankwart A. Rustow and Kenneth P. Erickson, eds., *Comparative Political Dynamics: Global Research Perspectives* (New York: HarperCollins, 1991), pp. 16–17; Arend Lijphart, "The Comparable-Cases Strategy in Comparative Research," *Comparative Political Studies* 8, no. 2 (1975): 132–157; Adam Przeworski and Henry Teune, *The Logic of Comparative Social Inquiry* (New York: Wiley-Interscience, 1970), pp. 34–35; and Peter H. Smith, "The Changing Agenda for Social Science Research on Latin America," in Peter H. Smith, ed., *Latin America in Comparative Perspective: New Approaches to Methods and Analysis* (Boulder: Westview Press, 1995), pp. 4–6.

PART ONE

The Design of Electoral Systems

CHAPTER TWO

———————— ■ ————————

Initiation of New Democratic Institutions in Eastern Europe and Latin America

Barbara Geddes

IN A SERIES OF ARTICLES and an influential book, Kenneth Jowitt has argued that forty years of rule by Leninist regimes has resulted in a cultural legacy in Eastern Europe that can be expected to undermine both democracy and capitalism.[1] Beginning with completely different assumptions, other observers have suggested that the economic costs to much of the population that are inherent in the transition to capitalism can be expected to jeopardize the survival of democracy in formerly Communist countries.[2]

We do not know whether most transitions from Leninism will, perhaps after a period of turbulence, result in competitive regimes; we also do not know how many of the currently democratic, formerly Leninist polities will suffer interludes of authoritarianism. Consequently, we cannot judge the various predictions of disaster. We can, however, examine the recent behavior of political elites and masses in Eastern Europe to see if they display signs of either the Leninist cultural legacy described so persuasively by Jowitt or the lack of support for democracy in the face of high economic costs predicted by a number of scholars. And we can compare the behavior of Eastern Europeans with the behavior of Latin Americans in similar circumstances as a means of identifying what is truly unique about the Leninist legacy.

In this chapter I respond to the claims about the incompatibility between democracy and various features of Eastern European reality through a concrete and quotidian investigation of the initiation of new democratic institutions in four East European countries: Poland, Hungary,

15

Romania, and Bulgaria. Much of the scholarly literature on Eastern Europe has been written by observers who have had little experience studying true democracies and who hence have somewhat unrealistic expectations. This study, in contrast, draws its assumptions and basic theoretical framework from the literature on democracies in the United States and Western Europe.

In the first part of the chapter I sketch a set of assumptions and predictions about the behavior of political elites in a stylized but not idealized democratic polity. I then compare these predictions to the behavior of contemporary politicians in Eastern Europe. To the extent that these politicians act like politicians in any other democratic setting, this investigation undermines claims about the importance of a distinctive Leninist legacy for elite political behavior in post-Leninist democracies. In the third section I compare the situation in Eastern Europe with that in Latin America during transitions from authoritarianism by examining both the politics of institutional choice and the interaction between economic hardship and mass political behavior. The comparison between Eastern Europe and Latin America suggests that although they have received little attention from observers, certain elements of the Leninist legacy have immediate political relevance.

I focus on negotiations over, and choices among, specific new democratic institutions. Other policy areas might have been chosen, but several analysts have suggested that the specific institutional characteristics of new democracies influence their ability to pursue effective economic policy and hence their long-term political stability.[3] Institutions thus seem to have special relevance for the questions raised earlier.

The four cases studied—Poland, Hungary, Romania, and Bulgaria—were selected first to exclude the effect of extreme ethnic nationalism on institutional outcomes. Although ethnic nationalism is an important cause of institutional choice in Eastern Europe, I excluded countries likely to split or disintegrate into civil war in order to increase cross-regional comparability. The level of ethnic strife experienced in the four selected cases is more typical of other developing countries than is the level in the former Yugoslavia. Within this set of cases, considerable variation exists in the level of development, the role of mass participation in the overthrow of the old regime, and institutional outcome. The Latin American material draws primarily on the experiences of Argentina, Brazil, Chile, Colombia, Peru, Uruguay, and Venezuela—countries at levels of development comparable to the range in the Eastern European cases and that have all experienced at least one transition to democracy since World War II. □

EXPLANATIONS OF INSTITUTIONAL CHOICE

How are new democratic institutions chosen in transitional and post-Leninist political systems? Two central questions to be answered are whether the norms, logic, or incentives that motivate politicians in post-

Leninist systems lead to different outcomes than would be expected in countries with longer democratic histories and whether institutional choice is affected by economic hardship or imperatives of the transition to capitalism.

Past Efforts to Explain Institutions

Two literatures on the emergence of political institutions currently exist. The first, pioneered by Seymour Martin Lipset and Stein Rokkan, links party systems and electoral laws to major historical events and to ethnic, religious, and economic cleavages resulting from them.[4] Recent work by Michael Coppedge and Timothy Scully has used a similar perspective to explain different kinds of party systems in Latin America.[5] Although this literature has some relevance to events in the post-Communist world, its direct utility for explaining the emergence of new political institutions in Eastern Europe is limited.[6] Industrialization under Communist auspices created neither the basic capital-labor cleavage nor the autonomous mass-participation, interest-based organizations (except in Poland) assumed by Lipset and Rokkan. Therefore, few parts of the model can be directly transferred to Eastern Europe.

The second literature has been developed primarily by economists. Economic explanations of institutional change rely on efficiency gains, often taking transaction costs into account, to explain the evolution of new institutions.[7] Since they have generally not considered collective-action problems or other issues involving the distribution of gains from efficiency, they have failed to explain the persistence of inefficient institutions.[8] Furthermore, these arguments have generally sought to explain institutions at a fairly abstract level (firms as a form of organization, efficient property rights with the details unspecified), rather than explaining concrete differences among institutions. When it is unclear which institution is more efficient (e.g., presidentialism or parliamentarism), economists' arguments offer little help in understanding outcomes.

In short, attempts to explain the emergence of concrete political institutions in Eastern Europe fail to fit well into conventional paradigms. It is often not obvious which economic interests will benefit from one form of political system as opposed to another; nor is it clear which set would be more efficient or even what efficiency would mean in this context.

In contrast to abstract economic arguments, two political arguments of considerable analytic sophistication seek specifically to explain a particular institutional outcome—the strength of the presidency. Matthew Shugart and John Carey have noted a correlation between weak parties and strong presidencies in Latin America and have argued that legislatures made up of weak parties tend to delegate powers to the president as a way of overcoming immobilism.[9] Shugart has suggested an extension of this argument to Eastern Europe.[10] Arend Lijphart, drawing on East European case materials, has argued that presidentialism is a response to uncertainty about the future, an attempt to hedge bets by creating more than one possibility of winning office.[11] These arguments are plausible, but some of the details posited do not fit the historical sequence of events in East European countries.

Most descriptions of the current round of institutional choice in Eastern Europe stress either the imitation of foreign institutions or the relationship between the continued power of Communist successor parties and the deviation from democratic principles. These discussions capture an aspect of reality, but they miss much. The continued importance of Communist successor parties in some countries explains the existence of a number of undemocratic features in constitutions, but it fails to explain the main features of East European political systems.

Discussions of borrowing offer no explanation for why certain systems are copied rather than others or why all East European countries have revised and adapted the systems they have borrowed. One might expect that in a situation in which the effects of decisions on material interests are not obvious, East European constitution writers—concerned about stability and economic performance—might choose to copy a successful system such as the West German system. Only Hungary has done so, however, and even there apparently minor revisions to the electoral system greatly reduce its proportionality and thus lead to a system of representation that is fairly different from the German one.[12]

Institutions as Weapons in the Struggle for Political Survival

In contrast to the various literatures discussed earlier, my attempt to explain institutional change and resistance to change begins with two assumptions drawn explicitly from standard treatments of democratic politics:[13] that those who make the changes—that is, the members of roundtables, constituent assemblies, and legislatures who must make the choices that determine electoral procedures—pursue their own individual interests above all else, and that their interests center on furthering their political careers. This political self-interest predisposes them to favor some institutional arrangements and oppose others. In advancing this argument, I do not deny that political leaders represent the interests of constituents and prefer some policies to others. But for politicians considering institutional changes, interest in furthering their careers usually converges with interest in achieving the policy goals of their constituents. The same institutions that will improve their chances of winning elections will also improve their chances of achieving policy goals, since the greater the likelihood that they and their party allies will be elected, the greater the chance of passing the legislation they favor.

The institutional preferences of the self-interested politicians who create new democratic political systems depend on their roles (e.g., legislator), which societal interests their parties represent and rely on for votes, and whether their parties are rising or declining relative to others. Most obviously, for example, members of small parties, declining parties, and parties with an uncertain future prefer proportional representation. The preexisting institutional context and the distribution of strength among parties determine the feasible alternatives from which they have to choose.

This approach, which effectively explains institutional change in Latin America, faces potential problems when applied to contemporary Eastern Europe. Foremost among these is the extreme volatility of the political and party contexts at the time of institutional choice. As transition began, Communist parties in the four countries discussed in this chapter had tremendous advantages over other parties in regard to local organization, control of government resources and patronage, and control of the media. Between 1989 and 1992, however, support for Communist parties and their successors declined—dramatically in most countries—as did these parties' control of political resources.[14] Meanwhile, new parties arose as if by spontaneous generation—in some countries over two hundred appeared. New parties were born, split, fused, died, survived, and in some cases prospered. The distribution of power among them changed rapidly, as did the institutional environment in which they operated.

Nevertheless, even though political circumstances changed quickly and at first unpredictably, institutional choices were made at certain moments. At any particular moment it is possible to identify the preexisting institutional context, as well as the parties and individuals who influenced choices. It is also possible to observe which parties were declining and which were growing and what preferences were expressed in negotiations and votes.

The extreme fluidity of the East European political context thus does not preclude explanations based on political interests of politicians, but it does require incorporating timing into the explanation. In all of the cases examined, initial institutional design resulted from negotiations between the Communists and their successors on the one hand and one or more opposition groups on the other. Outcomes varied with the perceived strength, and hence the bargaining power, of the two sides, which changed as Communist parties declined. Particularly in the second round of institutional changes, the degree of fragmentation and other characteristics of the opposition parties also influenced outcomes. Fragmentation of both Communist and opposition parties tended to increase over time.[15]

Timing, Misperception, and Uncertainty

Communist parties enjoyed their greatest negotiating power when uncertainty prevailed about possible Soviet intervention in the internal affairs of East European countries, that is, prior to fall 1989. When the round-table discussions took place in Poland in early spring 1989, the Communists were able to obtain most of what they wanted in the institutional domain in return for allowing the opposition the right to legal organization and participation in the political process. As a result, "Solidarity did not seriously press for the holding of completely free elections in June, 1989."[16]

Once Soviet withdrawal had become certain, the situation regarding both bargaining strength and information about party strength underwent a dramatic change. Communist parties had to assess their ability to compete in electoral systems, an area in which they had no practical experience (with the partial exception of Hungary) and little information. Prior to the first elections and the freeing of the media, both Communist and opposition parties systematically overestimated support for the Communists.

As long as the media is controlled and opposition parties are not permitted to mobilize campaigns that disseminate their views to large numbers of people, most people's opinions, as expressed in surveys and votes, will reflect the views carried in the controlled media.[17] All political leaders depend to some extent on votes and polls to judge public opinion and their own political standing; Communist leaders, however, were especially dependent on them because, as a rule, local party organizations failed to transmit expressions of discontent to the leadership, and public expression of opposition was strongly discouraged. Opinions shaped by a controlled media are highly volatile, however, and are subject to rapid and radical change when people are exposed to competing points of view.[18] Political elites in Eastern Europe, like military rulers in Latin America before them, were surprised by the rapid disintegration of regime support once opposition views were allowed to be articulated.

Prior to 1989, only in Poland had Solidarity's earlier success and the quasi legalization of what had been samizdat publications during the economic reforms of the 1980s created an opposition information flow that reached a significant part of the population.[19] As a result, popular opposition to the Communist regime in Poland became widespread and highly visible. Polish Communist leaders were aware that they were unlikely to win open elections and thus demanded institutions that would safeguard their control in spite of their lack of popularity: the reservation of 65 percent of the seats in the Sejm for themselves and their allies, along with a strong president elected by the legislature, which—given guaranteed control of 65 percent of the lower house—they thought they were sure to control. Neither Solidarity nor the Communist Polish United Workers' Party (PZPR) predicted the extent of Solidarity's victory. According to Voytek Zubek, "Even the worst predictions [by the Communists] saw Solidarity winning half of the [contested] seats, the PZPR's coalition a third of them ."[20]

In the rest of Eastern Europe, opposition information flows had reached only a few outside the most well-educated stratum. Communist leaders in these countries overestimated the depth and resilience of the opinions they had helped to create through control of the media. In consequence, when negotiations took place before the first free elections, Communist parties tended to demand institutional arrangements—such as a strong elected presidency and majoritarian forms of representation—that would benefit a dominant party. Opposition parties underestimated their own strength and settled for less than they might have received if perceptions on all sides had been more accurate.

As elections occurred throughout the formerly Communist world, assessments of Communist strength became more accurate, but uncertainty about which of the competing opposition groups would survive to become major players remained very high. Institutions designed or redesigned after the first round of elections tended to reflect this uncertainty. As noted by Lijphart, proportional representation, which protects small parties from annihilation, was the universal response to this uncertainty in countries that devised new electoral rules following the first open election.[21]

In every bargaining situation after fall 1989, Communists faced much higher costs for delay in coming to an agreement over institutions than did opposition parties. Except in Poland, the opposition initially lacked a grassroots organization, and the Communists controlled the official media and local government.[22] These differences gave the Communists important but eroding electoral resources. Holding early elections was a priority for the Communists, since this would increase in their probability of controlling the government during the transitional period. At times, Communist and successor parties traded early elections for less desirable institutional features.

Preferences of Parties and Politicians in Eastern Europe

As parties began to negotiate new institutional arrangements, each sought choices that would give it an advantage over the competition or, at a minimum, ensure survival. Different parties tried to maximize the usefulness of their characteristics and minimize the damage that would be caused by their weaknesses.

Initially, Communist parties preferred strong presidencies, which they expected to win or appoint, and majoritarian electoral systems.[23] In all cases, Communist negotiators favored the institution of the presidency. Where they expected to win (Hungary in late 1989 and in Romania), they preferred a popularly elected president, since popular election would confer more power and legitimacy on the holder of the office in any struggles with an unpredictable elected legislature. Where mass opposition had already become apparent, as in Poland, or where the presidential election was expected to occur in the unpredictable future, as in Bulgaria, the negotiators preferred a president elected by Parliament.

Communists' preference for majoritarian systems had three sources: overestimation of their own popularity; the desire of many successor party politicians to run as individuals, unhampered by the party label; and Communist control at the local level, intact in all cases, which provided Communist candidates with a preexisting local political machine and patronage network. Redrawing electoral districts, which would be necessary if proportional representation were to be adopted, would threaten these local electoral resources. If the electoral system remained unchanged, incumbents hoped to benefit from their local entrenchment.

Smaller parties and parties uncertain about their future preferred proportional representation. This category includes almost all opposition and Communist parties after the first round of elections.[24] The exceptions among opposition parties were the largest Hungarian opposition parties and Lech Walesa's supporters in Poland in fall 1990 and spring 1991. Because Hungary had allowed multicandidate elections after 1985, a number of opposition and reform-Communist members of Parliament had been elected in single-member districts. By 1989, they enjoyed the incumbency advantage in their districts and preferred to maintain the same system. During debates in Poland, whichever faction of the Solidarity movement supported Walesa at any particular time favored half majority and half proportional representation. The mixed system was originally proposed by the Citizens' Parliamentary Caucus (the leaders of which later formed the Democratic Union) in September 1990.[25] In March 1991, however, one observer noted:

> While the unity of the nationwide citizens' committee movement seemed to promise a repetition of the victory of "Walesa's team" as in June 1989, such an electoral system seemed good to the leaders of today's Democratic Union Caucus; now that "Walesa's team" has split and the citizens' committee movement and the Solidarity labor union seem set to serve as an efficient electoral machine for the pro-Walesa Center Alliance of right-of-center groups and parties, the alliance is interested in its adoption, while the Democratic Union fears finding itself at a disadvantage and supports a proportional electoral system.[26]

Parties that contained charismatic personalities, who had gained name recognition and popular respect for their opposition to the communist regime, favored open-list proportional representation. A large number of votes for certain well-known names on the party list can elect other, unknown candidates. In October 1995, Jan Krzysztof Bielecki's 115,002 votes, for example, also elected Liberal candidates Pavel Piskowski, with

589 votes, and Jacek Kurczewski, with 588 votes.[27] Parties with fewer well-known personalities and disciplined parties with an entrenched, dominant leadership preferred the more standard closed-list system.[28] Closed-list proportional representation enhances party discipline and the power of party leaders relative to members, since leaders determine the order of the list and hence candidates' electoral chances. The Democratic Union in Poland, which included most of the famous Solidarity activists except Walesa, and a number of other small Polish opposition parties favored the open list. Almost all Communist and successor parties and most other opposition parties favored the closed list.[29] Poland is the only country in this set in which the opposition was sufficiently widespread and effective to have produced well-known and highly regarded political figures. In Hungary, where the opposition also had a long and honorable history, the best-known reformers were concentrated inside the Communist Party and thus were unavailable as opposition heroes. A single-member–district system would seem to serve reform Communists better than would open-list proportional representation, since single-member–district systems lead to an emphasis on the individual politician while downplaying the party label. □

INSTITUTIONAL CHOICES IN THE REAL WORLD

Given these preferences and the pattern of change in relative bargaining power, we would expect stronger presidencies and more majoritarian systems of legislative representation to be associated with Communist parties that were relatively strong at the time the institutions were chosen. As Table 2.1 shows, these expectations are consistent with reality.

The left-hand column of Table 2.1 shows the fora within which institutional decisions were made, in chronological order for each country. The next column describes the strength of the Communist Party or its main successor *in the relevant forum* at the time when decisions were being made and lists the most important historical factors that affected Communist or successor party strength. In Poland, for example, Communist strength in spring 1989 is considered high because of uncertainty about the Soviet threat to intervene, even though widespread popular opposition to the PZPR was apparent. I judged Communist strength to be medium between June 1989 and October 1991, even though the June electoral results and public opinion polls showed public support to be low, because the PZPR and its successors continued to control the largest bloc of votes in the Sejm as a result of the roundtable agreement. Similar criteria were used in the other cases. Although an element of subjectivity necessarily enters into these categorizations, I have made every effort to base them on contemporary statements and descriptions by participants and observers rather than inferring them post hoc from known outcomes.

TABLE 2.1 Relationship Between Communist Strength and Institutional Outcome

Decision Forum	Communist Strength	Presidency	Parliament
Poland			
Roundtable (Feb.–Apr. 1989)			
	High: Uncertain Soviet threat	Elected by legislature, broad powers	Majoritarian with 65 percent of Sejm reserved for Communist Party (CP) and its allies
Sejm and Senate (Jun. 1989–Oct. 1991)			
	Medium: CP majority in Sejm	Popular election, majority runoff	Proportional representation (PR)
Sejm and Senate (Oct. 1991–Sep. 1993)			
	Low: CP small party in legislature, popular support low	Some compromise on presidential powers	No change
Hungary			
Roundtable (Jun.–Sep. 1989) and National Assembly (Oct. 1989)			
	High: National Assembly dominated by CP, Soviet threat declining, not gone	Popular election of president, powers unspecified	Half majoritarian with runoffs, half PR
Popular Referendum (Nov. 26, 1989)			
	Medium: no Soviet threat, popular opposition rising	Election postponed until after free election of Parliament	
National Assembly (Mar. 1990–Mar. 1994)			
	Low: CP small party in legislature, popular support low	Parliamentary election of president, powers limited	No change
Bulgaria			
Roundtable (Mar.–Jun. 1990)			
	High: No Soviet threat, but almost no organized opposition	Current CP president to continue, next to be elected by legislature, substantial powers	Half majoritarian with runoffs, half PR

TABLE 2.1 *(continued)*

Decision Forum	Communist Strength	Presidency	Parliament
National Assembly (Jun. 1990–Oct. 1991)			
	Medium-high: CP controls legislature, but popularity declining	Popular election, more limited powers	PR
National Assembly (Oct. 1991–Dec. 1994)			
	Medium: Union of Democratic Forces wins parliamentary and presidential elections, CP largest opposition	No change	No change
Romania			
National Salvation Front (NSF) (Dec. 1989–Jan. 31,1990)			
	High: Opposition unorganized, not included in NSF	Popular election, substantial powers	Majoritarian, fifteen officers appointed to Senate
Provisional National Unity Council (Feb.–May 1990)			
	Medium-high: Demonstrations forced inclusion of opposition	Majority, runoff	PR
Chamber of Deputies and Senate (May 1990–Sep. 1992)			
	Medium-high: NSF controls legislature and presidency, popularity declining slowly	No change	No change

The third column notes the most essential features of the presidency, and the fourth indicates the system of representation in the legislature.

As the fourth column shows, in the initial stage of reform when the Communist Party was at its strongest, all electoral systems were at least partly majoritarian. In the systems with the strongest Communist or successor parties (Poland in spring 1989 and Romania in winter 1990), the first systems announced were not only entirely majoritarian but were not fully democratic. Poland's arrangement reserved 65 percent of the seats in the lower house for the PZPR and its coalition partners. Romania's Senate included seats for fifteen appointed military officers. Poland's first partially competitive election took place under these rules before Soviet withdrawal became certain. In Romania, however, where the Soviet threat no longer existed and Nicolae Ceau4escu had recently been overthrown by massive street demonstrations, new protests forced the Communist successor National Salvation Front (NSF) to include opposition parties in a newly formed Provisional Council for National Unity and to negotiate with them over electoral rules, which resulted in the abandonment of the majoritarian system.[30]

In both Bulgaria and Hungary, initial institutional arrangements were negotiated at roundtables in circumstances in which reform Communists controlled nearly all of the political resources in the country but faced growing opposition and could no longer expect Soviet protection.[31] In an obviously deteriorating situation, Communist negotiators compromised on institutional details in exchange for a timely agreement and early elections.[32] The Hungarian roundtable agreement was modified in the direction of greater majoritarianism by an activist National Assembly dominated by reform Communists.[33] The original agreement had included an equal number of single-member and district-level proportional seats, with the remainders from the single-member districts distributed proportionally among national lists. This system, like the German one, would have resulted in a highly proportional system in spite of the existence of a large number of single-member districts. The final version of the agreement increased the number of single-member districts in response to legislators' demands and changed the basis for calculating the distribution of the national list to include remainders in the proportional contests, thus substantially increasing the majoritarian bias in the system.

In all but Hungary, after the first round of elections or demonstrations led to the realization of their own potential weakness by Communist successor parties still in control of legislatures, initial or partly majoritarian systems were abandoned in favor of proportional representation. The weak opposition parties in Bulgaria and Romania, as well as the highly fragmented opposition parties in Poland, also favored proportional representation.[34]

Only in Hungary did the opposition win control of the legislature in the first election, a victory magnified for the top party by the majoritarian features of the system. The Hungarian Democratic Forum received 24.4 percent of the votes in the first-round proportional districts but obtained nearly 43 percent of the seats when the single-member districts and runoffs were added. The Alliance of Free Democrats, which came in second with 21.7 percent of the proportional vote in the first round, also benefited slightly from the system, whereas all other parties—including the Communist successor Socialists—were disadvantaged.[35] Not surprisingly, the majority in the Hungarian National Assembly saw no reason to change a system that had treated it well.

We see a similar pattern with respect to the presidency, of politicians favoring institutions expected to contribute to their own electoral success. Communist and successor parties initially favored a presidency with substantial powers to act as a brake on a potentially unruly or unpredictable elected legislature.[36] In all cases, the Communists either already controlled the presidency or expected to win proposed elections. With the Sejm elections rigged by the roundtable agreement, Polish Communists could count on General Wojciech Jaruzelski's election by the combined legislature. Hungarian reform Communists confidently expected the election of one of their number—the popular Imre Pozsgay—and no other equally popular figure had emerged from within the opposition. In Bulgaria, the prereform National Assembly had elected reform Communist Petar Mladenov to the presidency for a period expected to run throughout the term of the first elected legislature.[37] In Romania, it was expected that former Communist Ion Iliescu, who occupied the presidency of the Council of the National Salvation Front when negotiations with the opposition began, would win a popular presidential election.

Only in Romania did events conform to successor party expectations. Iliescu won presidential elections, first in May 1990 and again in September 1992. The Romanian constitution, drafted by the National Assembly, which was dominated by the NSF, reaffirmed the powers of the presidency in 1991.[38]

Communist plans for the presidency first went awry in Bulgaria and Hungary. In Bulgaria, reform Communist President Mladenov was unexpectedly forced to resign as a result of popular demonstrations, making it necessary for the National Assembly to elect a new president a year ahead of schedule. The Communist successor Bulgarian Socialist Party lacked the two-thirds majority required in the legislature to elect one of its own number. Zhelyu Zhelev, leader of the opposition Union of Democratic Forces, was the compromise solution.[39] The constitution adopted in July 1991, written by the elected National Assembly and also requiring a two-thirds majority, provides for a popularly elected president with limited powers. Zhelev won the first competitive presidential election by a narrow margin in January 1992.

In Hungary, two opposition parties refused to sign the roundtable agreement and led a campaign for a referendum to postpone presidential elections until after the election of a democratic Parliament.[40] The referendum passed, and as a result, not only was the election postponed but the power to define the scope of the presidency and the mode of election passed to the new legislature. Jealous of its own prerogatives, the legislature decided to elect the president itself and to limit the powers of the presidency. Hungary thus has the weakest presidency of the four countries, with Bulgaria's the next weakest.

In Poland, Communist plans for the presidency went awry even more spectacularly. Not only did the Communists lose control of the office, but the presidency remained strong in the hands of their most famous opponent. Approximately one year after his election, General Jaruzelski was persuaded to resign by a popular campaign for a freely elected presidency mounted by Lech Walesa and one faction of Solidarity. After Walesa's election in December 1990, the Roundtable Sejm struggled to limit presidential powers.[41] It fought Walesa to a standstill on many issues but never managed to curtail his powers. The Little Constitution, promulgated in fall 1992, clarified the roles of the president, the prime minister, and the legislature; it was expected to reduce conflict, but it left the Polish presidency relatively strong.[42]

Parties that support a strong presidency in Poland have evolved with the shifting winds of Walesa's alliances. In the months following Walesa's election, the Center Alliance (Centrum), the faction of Solidarity that had supported his presidential campaign, fought for a strong presidency whereas the Democratic Union—the faction of Solidarity that had supported Tadeusz Mazowiecki in the presidential elections—sought to limit the powers of the presidency. In late 1991, when Walesa reestablished cooperation with the Democratic Union, these positions were reversed. In short, the party or alliance that controls the presidency or expects to control it in the near future supports broad powers for the president, whereas parties opposed to the president seek to limit presidential powers.

The evidence from these cases thus offers support for some but not all of the arguments proposed by Lijphart and Shugart and Carey. As Lijphart has suggested, Communist negotiators attempted to create presidencies with substantial powers as a hedge against future uncertainty. Their aim was to create a strong executive office under their own control for the duration of the transition period and thus to limit change.[43] In the words of an observer of the Polish roundtable, "This arrangement was intended to guarantee communist control over political developments at least until the next elections, which were expected to take place in four years."[44]

Communists may also have sought to multiply the number of offices for which they could compete in the future. Strong presidencies have been maintained in countries in which the president has the support of the strongest party and the legislature—which in all countries has contested presidential power—is relatively weak.[45] In other words, strong presidencies are supported by the parties that benefit from their alliance with the president; they are opposed by parties that do not benefit and by legislators who have an interest in defending the powers and prerogatives of their own institutions. There is no evidence from these cases that the presidency is seen as a cooperative solution among parties to a shared problem of uncertainty.

Shugart and Carey have argued that strong presidencies tend to be associated with weak parties.[46] These cases support their argument. Poland and Romania have both the weakest parties (or at least the weakest opposition parties) and the strongest presidencies. Shugart and Carey's suggestion that this association comes about through delegation of powers by the legislature to the president, however, is not supported by the evidence. Strong presidencies, where they exist, were established prior to, or at the same time as, freely elected legislatures. In all cases, legislatures have made efforts to curtail the independent powers of the presidency. They have had more success in doing so in countries in which opposition parties in the legislature (that is, parties other than that of the president) are relatively large and strong.

Opposition parties may be weak either because of general fragmentation and weakness in the party system or because of the great strength of the president's party, a condition that is likely to occur only in Eastern Europe as a result of the continued strength of the Communist successor party. I would suggest that an extremely fragmented party system makes for a weak legislature, as does the continued domination of a Communist successor party over small, weak opposition parties. An alternative explanation, then, for the association between weak parties and strong presidencies found by Shugart and Carey is that weak, fragmented parties undermine the legislature's ability to pursue its own aggrandizement at the expense of the presidency and thus contribute to the accretion of presidential powers.

Up to this point, I have focused on demonstrating a strong and direct relationship between politicians' desire to improve their own electoral chances and their choices with regard to new democratic political institutions. Incentives created by electoral competition have affected East European politicians—including those whose entire careers had been spent in Communist Party politics—in exactly the same way they would affect a politician in any other setting who was faced with the same choices. One might argue that post-Leninist politicians made more mistakes in their institutional choices than politicians with more democratic political experience would have, either because circumstances were changing too quickly or because they lacked a feel for democratic politics. One could not argue, however, that the basic underlying logic of their choices derived from norms or a worldview distinctive to the Leninist experience. In this regard, the behavior of political elites shows no evidence of the persistence of a special Leninist legacy. ☐

COMPARISON OF EASTERN EUROPE AND
LATIN AMERICA: THE OTHER LENINIST LEGACY

A comparison of negotiations over institutional choice in Eastern Europe with those in Latin America emphasizes the strong similarities in the institutional preferences of similar political actors in the two areas. Most obviously, dominant parties (e.g., the Partido Revolucionario Institucional in Mexico and the nineteenth-century Partido Autonomista Nacional in Argentina) have preferred majoritarian systems of legislative representation, whereas smaller parties and parties uncertain of their future electoral strength have preferred proportional representation. Parties that control or expect to control the presidency and individual politicians who hold or hope to hold the office (what Latin Americanists call the *presidenciables*) have been the strongest advocates of extending presidential powers and continuing the presidential form of the executive.[47]

Differences in outcomes between the two regions derive more from differences in preexisting institutional arrangements than from norms or motivations of political elites. A full catalog of such differences would be long and complicated, but two of the most important can be discussed here: the institutional blank slate left by the "Leninist extinction," to use Jowitt's phrase, and the near absence of autonomous interest groups (with the partial exception of labor in Poland) that either are or could quickly be linked to class- or interest-based parties.

A striking difference between Eastern Europe and Latin America is the much greater influence of the preauthoritarian institutional legacy on the choice of new institutions during transitions to democracy in Latin America as compared with Eastern Europe. Transitions to democracy would seem to offer an opportunity for relatively easy institutional change. Such transitions are periods of great political ferment and creativity and are a time for political soul-searching about the causes of previous democratic breakdowns. It seems natural to write new constitutions and electoral rules during democratic transitions, as a means of both ridding the polity of laws decreed by the authoritarian regime and fortifying the new democratic system. Yet notwithstanding the apparent fluidity of the transition phase, in Latin America little institutional change has occurred during redemocratizations. Rules and procedures of the earlier democratic period, although sometimes long suppressed, are often simply revived.[48]

Past institutions resurface during transitions when they are useful to the politicians competing in the new political context. Parties that dominate political life in a democracy at any particular time will tend to be those that are well adapted to functioning in the institutional environment and that can benefit from its idiosyncrasies. This is one reason such institutions are "sticky," that is, difficult to change. When a military or other authoritarian regime comes to power and simply outlaws parties, as most did in Latin America during the 1960s and 1970s, the parties go underground. They continue to function, although in a much reduced fashion. The parties lose contact with casual adherents, but committed activists maintain clandestine organizations, at least as long as the original generation of activists survives. Consequently, when the dictatorship, in preparing to relinquish power, allows the reemergence of parties, the old party system rises phoenixlike from the ashes of repression. These parties still have essentially the same interests they had before, and they represent the same societal groups and benefit from the same features of the institutional environment; thus, they have little to gain from making risky changes in political rules.

Modern military regimes in Latin America have lasted twenty-one years at most, and in all but Brazil the continuity between pre- and postauthoritarian parties is striking. Even in Brazil, where military manipulation changed the party system, many individuals who had established themselves as important political actors during the 1946–1964 democratic period either continued to have an active political life in the military government or played an important role during the long period of redemocratization (1974 –1985) and reemerged—along with their informal followings—as major political actors in the new democratic regime.[49]

In Eastern Europe, in contrast, the forty-year period of Leninist rule and the more systematic attack by Leninist rulers on virtually all autonomous organizations resulted in a more thorough destruction of traditional parties. At the same time, the Communist parties, like the parties established by the military in Brazil, created a channel of upward mobility and a road to political power that diverted many individuals with a vocation for politics away from the old parties and into the new ones. In none of the cases examined here did the historical parties reemerge as major political forces. New parties that have arisen during the dictatorship, as either supporters of or opposition to the regime, have no stake in the rules and institutions of the preauthoritarian regime. Consequently, current institutional choices in Eastern Europe, in contrast to those in Latin America, show relatively little continuity with pre-Leninist institutions.

The second striking difference between Eastern Europe and Latin America follows from the effects of industrialization in different contexts on the creation of interest groups in society and on the links between those interest groups and political parties. In most capitalist countries, industrialization has resulted in the dominance, as expressed in the party system, of the capital-labor cleavage over other potential sources of cleavage (ethnic, religious, urban-rural). There are some obvious and well-known exceptions, but in most industrialized countries—even those in which two parties converge at the center of the political spectrum—it is possible to array most parties on a left-right continuum that ranges from representatives of those who own no capital to representatives of those who own much capital.

East European parties can also be arrayed from left to right in terms of their economic policy preferences, but their linkages to interest groups are not well established, long-standing, or, in many cases, even apparent. Early survey research done in Hungary, for example, showed no relationship between class and party preference. Working- and lower-class background was associated with support for a strong state role in the provision of welfare, intolerance for income inequality, and aversion to capitalism, as would be expected. And different parties gave promises about welfare, equality, and the rapidity of the transition to capitalism a prominent place in their campaigns. Nevertheless, party preference was unrelated to any of these attitudes or to either self-defined or objectively measured class.[50]

In the Leninist regimes, the principal political cleavage was that between party apparatchiks and managers on the one hand and ordinary people on the other. In Jowitt's words, "For forty years . . . ruling Leninist parties persistently defined and asserted themselves . . . as the exclusive autarchic locus of political leadership and membership. The political consequence was to reinforce the traditional stark gap between a privileged domineering official realm, and a private realm characterized by mutual suspicion."[51] With the destruction of the Leninist systems, this cleavage has declined in salience (although it has not disappeared, since the managers and bureaucrats have not disappeared), but the capital-labor cleavage has yet to emerge in full force. With the partial exception of Poland, interest groups have not yet made the transition from Communist-controlled to independent organizations capable of exerting political influence. In fact, since it ceased to be compulsory, union membership has declined. In Hungary, the number of members in the pretransition union dropped from about 4.5 million to 2 million during the first two years, whereas newly created unions attracted only three hundred thousand to four hundred thousand members.[52]

It may be that objectively the most important economic cleavage in most post-Communist countries is that between the declining public sector and the rising private sector, rather than the cleavage between capital and labor. This dichotomy, too, lacks organization and political representation.[53]

The difference in the underlying structure of interests leads to differences in the party system. In transitional periods, party leaders search especially actively for policies and specific benefits they can use to attract the support of societal groups and thus assure their own political survival. When the parties are new, as in Eastern Europe, they are relatively unconstrained by past commitments and reputation effects in their search for support.

Society offers the raw material for multiple but not unlimited dimensions along which to organize party competition. At any time, but especially at times of great political and economic ferment and fluidity—such as in Eastern Europe today—multiple potential ways of defining societal interests and divisions exist. Not all potential divisions will become politicized, and self-interested politicians play a role in determining which ones do. In contrast to recent East European experience, it is striking that ethnicity remains largely unpoliticized in Latin American democracies. Only in Bolivia has a significant political party used an appeal to disadvantaged ethnic groups (which form substantial parts of the populations of several countries) as a basis for electoral mobilization.

Furthermore, not all politicized divisions survive the passage of time. Such divisions are far more likely to remain politically central if they become enshrined in political institutions chosen during the brief periods of rapid institutional evolution that punctuate the much longer and more common periods of institutional stability and resistance to change. Politicians, as shown earlier, often make these institutional choices based on immediate electoral calculations with little regard for, or understanding of, their probable long-term effects.

In Eastern Europe, politicians have moved quickly to mobilize ethnic differences into party support (the Movement for Rights and Freedom that represents Turkish interests in Bulgaria; the Hungarian Democratic Union of Romania; numerous small, ethnically based parties in every country; and the Croatian Democratic Union and Slobodan Milosevic's Socialist Party of Serbia) and, to a lesser extent, urban-rural differences (significant peasant parties in all four countries discussed this chapter). Communist successor parties are attempting to establish themselves as representatives of working-class interests, but the transition from autocrat to representative is difficult to make, especially in countries with relatively well-educated and politically sophisticated populations. So far, Communist successor parties have drawn support from fluid coalitions of those who have lost as a result of economic reform.[54] Powerful West European-style labor or social democratic parties linked to organized labor have not arisen, even though a larger part of the population works in blue-collar industry in Eastern Europe than in either Western Europe or Latin America.[55]

The result of the disorganization of interest groups and the weak linkage between urban labor and political parties has been that the populations most hurt by the transition to capitalism have had only limited ability to make effective demands for policy changes. This is not to say that they are totally powerless. They have strikes, demonstrations, and the vote—which can be used as a blunt instrument with which to punish incumbents held responsible for policies that have caused welfare losses. District-level electoral data from Poland and Bulgaria strongly suggest a connection between real wage declines and unemployment and votes against incumbents—as would be expected. The victory of the Communist successor Democratic Left Alliance in the Polish parliamentary elections in September 1993 has been attributed to that group's appeal to state employees, pensioners, and industrial workers in state firms hurt by economic reforms.[56] Its victory has resulted in greater concern for the distribution of the costs and benefits of reform but not in radical changes in economic policy.

Without party leadership to articulate an alternative economic ideology and to coordinate an alliance of multiple interests that could benefit from an alternative set of economic policies, the ability of losers to interfere with the transition to capitalism is limited. They can slow it down, but they cannot divert it onto an altogether different road. Economic hardship seems to be creating less predictability about which parties will consolidate mass support, as voters punish one set of incumbents after another. But in none of these countries do we see the emergence of populist parties or coalitions capable of winning elections and reversing the transition to capitalism; nor do we see organizations representing owners who are frustrated by their inability to secure economic policies they consider tolerable and who are therefore willing to back an authoritarian intervention. In other words, the Peronist alternative that many, including myself, initially thought would be a likely outcome in Eastern Europe now seems more remote. The threat of authoritarianism seems linked more closely to the mobilization of ethnic nationalism and fear than to economic hardship alone.

The transition to capitalism is moving slowly in Eastern Europe, not in those countries in which competitive political systems give injured interests the greatest opportunity to resist reforms but in the least democratic countries in which renamed Communist parties have retained the greatest power. The impediment to reform in these countries comes not from injured interests empowered by democracy but rather from vested interests within and allied to regimes that have been modified but not fundamentally changed by recent political events. Eastern Europe's experience with economic liberalization thus does not differ greatly from that of Latin America or Southern Europe. In all three regions, democratic countries have carried out important steps in the direction of economic liberalization that entailed significant costs to substantial parts of the population without causing regime breakdown, although about half of the initial incumbents have been defeated in subsequent elections.[57] The current crop of Latin American democracies has proven far more resistant to breakdown, despite catastrophic economic conditions, than observers initially predicted.

Although it is too early to speak with certainty, there is little evidence so far of inconsistency between democracy and capitalism in Eastern Europe. The survival of democratic institutions has not been threatened by withdrawal of support caused by disillusionment with capitalism.[58] The greater threat to the establishment of democracy seems to have come in countries in which former Communists were able to mobilize widespread support on the basis of ethnic nationalism and thus to derail the initial creation of democratic institutions. These are the countries in which predictions of turbulence, tumult, and breakdown seem to have been most apt. □

INSTITUTIONS AND CULTURE

Where democratic institutions have taken root, however shallowly, during post-Leninist transitions, they have created compelling incentives that structure the behavior of political elites and thus lead to outcomes similar to those that would occur in other democratic settings. Among the dynamics inherent in even seriously flawed competitive systems are the tendency of aspiring political leaders to mobilize previously excluded groups into the political system to support their own challenges to established leaders and the tendency of leadership competition within parties to result in party cleavages, even when these splits undermine party dominance or reduce the probability that the party will win the next election. Such a split undermined the continued dominance of the Communist successor party in Romania (where opposition parties had shown no sign of being able to dislodge it). As a result, even narrow and flawed democracies contain within them forces that often lead to more inclusive and competitive political systems over the long term.

The cultural legacies of Leninism that are hostile to democracy will not disappear overnight, although cultural traits are neither static nor indefinitely self-perpetuating. To persist, they must be reinforced by formal and informal institutions.[59] To the extent that the cultural legacies of the Leninist experience are inconsistent with democratic institutions, they are currently being eroded in the countries of Eastern Europe in which democracy holds sway. And the longer these institutions persist, the greater the erosion will be. Some of the currently democratic countries of Eastern Europe will probably suffer future authoritarian interludes, although these interludes will not wipe away the legacy of democracy now being created, any more than authoritarian interludes in Latin America have done so.

Periods of rapid institutional change occur rarely. In general, institutions, like species, change only incrementally. Vested interests in political institutions develop with amazing rapidity, quickly ending periods of change. The current spate of institutional creativity can thus be expected to have long-term consequences. As can be seen in the final time period for each country in Table 2.1, the pace of institutional change in Eastern Europe seems already to be subsiding. There will undoubtedly be upheavals in some countries, but it appears that a period of greater institutional stability has arrived. For countries able to maintain competitive systems, the institutions created during the past few years are likely to structure politics for a long time to come. For countries that undergo periods of authoritarianism, redemocratization can be expected to bring in its train a return to many of the institutions recently created. □

NOTES

I am very grateful to Lyubov Mincheva, Dick Anderson, Iván Szelényi, Jerzy Wiatr, Andrzej Korbonski, and John Zaller for their help, information, and advice, and to Kimberly Niles for research assistance on this project. Matthew Shugart, Ellen Comisso, Akos Róna-Tas, Rein Taagepera, David Laitin, and Kaare Strom made very useful comments on earlier versions of this chapter. I owe even more to Ken Jowitt, who sparked my long-standing, although not previously public interest in Eastern Europe and whose ideas have influenced everything I have ever done. The Center on Institutional Reform and the Informal Sector (IRIS), the NSF, and the Center for German and European Studies at the University of California, Berkeley, and the Hoover Institution have made it possible for me to begin to conduct research on a part of the world I have hitherto neglected.

1. Kenneth Jowitt, "A Research Agenda for Eastern Europe," *East European Politics and Societies* 4 (1990): 193–197; Kenneth Jowitt, "A World Without Leninism," in Robert Slater, ed., *Global Transformation in the Third World* (Boulder: Lynne Rienner Publishers, 1991), pp. 9–27; Kenneth Jowitt, "The Leninist Legacy," in Ivo Banac, ed., *Eastern Europe in Revolution* (Ithaca: Cornell University Press, 1992); Kenneth Jowitt, *The New World Disorder: The Leninist Extinction* (Berkeley: University of California Press, 1992), pp. 207–224.

2. See, for example, Adam Przeworski, *Democracy and the Market: Political and Economic Reforms in Eastern Europe and Latin America* (New York: Cambridge University Press, 1991).

3. For example, Stephan Haggard and Robert Kaufman, "The Politics of Stabilization and Structural Adjustment," in Jeffrey Sachs, ed., *Developing Country Debt and Economic Performance: The International Financial System*, Vol. 1 (Chicago: University of Chicago Press, 1989), pp. 209–254; Stephan Haggard and Robert Kaufman, eds., *The Politics of Economic Adjustment* (Princeton: Princeton University Press, 1992); Juan Linz, "The Perils of Presidentialism," *Journal of Democracy* 1, no. 1 (Winter 1990): 51–69; Arturo Valenzuela, "Origins and Characteristics of the Chilean Party System: A Proposal for a Parliamentary Form of Government," Woodrow Wilson Center, Latin American Program, Working Paper no. 164 (Washington, D.C., Woodrow Wilson Center; 1985); Scott

Mainwaring, "Presidentialism, Multipartism, and Democracy: The Difficult Combination," *Comparative Political Studies* 26, no. 2 (1993): 198–228.

4. Seymour Martin Lipset and Stein Rokkan, "Cleavage Structures, Party Systems, and Voter Alignments: An Introduction," in Lipset and Rokkan, eds., *Party Systems and Voter Alignments: Cross-National Perspectives* (New York: Free Press, 1967).

5. Michael Coppedge, "Institutions and Cleavages in the Evolution of Latin American Party Systems," paper presented at the American Political Science Association, Washington D.C. (September 1991); Timothy Scully, *Rethinking the Center: Party Politics in Nineteenth and Twentieth Century Chile* (Stanford: Stanford University Press, 1992).

6. See, for example, Arend Lijphart, "Democratization and Constitutional Choices in Czecho-Slovakia, Hungary, and Poland, 1989–91," *Journal of Theoretical Politics* 4, no. 2 (April 1992): 207–223.

7. For example, Armen Alchian, "Uncertainty, Evolution, and Economic Theory," *Journal of Political Economy* 58 (1950): 211–221; Yoram Barzel, *Economic Analysis of Property Rights* (Cambridge: Cambridge University Press, 1989); Douglass North and Robert Thomas, *The Rise of the Western World: A New Economic History* (Cambridge: Cambridge University Press, 1973); Douglass North, *Structure and Change in Economic History* (New York: Norton, 1981); Oliver Williamson, *Markets and Hierarchies* (New York: Free Press, 1975); Oliver Williamson, *The Economic Institutions of Capitalism* (New York: Free Press, 1985).

8. Douglass North, especially *Institutions, Institutional Change, and Economic Performance* (Cambridge: Cambridge University Press, 1990), is an exception, as is Margaret Levi, *Of Rule and Revenue* (Berkeley: University of California Press, 1988), who draws on this economic literature to build a political argument.

9. Matthew Shugart and John Carey, *Presidents and Assemblies: Constitutional Design and Electoral Dynamics* (Cambridge: Cambridge University Press, 1992).

10. Matthew Shugart, "Of Presidents and Parliaments," *East European Constitutional Review* 2 (1993): 30–32.

11. Lijphart, "Democratization and Constitutional Choices."

12. For details on the translation of votes into seats in Hungary, see John Hibbing and Samuel Patterson, "A Democratic Legislature in the Making: The Historic Hungarian Elections of 1990," *Comparative Political Studies* 24, no. 4 (January 1992): 430–454.

13. Anthony Downs, *An Economic Theory of Democracy* (New York: Harper, 1957); Morris Fiorina, *Congress: Keystone of the Washington Establishment* (New Haven: Yale University Press, 1977); Gary Jacobson and Samuel Kernell, *Strategy and Choice in Congressional Elections*, 2d ed. (New Haven: Yale University Press, 1983); David Mayhew, *Congress: The Electoral Connection* (New Haven: Yale University Press, 1974).

14. Kjell Engelbrekt and Rada Nikolaev, "Bulgaria: Socialist Party Elects New Leader," *RFE/RL* [Radio Free Europe/Radio Liberty] *Research Report* (January 17, 1992): 27–30; Michael Shafir, "Public Opinion One Year After Elections," *RFE/RL Research Report* (June 14, 1991): 22–28; Voytek Zubek, "The Threshold of Poland's Transition: 1989 Electoral Campaign as the Last Act of United Solidarity," *Studies in Comparative Communism* 24 (1991): 355–376.

15. Kjell Engelbrekt, "Cracks in the Union of Democratic Forces," *RFE/RL Report on Eastern Europe* (May 17, 1991): 1–8; Kjell Engelbrekt and Duncan Perry, "The Run-up to the National Elections: Politics and Parties," *RFE/RL Report on Eastern Europe* (October 11, 1991): 4–9; Lyubov Grigorova Mincheva, "Political Institutions and Party System in Bulgaria: 1989–1992," unpublished manuscript, Sofia University, Bulgaria; Duncan Perry, "Bulgaria: A New Constitution and Free Elections," *RFE/RL Research Report* (January 3, 1992): 78–82; Michael Shafir, "'War of the Roses' in Romania's National Salvation Front," *RFE/RL Research Report* (January 24, 1992): 15–22; Gabriel Topor, "The National Salvation Front in Crisis," *RFE/RL Report on Eastern Europe* (August 16, 1991): 24–29; Louisa Vinton, "Solidarity's Rival Offspring: Center Alliance and Democratic Action," *RFE/RL Report on Eastern Europe* (September 21, 1990): 15–25; Zubek, "The Threshold."

16. Zubek, "The Threshold," p. 361.

17. Barbara Geddes and John Zaller, "Sources of Popular Support for Authoritarian Regimes," *American Journal of Political Science* 33, no. 2 (May 1989): 319–347.

18. Ibid.

19. Zubek, "The Threshold," pp. 356–357.

20. Ibid., p. 363.

21. Lijphart, "Democratization and Constitutional Choices."

22. Mincheva, "Political Institutions"; Vladimir Socor, "Political Parties Emerging," *RFE/RL Report on Eastern Europe* (February 16, 1990): 28–35; Luan Troxel, "Socialist Persistence in the Bulgarian Elections of 1990–1991," *East European Quarterly* 26 (1993): 407–430. For discussions of later efforts to democratize local governments in various countries, see Dan Ionescu, "Government Moves to Recentralize Local Administration," *RFE/RL Report on Eastern Europe* (September 7, 1990): 19–24; Jan Kubik, "Local Government: The Basic Laws and Most Common Problems," *RFE/RL Report on Eastern Europe* (May 31, 1991): 19–22; Judith Pataki, "Local Elections Expected to Complete the Political Transition," *RFE/RL Report on Eastern Europe* (October 5, 1990): 18–22; Anna Sabbat-Swidlicka, "Local Self-Government: The Legal Framework," *RFE/RL Report on Eastern Europe* (May 4, 1990): 24–27; Michael Shafir, "Romania Prepares for Local Elections," *RFE/RL Research Report* (January 31, 1992): 15–22; Michael Shafir, "Romanian Local Elections Herald New Political Map," *RFE/RL Research Report* (March 13, 1992): 18–23; Louisa Vinton, "Political Parties and Coalitions in the Local Government Elections," *RFE/RL Report on Eastern Europe* (June 29, 1990): 26–29.

23. Rada Nikolaev, "Preparations for Free Elections of a Grand National Assembly," *RFE/RL Report on Eastern Europe* (June 15, 1990): 6–10.

24. Ibid.; Louisa Vinton, "The Debate over the 'Political Calendar,'" *RFE/RL Report on Eastern Europe* (November 2, 1990): 13–19.

25. David McQuaid, "The 'War' over the Electoral Law," *RFE/RL Report on Eastern Europe* (August 2, 1991): 12; Vinton, "The Debate," p. 16.

26. Anna Sabbat-Swidlicka, "Sejm Rejects President's Proposals for Early Elections," *RFE/RL Report on Eastern Europe* (March 22, 1991): 19.

27. Frances Millard, "The Polish Parliamentary Elections of October 1991," *Soviet Studies* 44 (1992): 851.

28. McQuaid, "The 'War' over the Electoral Law."

29. The successor party in Poland was divided and took no official position. The argument in favor of the open list in Poland was that, given the extreme

fragmentation of the party system and the near absence of party loyalties in the population, the additional personal accountability implied by the open-list system would aid party building. It was expected, on the one hand, to give legislators a strong incentive to pay attention to constituents and, on the other, to allow voters to punish candidates who had not lived up to their expectations without necessarily punishing the candidates' parties. My thanks to Jerzy Wiatr for helping me to understand this aspect of the debate in Poland.

30. Michael Shafir, "The Provisional Council of National Unity: Is History Repeating Itself?" *RFE/RL Report on Eastern Europe* (March 2, 1990): 18–24; Michael Shafir, "The Electoral Law," *RFE/RL Report on Eastern Europe* (May 4, 1990): 28–32.

31. Vera Gavrilov, "Communist Party and Opposition Sign Key Political Agreements," *RFE/RL Report on Eastern Europe* (April 6, 1990): 1–4; Vera Gavrilov, "National Assembly Elects Mladenov President and Sets Stage for Elections," *RFE/RL Report on Eastern Europe* (April 27, 1990): 9–10; Mincheva, "Political Institutions"; Alfred Reisch, "Cliffhanger Referendum Changes Political Timetable," *RFE/RL Report on Eastern Europe* (January 12, 1990): 9–13.

32. Nikolaev, "Preparations for Free Elections."

33. Judith Pataki, "Hungarian Electoral Law Complicates Elections," *RFE/RL Report on Eastern Europe* (March 9, 1990): 33–35.

34. McQuaid, "The 'War' over the Electoral Law"; Sabbat-Swidlicka, "Sejm Rejects"; Vinton, "The Debate." For details of the Polish electoral law, see Millard, "The Polish Parliamentary Elections."

35. Hibbing and Patterson, "A Democratic Legislature," pp. 436–437.

36. Anna Sabbat-Swidlicka, "The Powers of the Presidency," *RFE/RL Report on Eastern Europe* (November 2, 1990): 20–23; Michael Shafir, "Romania's New Institutions: The Parliament," *RFE/RL Report on Eastern Europe* (October 19, 1990): 31–37.

37. Gavrilov, "National Assembly Elects Mladenov"; Mincheva, "Political Institutions."

38. Michael Shafir, "Romania's New Institutions: The Draft Constitution," *RFE/RL Report on Eastern Europe* (September 20, 1991): 22–33; Michael Shafir, "Romania: Constitution Approved in Referendum," *RFE/RL Research Report* (January 10, 1992): 50–55.

39. Mincheva, "Political Institutions"; Rada Nikolaev, "The Bulgarian Presidential Elections," *RFE/RL Research Report* (February 7, 1992): 6–10; Duncan Perry, "Dissident Becomes New President," *RFE/RL Report on Eastern Europe* (August 17, 1990): 3–6.

40. Alfred Reisch, "The New Coalition Government: Its First 100 Days and Beyond," *RFE/RL Report on Eastern Europe* (October 12, 1990): 10–18; Reisch, "Cliffhanger Referendum."

41. Louisa Vinton, "Walesa, 'Special Powers,' and the Balcerowicz Plan," *RFE/RL Report on Eastern Europe* (July 19, 1991): 15–23; Louisa Vinton, "A Postcommunist Parting Shot: Roundtable Sejm Rejects 'Special Powers,'" *RFE/RL Report on Eastern Europe* (October 4, 1991): 10–16.

42. Louisa Vinton, "Poland's 'Little Constitution' Clarifies Walesa's Powers," *RFE/RL Research Report* (September 4, 1992): 19–26; "Special Reports: A 'Little Constitution' in Poland," *East European Constitutional Review* 1, no. 3 (Fall 1992): 12–14.

43. Lijphart, "Democratization and Constitutional Choices."

44. Anna Sabbat-Swidlicka, "Poland in 1989," *RFE/RL Report on Eastern Europe* (January 5, 1990): 25.

45. Matthew Shugart has pointed out that only the Polish president is strong in the sense of having veto power. Nevertheless, the continuous struggles among the president, the government, and parliament in all of the cases in which the president is popularly elected attest to the real power of presidents in these countries to block legislative initiatives at least some of the time. Even in Hungary, the president's struggle to increase his range of influence has not been trivial. See Shugart, "Of Presidents and Parliaments," *East European Constitutional Review* 2 (1993): 30–32.

46. Shugart and Carey, *Presidents and Assemblies.*

47. Barbara Geddes, "Democratic Institutions as Bargains Among Self-Interested Politicians," paper presented at the annual meeting of the American Political Science Association, San Francisco, California, August 30–September 2, 1990.

48. Ibid.

49. Frances Hagopian, "The Compromised Consolidation: The Political Class in the Brazilian Transition," in Scott Mainwaring, Guillermo O'Donnell, and Samuel Valenzuela, eds., *Issues in Democratic Consolidation* (Notre Dame: University of Notre Dame Press, 1992): 243–293.

50. László Bruszt and János Simon, "The Great Transformation in Hungary and Eastern Europe," paper presented at the Southern California Workshop on Political and Economic Liberalization, University of Southern California, Los Angeles, 1992.

51. Jowitt, *The New World Disorder*, p. 287.

52. Bruszt and Simon, "The Great Transformation," p. 196.

53. Survey results reported in Miroslawa Grabowska, "Political Action of Social Groups," in Richard Staar, ed., *Transition to Democracy in Poland* (New York: St. Martin's Press, 1993), p. 45, show virtually no difference in party preference between public- and private-sector employees.

54. Communist successor parties have been most successful where they have based their appeal on nationalism, most notably in Serbia and Romania, and where they have successfully attracted votes from the least educated and sophisticated segments of the population in rural areas, especially in Bulgaria and Romania.

55. A social democratic party exists in the former East Germany as a result of unification. East German workers, however, have tended to vote for the Christian Democrats.

56. To keep the victory of the Democratic Left Alliance (DLA) over the Democratic Union in perspective, we should note that between 1991 and 1993 the DLA increased its share of the vote from 11.9 percent to 20.4 percent, whereas the Democratic Union's share decreased from 12.3 percent to 10.6 percent. In the very fragmented Polish party system, it is not necessary to receive even close to a majority of the vote to win an election. The top vote-getting party has to be able to put together a coalition in order to govern. (For election results, see *The Economist* [September 25, 1993], p. 64.)

57. Substantial reforms have been carried out by Spain, Turkey, Argentina, Bolivia, Colombia, Costa Rica, and Ecuador—all democratic by standard

definitions. See Barbara Geddes, "How Politicians Decide Who Bears the Cost of Economic Liberalization," in Ivan Berend, ed., *Transition to a Market Economy at the End of the Twentieth Century* (Munich: Südosteuropa–Gesellschaft, 1994), for discussions of the effects of economic liberalization on the urban working class in eleven countries, the political factors conducive to privatization in democratic and partially democratic countries, and an explanation of why the social groups injured by economic reform have often been unable to impede such reform even in fully competitive democracies.

58. Low levels of voter turnout are often cited as evidence of declining support for democracy in Eastern Europe, but there is no real evidence that low turnout makes regime change more likely. This interpretation of turnout in Eastern Europe seems especially problematic, since turnout is much higher in Romania and Bulgaria than in Poland and Hungary.

59. Kenneth Jowitt, "An Organizational Approach to the Study of Political Culture in Marxist-Leninist Systems," *American Political Science Review* 68 (1974): 1171–1191.

CHAPTER THREE

—————————— ■ ——————————

Electoral Systems and Electoral Reform in Latin America

Dieter Nohlen

SINCE THE REDEMOCRATIZATION of Latin America, academics and policy-makers south of the Rio Grande have been reexamining three critical aspects of Latin America's political structures:

1. The *political system*, in regard to the structure and functioning of Latin American presidentialism and the possibility of a parliamentary alternative.[1]
2. The *electoral system*, understood in the broadest sense as the electoral regime—suffrage, organization, and the electoral system (in the strict sense, that is, the method of translating votes into seats).[2]
3. The *state structure,* in regard to political or administrative decentralization, regionalization, and local autonomy.[3]

The academic and political debate arising from this reexamination is noteworthy because it breaks with a deeply rooted theoretical tradition and long-observed political practices.

First, the debate highlights the importance of the institutional aspects of politics, which stands in sharp contrast to the historical disdain in Latin America for analysis of the institutional structures of political processes. This new trend is especially pertinent for Latin American social science, whose structuralism—whether cut from the cloth of Marxist, dependency, or modernization theory—had traditionally left no room for thinking about politics from a political-institutional perspective. In its denial that politics was autonomous from economics and socioeconomic processes, the structuralist perspective was true to its own internal logic and was consistent with its own premises.

43

Second, it is important to emphasize the profound reorientation involved in the reconsideration of these issues. In Latin America, political power has traditionally been perceived, conceived, and organized in a strong and centralized fashion. Thus, the discussion of presidentialism and state decentralization calls into question basic characteristics of both the constitutional order and the political-institutional process. Undertaking reforms that move toward the alternatives under discussion here would constitute a true break with long-term political traditions that are anchored in Latin American political culture. In other words, these profound changes occur not only in the political-institutional sphere, they also *originate* there, and thus they may influence political culture. In regard to electoral issues, reforms that attempt to create conditions conducive to the true exercise of universal and equitable suffrage and clear and honest elections are equally noteworthy. The question is how to imbue elections with their full potential for "legitimacy by procedure," a very important issue in the process of democratic consolidation in Latin America.

Although the debate about electoral systems (in their strict sense) does not represent such a historical reorientation, this issue is perhaps the one that has played and will continue to play a preeminent role in the discussions of political-institutional reform. It is legitimate to question the importance attributed to the electoral process, however; in fact, behind the placement of this issue as a top priority we find many myths, much misunderstanding and confusion, and too much short-term political calculation. Nevertheless, regardless of the wide variety of political-historical situations that underlie different democratic consolidations, one must recognize that electoral system reform is perceived as a key—or perhaps *the* key—to reforming the political system. Thus, the discussion of electoral system reform covers the spectrum from Uruguay's pure proportional representation in a political system with a long democratic tradition (embedded in a "hyperintegrated" society) to Mexico's bifurcated system of majoritarian control within a semi-authoritarian regime.[4]

In this chapter I first briefly cover the relations between institutionality and the electoral process on the one hand and political development on the other. Second, I present an overview of Latin America's electoral systems in order to study their effect on political systems. And finally, I consider the electoral reform debate, offering—by way of conclusion—some reflections of a "sociotechnological" nature. □

THE ELECTORAL SYSTEM
AS AN INSTITUTIONAL PHENOMENON

I make three assertions about the importance of the electoral process as an institutional phenomenon and about the limits of its autonomy as an independent variable in the areas of the polity, politics, and policies.

1. Institutions play an important role in the development of politics and in sociopolitical relations. Beginning with Max Weber, intellectuals have viewed modernization as a process of institutionalization. At the same time, institutions delimit political behavior. Basic underlying values about political behavior are shaped by their interdependence with institutions, such that political culture and political institutions influence and mutually condition one another. Finally, institutional regulation is a powerful variable in explaining a government's performance and for understanding differences in performance across nations. At the level of policymaking, institutional reforms are thus more than merely symbolic. They may involve changes in the political order aimed at improving governmental performance.

2. The electoral system's importance for shaping political parties is obvious and, in turn, largely determines the effectiveness of the political system, whether presidentialist or parliamentary. The electoral system also affects governmental performance, a relationship that has only recently gained attention through the debate about "governability."[5]

3. Nevertheless, no monocausal or unilinear relationship exists between the electoral system and the party system. Despite its apparent obviousness, it is important to point this fact out, given that the electoral reform debate does not always recognize the complex interdependence of the countless variables that influence the shape of party systems. Such complexity is difficult to analyze; in other words, it is difficult to adequately discern the effects of the different variables as a set. In systematic terms, we must at a minimum consider:

- Multicausality—the electoral system is only one factor among many to be considered;
- The circular causal relationship—the selection of the electoral system itself depends greatly on the party system as it exists when decisions are taken about its restructuring;
- Historical and sociopolitical contingencies—electoral systems have effects that result directly from their structure and from the interaction of the electoral process with conditions under which elections occur.

This is where my differences with Maurice Duverger and Giovanni Sartori and their widely accepted sociological laws lie.[6] My hypothesis does not dismiss the possibility of determining the effect the electoral process has as a result of its own logic. Sartori's laws come close to mathematical affirmations, whose content cannot be denied but that lack information and are at times even trivial.[7] My position is based on the importance of considering electoral systems in terms of the contingent conditions in which they arise, and it allows for contextualizing the causal relationships under study. This means we must examine electoral system variables within the context of structural variables and of the behavior that characterizes each historical situation in both time and place. □

LEGISLATIVE ELECTORAL SYSTEMS IN LATIN AMERICA

To gain an overview of Latin American electoral systems, I examine certain characteristics of legislatures in unicameral systems and chambers of deputies in bicameral systems. First, of the two overarching alternative arrangements, which form predominates: majority or proportional representation systems? In Latin America the proportional representation system is the standard; Mexico and Chile are the only exceptions.

Second, which of the proportional representation subtypes is the most common in the region? The answer is a system of proportional representation with imperfect remainders in which an exact proportionality between votes and representatives is not the goal. The only exception is Uruguay, with its system of integral proportional representation.[8]

The next questions focus on particular electoral systems. Here we can distinguish among issues related to electoral districts, candidates, the system of voting, and the procedures for counting the votes.

Third, we can examine the characteristics of Latin American electoral districts. Are they large, medium, or small; heterogeneous or uniform? The answer is that electoral districts are multimember in form, and they vary in size. Their distributional structure is different across countries. A deciding factor is the shape of a nation's political-administrative subdivision, since national territories are always broken up into electoral districts delimited by province, department, or state (or, in some cases, territory or federal district). Variability refers to the number of seats in a given district. Proportional representation systems are notable for their many small districts ("small" being defined here as those with no more than five representatives). This observation excludes the special case of Venezuela, where half of the representatives are chosen in single-member districts in a system of personalized proportional representation that took effect in 1993. This is particularly important since in almost every country seats are awarded exclusively at the district level, which means seats are not awarded proportionally at higher levels and compensation procedures do not exist.[9]

The fourth question refers to the selection of candidates and the voting system, which can be examined together since they often mutually condition each other. In proportional representation systems, nomination generally occurs through a list of candidates proposed by each party. One must keep in mind that because of the great number of small electoral districts in the Latin American proportional representation systems, this practice often produces a single- or two-member district. The electoral lists are closed in all cases, and in most cases they are also blocked.[10] The exceptions are Brazil and Peru. In Uruguay, it is debatable whether the candidate list should be described as blocked or not blocked, because legal documents (which many authors accept as a guide) mention both. But the system allows for assorted *sublemas*, that is, lists of candidates created within the main lists. The voter may choose among them but is not permitted to express a preference within a single *sublema*.[11]

Regarding voting, a Latin American voter typically has one vote. Brazil deviates somewhat from the norm: Voters can vote for a list of candidates *or* for an individual candidate. Peru and Venezuela (following reforms in 1989) are also exceptions, since voters in these two countries select one party's complete candidate list rather than voting for individual candidates. In Peru, voters select a list of candidates and can vote preferentially for two candidates. In Venezuela, voters choose one party's candidate for the one seat in their district and with a second vote select a party list in a multimember district. Guatemala is another exception. By means of their votes in the presidential election (which occurs simultaneously with legislative elections), voters choose a quarter of the deputies in the assembly.

One can also ask whether voters are able to vote more than once in the elections for different constitutional organs. In Argentina, Bolivia, the Dominican Republic (until 1990), Honduras, and Uruguay, voters have only one vote for both executive and legislative posts. We thus need to consider whether this linked vote influences electoral outcomes.

The fifth and final question—about the procedures for counting votes—can be divided into two components.

1. Level at which the vote is counted: In most countries the assignment of legislative seats occurs exclusively at the district level. Exceptions include Uruguay, where seats awarded in district elections are linked to an allocation of seats at the national level; Ecuador, where twelve deputies are "national" officials who are elected on a nationwide ballot; Guatemala, where a quarter of the deputies are elected at the national level; El Salvador, where (since the electoral reform of 1993) twenty deputies are selected at the national level; and Venezuela, where (also since 1993) half the deputies are elected in single-member districts established in 1990 within multimember districts (and some additional seats are assigned at the national level).

2. Procedures for counting the vote (the electoral quota or the d'Hondt method): Half of the countries in Latin America utilize the quota method, whereas the other half use the d'Hondt method.[12] The quota method is usually based on a simple calculation (valid votes counted divided by the

number of seats to be distributed). Ecuador and Nicaragua are exceptions for small districts of up to three representatives. Going deeper, however, one finds differences in the electoral quota because of the use of different kinds of data in the calculation. For example, in Brazil the calculation is based on valid votes *and* blank votes. The electoral quota method requires new processes for the assignment of remaining seats. Generally, the rule of the largest remainder is used; in the case of Brazil, the rule of the higher average is used.

In Ecuador (and in Bolivia until 1989), two electoral quotas are used. The first determines the parties that are to be awarded seats. Only then are posts distributed by means of a second use of the electoral quota, calculated now on the basis of a count of only those votes for the selected parties. In the case of Ecuador, however, small parties that win 60 percent of the vote in the first calculation (the quota for elimination) participate in the assignment of remaining seats. This double application of the electoral quota increases the barriers to participation of small parties in the distribution of seats.

Legal barriers to small-party participation, however, are almost unknown in Latin America. The only exception is Argentina, which has a legal lower limit of 3 percent at the district level, calculated on the basis of registered voters (until 1973 the limit was 8 percent). This threshold is so low that it is meaningful only in the two largest districts, the province of Buenos Aires and the Federal district.

In summary, the standard Latin American electoral system is a proportional system with districts of varying sizes. The development of this type of organization appears to depend on the evaluation that may be made about the system's different elements, which determine the specific national features of each system—such as district size, voting practices, mechanism of seat distribution, and entrance barriers. For an accurate evaluation, it is important to take into account the actual effects of electoral systems on political representation. □

ELECTORAL SYSTEM EFFECTS ON THE PARTY SYSTEM

In Latin America, the effect of the proportional system on the party systems is of great interest because of the frequent relationship—found, for instance, in Brazil—among proportional representation, multipartism, the inability of party systems to generate one-party or stable legislative majorities, and governability problems. This holds true in presidential systems as well, even when this form of government—in contrast to parliamentary systems—does not produce an executive that is dependent on the legislature for its inception and its political action. Moreover, some political scientists maintain that proportional representation systems are to some degree responsible for the political problems that have plagued Latin America for decades. They claim it cannot be coincidence that throughout the region proportional representation coexists with political instability and that the combination of presidentialism and proportional representation is the worst of all possible scenarios.[13] In this regard, analysts have established this ranking of efficiency, from most to least efficient: parliamentary system and proportional representation, parliamentary system and majoritarian system, presidentialism and majoritarian system, and finally, presidential system and proportional representation system.[14]

Electoral system effects can be delimited more easily and directly in regard to the votes-seats relationship. What is the degree of proportionality following the conversion of votes into seats, and what consequences does this have for political representation? Are some parties excluded? Do other parties gain legislative majorities, which results—in the case of the presidentialist system—in a legislative majority for the president's party in the national congress?

First, every electoral system exhibits reductive effects; the issue lies in the scope or intensity of these effects, which can be measured by the number of parties competing compared with the number of parties that win legislative seats. A comparison of Latin American data from the 1980s shows that reductive effects vary across countries and that these effects always depend on the electoral system and also on the party system, whose shape is not solely determined by the electoral system.[15] In some countries, it is difficult to make accurate calculations because of the complexity of voting (multiple regional parties, district-level electoral alliances, and so forth). (See Chapter 5 for an example of complexity.) In other countries, the structural complexity of both the parties (internal factionalism) and the electoral system makes analysis difficult (Uruguay and Honduras in 1985 provide examples). In Peru, party alliances, which do not lead to the formation of new legislative groupings, escape the system's possible reductive influence; thus, the number of groups may be greater than the number of parties or alliances that have run in the elections. The reductive influence of the electoral process on the scope of parties disappears. In other words, the possibility of forming electoral alliances in proportional representation systems in districts having reductive effects may erase such effects.

In Nicaragua and also in Guatemala, the reductive effect is negligible. It is somewhat stronger in Ecuador and is considerably stronger in Costa Rica and also—with the reforms of 1986—in Bolivia, where half or fewer than half of the parties won seats in the 1989 election. The reductive effect is strongest in Venezuela, although this is an example of how electoral systems can initially increase the number of parties participating in elections by providing opportunities to mini-parties—in this case, by means of additional seats awarded at the national level. In spite of the party system's natural tendency toward a two-party structure—and the electoral system's collaboration in this tendency—numerous parties win seats in the legislature, albeit with only a few representatives each. In 1983, forty-nine parties took part in the elections, and in 1988, sixty-eight parties participated. In each case, eleven parties won legislative seats.

Second, in regard to the creation of majorities, my analysis of elections occurring during the 1980s in fourteen Latin American countries (in which a minimum of two elections took place) revealed the following: From a total of thirty-nine elections, a party majority was achieved on twenty occasions. These twenty elections occurred in eleven of the fourteen countries (all but Bolivia, Ecuador, and Uruguay). In twelve cases the respective parties won an absolute majority of votes; in eight cases the majorities were created through the electoral system. The lowest percentage of the total vote—but one still sufficient to win an absolute legislative majority—was 38.6 percent in Guatemala's 1985 election. All other percentages exceeded 44 percent, with three exceeding 48 percent.

Concerning party system effects on legislative majorities, it is important to focus more on the concrete results than on generalized impressions, which are always cropping up even though they have no base in empirical fact. Above all, it is clear that bipartisan systems—in which two large parties exist alongside many much smaller parties—create strong antecedents for absolute party majorities in the legislature. This is almost inevitable, mathematically speaking, and comes as no surprise. For that reason, we must not place too much emphasis on such results, especially in those situations where two-party systems, combined with proportional representation, lead to an inherent tendency toward legislative party majorities. During the period of analysis, fourteen of twenty majorities of this kind were produced in two-party systems or incipient two-party systems.

But tripartite systems (which, in terms of numbers, most closely resemble bipartisan systems) seem to guarantee that a sole party will *not* win a majority, regardless of the level of proportional representation. For examples we have Bolivia, the Dominican Republic in 1990, and Uruguay—although changes underway in the party systems in the last two countries have coincided with a shrinking capacity to create party majorities. During the process of constitutional reform, in which part of the former guerrilla movement participated and agreed to electoral competition, it was interesting to speculate whether Colombia would follow a similar path. In the 1994 elections in Colombia, however, the traditional two-party system was reestablished in its entirety.

In any case, Latin American elections in recent years have revealed that a great deal depends on the way in which the spectrum of parties can participate in elections. For example, is the left or the right able to make alliances? Do established parties experience splintering? Much also depends on the volatility of the electorate, which has exhibited extraordinary behavior in certain countries—most notably in Peru. Volatility, whether great or mild, can arise from a variety of causes; noninstitutional factors will be present in any discussion of variables underlying the creation of majority parties (e.g., the problem of issues and candidates in the presidentialist systems that do not allow the reelection of the government in power).

Empirical observations lead us, from the comparative angle, to two hypotheses about tripartite and bipartisan situations. In tripartite systems with relatively nonvolatile, stable structures, it is very difficult for a sole party to attain a legislative majority—unlike presidential elections where, through the mechanism of runoff elections, it is possible for one candidate to achieve an absolute majority. On the other hand, in unstable multiparty systems with significant volatility, a majority is possible, in fact, it is more probable than in a tripartite situation (Guatemala in 1982 and Brazil in 1986 provide examples). Thus, volatility plays the role of an intervening variable, with clear implications for the relationship between the shape of the party system (two party, tripartite, or multiparty) and its ability to produce one-party or stable majorities in support of government action.

On the issue of governability, my findings about the effect of electoral systems on party systems can be summarized as follows.

1. Latin American electoral systems in general have a significant effect, whether reductive (by limiting the number of parties) or disproportional. Thus, without definitively and categorically determining party system structure, electoral systems undoubtedly influence the party system.
2. The capacity of the electoral system to structure the party system depends not only on the reductive effect of the electoral system or its influence on disproportionality but also on the shape of the party system. In other words, the shape of the party system actually affects the repercussions of the electoral system. This is particularly clear when the shape of the party system shifts because of factors not related to the electoral system. One very important variable is the volatility of the electorate, which—thanks to institutional factors such as no-reelection rules, the lack of well-structured parties, and the political culture and conduct (*personalismo*, political erosion)—turns out to be rather prevalent in Latin America compared with highly industrialized nations.
3. Nevertheless, the confluence of all these factors—institutional, structural, political-cultural, behavioral, conjunctural—results in Latin American electoral outcomes that largely resemble those in other parts of the world. If, in about half of the Latin American elections that occurred during the 1980s, the party of the president in power won the absolute majority of legislative seats, the argument that a lack of an

institutional majority would determine the critical relationship between proportional representation and governability within a given Latin American presidentialist system is not convincing.

4. In spite of the fact that in proportional representation systems the shape of the party system is determined in a very limited manner by the electoral system, one must not overlook the possibility, however limited, of political engineering. For example, in Bolivia the trend toward a tripartite organization has been reinforced through the modification of the method of electoral quota. Venezuela is also worth mentioning: Here, a possible trend toward a tripartite system, inserted into the municipal elections by means of the nonblocked list, was checked by the introduction of a personalized proportional representation system—that is, a system with more majoritarian elements in party competition. The crisis of Venezuelan democracy—the total breakup of the two-party system—made it impossible to test the effects of the new electoral system.

5. When we consider the effects of electoral systems on the problem of governability in presidentialist democracies, a question remains about the structure of party factions within the legislatures. In the case of the United States, some scholars claim the presidentialist system lacks incentives for the parties to maintain congressional discipline because government stability does not depend on a congressional majority.[16] In spite of the basic plausibility of this argument, a review of presidentialist democracies in Latin America offers a very different picture, with strong legislative discipline in the cases of Venezuela and Chile and much less structured situations elsewhere, as in Brazil. Much appears to depend on variables both outside the electoral system and outside the system of government itself, even though institutionality doubtless plays an important role. In any case, in this area there may be no quick solution. The development of strong parties (and party systems) with the capacity to guarantee a factional discipline within legislatures requires certain institutional fundamentals, but above all else it will take time and experience. □

ISSUES IN THE DEBATE ON ELECTORAL REFORM

An analysis of the electoral reform debates occurring in many Latin American countries reveals two basic issues that go beyond the particulars of each country case. The first is the relationship of votes to the assignment of seats—in other words, of the greater or lesser degree of proportionality between the electorate's political preferences and the actual legislative composition. What is debated is the overall level of political representation: whether all of a country's active political players are represented. The controversy unfolds in terms of the disjuncture between electoral justice (that is, accurate representation of all of the political tendencies existing in the electorate), and representation as a political institution designed to facilitate, support, critique, and control a representative government.

The second issue is the relationship between the voter and the elected official, that is, representativeness measured by the electorate's degree of familiarity with, and knowledge about, its elected official and the elected official's level of commitment to those who voted for him or her. At a technical level, this distinction translates into the choice between voting for an individual versus voting by means of party lists. What is under discussion is personalized political representation, in which the voter feels represented and the elected official feels linked to the electorate and reacts responsibly to that perception.

The importance of these two issues varies with time and place. All the same, two trends exist that equate to two reform strategies, which in turn are linked to the technical elements necessary to bring these strategies to realization. Regarding the relationship between votes and seats, the first trend aims to maximize the degree of proportionality; its goal, in short, is to increase proportionality. Numerous technical mechanisms in the area of redistricting and the methods of calculating seat distribution can accomplish this goal. The second trend aims to rationalize the vote/seat relationship to facilitate governability. A variety of mechanisms can decrease proportionality or introduce thresholds of representation. These changes can shape the structure of the party system by reducing the number of parties in the legislature or by increasing the likelihood that the party that wins the largest number of votes will be awarded an absolute majority.

Regarding the relationship between the elected official and the voter, the first trend reinforces the vote for the party—a tendency that is exemplified, for example, in the introduction of large, multimember districts (in lieu of single-member or small, multimember districts) or of closed and blocked lists. The second trend reinforces voting for the individual by means of the introduction of single-member or small multimember districts, by means of lists that are open but not blocked, and by preferential or alternative voting (a two-vote system—one by list and the other by individual).

Building on this general conceptual foundation, we can differentiate the issues in the electoral reform debate:

- National debates are characterized largely by their focus on the point of departure, that is, the system currently in force.
- Where a majoritarian system exists, the alternative model under consideration is that of a proportional representation system (New Zealand and Chile are examples).

- Where a high measure of proportionality exists in a proportional representation system, the alternative model examines the possibility for limiting proportionality (Israel is an example).
- In a proportional representation system that uses a list of candidates and in which a weak relationship exists between the voter and the elected official, the alternative model is a system of personalized voting, that is, voting for individual candidates (Venezuela is the sole example).

Generalizing once again, the predominant trend in the current debate leans toward the rationalization of proportionality and personalization of the vote. In other words, in proportional representation systems, the trend favors majoritarian standards (or those traditionally identified with the majoritarian system). □

CONCLUSION

In closing, I formulate some recommendations for reform in Latin America. First, it seems preferable for reforms to be shaped and guided by Latin America's own experience. Without discarding possible innovation and insights garnered outside the region, we must keep in mind that too often problems of institutional transference and adaptation are underestimated. Latin America possesses its own valuable resources for developing electoral systems.

Second, transparency and ease of control of the electoral system must become basic criteria for reform. Sophisticated solutions are not especially valuable. The electoral system should be simple, reliable, and defensible in the face of criticism aimed at delegitimating the electoral outcome which is: political representation.

Third, another basic criterion imposed here is that of consensus. A nation's strongest political actors must agree to the reforms. The electoral system is a fundamental part of the rules of the democratic game: It must not serve as an instrument of power.

Fourth, the use of both incrementalism and functional adaptation of the system to institutional requisites is recommended.

As I established earlier, the standard Latin American electoral system is proportional, with variable-sized, multimember districts that correspond to the political-administrative division of a country. It is also characterized by voting through candidate lists and by a lack of thresholds of representation. I recommend a reform that improves political representation—taken to mean an egalitarian representation of the people by a candidate—which in many parts of Latin America is very distorted because of the way seats are distributed by district (for example, according to the constitutional minimums). It would be best to minimize criticism concerning effective representation by improving the relationship between voters and elected officials. Such a reform should not hurt political parties, and, for this reason, nonblocked lists or preferential votes do not appear to be the most effective reform measure, at least not at the level of national elections.

I propose as a foundation the mechanism of single-member districts within a proportional representation system. The electoral reforms in Venezuela (1990) and Bolivia (1993) have moved in this direction (as did those in New Zealand in 1993). They go a long way toward introducing a system based on the German electoral system, which is a personalized proportional representation system. In regard to the relation of votes to seats, because the great majority of the electoral systems fall within the subtype of restricted or rationalized proportional representation systems, it would not be wise to concentrate reform efforts in this area.

In summary, considering the criticisms of the current electoral systems in Latin America, the functioning of those systems, and the actual outcomes and normative standards available to guide the reform, an opening exists for electoral system transformation. That opening is small. It is reasonable to fear that because of the complexity of the problem, the lack of full understanding and evaluation of currently functioning systems, political agenda that underestimate institutional problems, and conjunctural political calculations, the attempts at electoral reform may fail. □

NOTES

Translated by Patricia Rosas.

1. See, for instance, Consejo para la Consolidación de la Democracia, *Reforma constitucional* (Buenos Aires: Eudeba, 1986); Juan J. Linz and Arturo Valenzuela, eds., *The Failure of Presidential Democracy* (Balimore: John Hopkins University Press, 1994); Dieter Nohlen, ed., *Reforma política y consolidación democrática* (Caracas: Nueva Sociedad, 1988); Dieter Nohlen and Mario Fernández, eds., *Presidencialismo versus parlamentarismo. América Latina* (Caracas: Nueva Sociedad, 1991); Dieter Nohlen and Liliana De Riz, eds., *Reforma institucional y cambio político* (Buenos Aires: CEDES/Legasa, 1991).

2. See, for instance, Fundación Friedrich Ebert/Instituto de Cooperación Iberoamericana (FFE/ICI), ed., *Sistemas electorales y representación política en América Latina*, 2 vols. (Madrid: FFE/ICI, 1986); Dieter Nohlen, ed., *Elecciones y sistemas de partidos en América Latina* (San José: Centro de Asesoría y Promoción Electoral/Instituto Interamericano de Derechos Humanos (CAPEL/IIDH), 1993); Dieter Nohlen, *Sistemas electorales de América Latina. Debate sobre la reforma electoral* (Lima: Fundación Friedrich Ebert, 1993); Dieter Nohlen and Juan Rial, eds., *Reforma electoral, ¿posible, deseable?* (Montevideo: FESUR/EBU, 1988).

3. See, for instance, Consejo Latinoamericano de Centros en Ciencias Sociales (CLACSO), ed., *¿Hacia un nuevo orden estatal en América Latina?* Vol. 6: *Centalización/descentralización del Estado y actores territoriales* (Buenos Aires:

CLACSO, 1989); Dieter Nohlen, ed., *Descentralización política y consolidación democrática. Europa-América del Sur* (Caracas: Nueva Sociedad, 1991).

4. The majoritarian nature of Mexican electoral systems was reformed through the elimination of the governability clause in 1993 (see Chapter 8). For a discussion of the nature of the Mexican electoral system after this reform, see Dieter Nohlen, *Elecciones y sistemas electorales* (Caracas: Nueva Sociedad, 1995).

5. See Dieter Nohlen, "Sistemas electorales y governabilidad," *Boletin Electoral Latinamericano 6* (San José: CAPEL/IIDH, 1992): 85-110.

6. See especially Maurice Duverger, *Les partis politiques* (Paris: Colin, 1951), and Giovanni Sartori, "The Influence of Electoral systems: Faulty Laws or Faulty Methods?" in Bernard Grofman and Arend Lijphart, eds., *Electoral Laws and Their Political Consequences* (New York: Agathon Press, 1986), pp. 43–68.

7. See Dieter Nohlen, *La reforma electoral en América Latina. Seis contribuciones al debate* (San José: CAPEL/IIDH, 1988), pp. 54–58, and Dieter Nohlen, *Sistemas electorales y partidos políticos* (Mexico City: Universidad Nacional Autónoma de México/Fondo de Cultura Económica, 1994), pp. 334–342.

8. It is true that some countries—Nicaragua, for example—achieve relatively proportional electoral results. For a typology of modern electoral systems, especially those that combine single-member districts with some kind of proportional list—as in the case of Bolivia (the reforms of 1994), Mexico, Venezuela, and, outside Latin America, Germany, Japan, Italy, New Zealand, Russia, and others, see Nohlen, *Elecciones y sistemas electorales.*

9. To some extent, Ecuador and Guatemala constitute an exception because of their parallel nationwide districts. Uruguay has a system of integral proportional representation in which the relationship between votes and representatives is set at the national level.

10. In Latin America, the term "closed list" is used to cover any list PR system in which a voter cannot cross party lines (for instance, by dividing his or her vote among two or more party lists). If, in addition, a voter cannot mark an order of preference or indicate at least one preferred candidate within a list, the lists are regarded as "closed and blocked" (that is, equivalent to what would simply be called a "closed" list according to standard terminology outside Latin America).

11. For a detailed analysis, see Nohlen, *Sistemas electorales y partidos políticos*, pp. 249–64.

12. According to the d'Hondt method, seats are awarded sequentially to parties having the highest numbers of votes per seat already won plus one. This method tends to yield somewhat less proportional results than the quota method. At times, reference is made to the *cifra repartidora* (distribution number), but in reality this is merely an extension of the d'Hondt method by means of certain calculations. See Arend Lijphart, "Electoral Systems" and "Proportional Representation," in Seymour Martin Lipset, ed., *The Encyclopedia of Democracy* (Washington, D.C.: Congressional Quarterly, 1995), Vol. 2, pp. 412–422, and Vol. 3, pp. 1010–1016, respectively.

13. See André Blais and Stephane Dion, eds., *The Budget Maximizing Bureaucrat: Appraisals and Evidence* (Pittsburgh: University of Pittsburgh Press, 1991).

14. Arend Lijphart, "Forms of Democray: North-South and East-West Contrasts," in Wolfgang Reinhard and Peter Waldmann, eds., *Nord und Süd In Amerika: Gegensätze, Gemeinsamkeiten, Europäischer Hintergrund,* Vol. 2 (Freiburg: Romback, 1992), pp. 933–942.

15. See Dieter Nohlen, ed., *Enciclopedia electoral latinoamericana y del Caribe* (San José: Instituto Interamericano de Derechos Humanos, 1993).

16. Gary Jacobson, *The Electoral Origins of Divided Government: Competition in U.S. House Elections, 1946-1988* (Boulder: Westview Press, 1990): Juan Linz, "The Perils of Presidentialism," *Journal of Democracy* 1, no. 1 (1990): 51-69: Scott Mainwaring, "Presidentialism, Multiparty Systems, and Democracy: The Difficult Combination," *Comparative Political Studies* 26, no. 2 (1993): 198–228.

CHAPTER FOUR

■

Proportional Representation Versus Majoritarian Systems: Free Elections and Political Parties in Poland, 1989–1991

Stanislaw Gebethner

THE POLITICAL CONSEQUENCES of electoral systems—especially the connection between proportional representation and the multiparty system, which can give rise to cabinet instability—have been debated ever since the 1950s when Maurice Duverger formulated his "iron sociological law."[1] According to this law, majoritarian (especially plurality) electoral systems produce two-party systems with stable governments, whereas proportional representation (PR) leads to fragmented multiparty systems and unstable governments.[2] As East European countries have undertaken the transition to pluralist democracy, old controversies over how electoral systems affect party systems have been reactivated.[3]

I support the view that a party system in general precedes the electoral system. Where multiparty systems already exist, PR tends to be adopted to eliminate the wide discrepancies between shares of votes and seats, to prevent one party from winning an overall majority in the parliament, or to save a minority party from possible exclusion from power. Electoral systems thus seem to express a society's deeper determinants.[4] Nevertheless, I must agree with Rein Taagepera and Matthew Shugart, who think politics and electoral systems interact in complex, bidirectional ways.[5] This means party politics and the socioeconomic situation of a given country affect its electoral system, just as the electoral system affects politics.

In this chapter I focus primarily on the outcomes of the first and second parliamentary elections in post-1989 Poland. I examine the reasons the Polish Parliament voted in 1991 for an electoral system based on PR for elections to the Sejm and for a plurality system for elections to the Senate. Because Poland is an extreme example of (more or less visible) fragmentation of the political arena, the Sejm's electoral rules have been fiercely criticized for causing that splintering, with the blame placed particularly on the adoption of the Hare method of seat allocation (i.e., of the largest remainder) with no legal threshold.[6] The inaccuracy of that criticism is discussed in detail here. □

PARTY SYSTEM FRAGMENTATION AND THE CHOICE OF ELECTORAL SYSTEMS

The final form of Poland's electoral law, passed in June 1991, was determined largely by the nature of previous elections and by the paucity of mature political parties sufficiently anchored in civil society.[7] Five national votes took place between 1989 and the adoption of the 1991 electoral law: the parliamentary elections of June 1989 (two rounds of voting), the municipal elections of May 1990, and the presidential election of November-December 1990 (also with two rounds of voting).

The essence of the 1989 roundtable agreement on Sejm elections was that seat allocation would take place prior to the voting. The agreement stipulated that the governing coalition (then composed of the Polish United Workers' Party [PZPR], the United Peasant Party [ZSL], the Democratic Party [SD], and three small Christian political groupings) would receive 65 percent of the seats, and nonparty candidates would compete for the other 35 percent. In practice, candidates supported by Solidarity could compete for the second bloc of seats, and, in fact, all of these seats were won by candidates who ran for election under the Solidarity label of the Civic Parliamentary Club (OKP). The 65 percent of seats in the Sejm were allocated to partners of the governing coalition according to a settlement reached by them. In the Senate election, in which no seats were preallocated, Solidarity candidates won all but one of the seats.

After the 1989 elections, both the domestic and the external scene changed radically. The international environment was altered as a result of the 1989 Autumn of Nations in Eastern and Central Europe. In Poland, the hegemonic party system collapsed, and the PZPR disappeared. The civic Solidarity movement gradually disintegrated, and its parliamentary representation was split. Similarly, deputies from the former PZPR created four separate parliamentary clubs in the Sejm.

After the presidential election, followers of the defeated candidate, Tadeusz Mazowiecki, dropped out of the OKP and created a parliamentary club, the Democratic Union. This reduced the OKP to only 106

TABLE 4.1 Political Groups in the Sejm Before Dissolution in 1991

	Number	Percent
Former Polish United Workers' Party (PZPR) deputies		
Parliamentary Club of the Democratic Left	103	22.39
(including twenty Social-Democracy deputies)		4.35
Polish Social-Democratic Union	41	8.91
Club of Independent Deputies	9	1.96
Militarymen's Independent Deputies	7	1.52
Party X	1	0.23
Former PZPR allies		
Polish Peasant Party	75	16.30
Democratic Party	21	4.56
Association PAX (Catholics)	10	2.17
Christian Social Union	8	1.74
Polish Catholic-Social Association	5	1.09
Solidarity deputies		
Civic Parliamentary Club	106	23.04
Democratic Union Club	43	9.35
Solidarity of Labor	6	1.30
Polish Peasant Party—small	4	0.87
Nonaffiliated	20	4.35

deputies, among whom splintering was already occurring. By 1991, the Sejm had fragmented significantly, which inevitably affected the choice of a future electoral system. The composition of the Sejm according to a division of deputies affiliated with different parliamentary groups before the dissolution of the Parliament in 1991 is shown in Table 4.1.

Given the parliamentary fragmentation, clearly nobody wanted a majoritarian (especially a plurality) system. Despite the political rhetoric, all blocs in the Sejm preferred PR rules. This system was selected by, and adopted for the benefit of, the fractured post-Solidarity political groupings.

On March 8, 1990, the Sejm approved the legal framework for local government reform. The constitution was revised, and the Soviet pattern of people's councils was replaced with municipal councils. These laws introduced two different electoral systems. Single-member districts were created in municipalities of fewer than forty thousand inhabitants, and council members were elected under the plurality system. In municipalities with more than forty thousand inhabitants, a PR system that used the Scandinavian Sainte-Laguë method of seat allocation was adopted.[8] To be nominated, candidates in single-member districts had to get at least 50 signatures. Candidates in multimember districts needed 150 signatures.

Some regions experienced a problem finding candidates to run in the elections. Ultimately, in forty-four single-member districts no nominations were made. In other districts only one candidate stood for election.

This was a strong signal of a lack of public interest, and it was a visible symptom of the weakness of political parties and civic organizations, in particular the Solidarity-sponsored Civic Committees. The low voter turnout of only 42 percent of registered voters attested to the widespread public apathy for democratic electoral procedures in the creation of local government bodies.

The overall majority of seats in municipal councils was won by Civic Committee candidates or other organizations under the Solidarity label. The general results of the 1990 local elections are presented in Table 4.2. Solidarity triumphed once again, but its popular support was reduced from its level in the 1989 parliamentary elections to only about 23 percent of the eligible voters. This was the first signal that Solidarity's constituency was melting away. □

THE 1990 PRESIDENTIAL ELECTION

The presidential election that took place in fall 1990 deeply influenced the shape of the electoral law adopted for the next parliamentary elections. The initiation of a new party system occurred simultaneously. Internal splits within the Solidarity camp had begun to appear, as was evident from the creation of factions within the framework of the OKP and in regional competition between rival Solidarity groups during local elections. In spite of these rifts, Lech Walesa—concerned about both his declining popularity and the increasing prestige of Prime Minister Tadeusz Mazowiecki—declared his candidacy for the presidency in April 1990. At the same time, there were signs of social tension and industrial labor unrest. Walesa distanced himself from the Mazowiecki government and launched his presidential campaign with a populist platform, which stirred up adversaries within the Solidarity camp to Walesa's potential election. To stop his presidential ambitions, these adversaries introduced constitutional amendments requiring the election of the president by universal suffrage, assuming that in direct universal voting Walesa would be defeated by Mazowiecki.

This move, however, reversed the tentative schedule for institutional transformation (first the adoption of a new constitution, then free parliamentary elections, and finally a presidential election). Instead, the presidential election preceded both the enactment of a new constitution and the parliamentary elections. By September 27, 1990, the Sejm and the Senate had approved the constitutional amendments and the Law on the Election of the President of the Republic, and President Wojciech Jaruzelski faced a curtailed term in office.

According to the electoral law, the nomination of presidential candidates required the support of at least one hundred thousand voters. To win election, a candidate had to obtain the overall majority of valid votes cast. If no candidate won such a majority, a second ballot became neces-

TABLE 4.2   Results of Polish Municipal Elections, 1990

	Percentage of Votes Cast	*Percentage of Eligible Electorate*
Civic Committees	50.0	21.2
Polish Peasant Party	4.8	2.0
Social-Democracy of the Republic of Poland	2.7	1.1
Autonomous Independent Trade Unions "Solidarity"	2.6	1.1
Democratic Party	2.1	0.9
Rural "Solidarity"	1.7	0.7
Confederation for Independent Poland	1.0	0.4
Trade unions, professional associations, and other civic organizations	5.9	2.5
Others	26.5	11.2

Note: Invalid votes and non-voters are not included in the percentages.

sary, with a runoff between the two candidates who had won the largest number of votes in the first balloting.

Solidarity groups believed almost unanimously that the presidential election would be an internal affair within the ruling establishment, consisting of competition between two Solidarity politicians, Mazowiecki and Walesa. Walesa expected he would win in one round with a comfortable majority of at least 75 percent. Many within Solidarity believed the Polish electorate was under the absolute control of Solidarity—and that the old political parties (representing the ancien régime), as well as new ones created outside Solidarity (like the Confederation for an Independent Poland [KPN]), were marginal and insignificant.

Given the weakness of political parties, many Solidarity politicians even doubted that any one group would collect the signatures required for a nomination. What is more, the period for collecting signatures was extremely short—only two weeks.

The most influential Solidarity politicians propagated the theory of an end to political parties as such, and they planned for the creation of two electoral machines (like early U.S. parties) that would be called into being by Solidarity and that would compete against each other in the next parliamentary elections. Former Prime Minister Mazowiecki eventually admitted that his government had seriously misread the existing social and political reality. But this error of judgment served, to some extent, to delay the establishment of a new multiparty system—a development that is now recognized as a major difference between Poland and Hungary. In the latter, the first free parliamentary elections, in March 1990, occurred when the new multiparty system was already fairly well formed. In

Poland, in contrast, the fully free parliamentary elections took place when the formation of the new multiparty system was still in its infancy.

At the end of 1990, there were sixteen contenders in the Polish presidential campaign. However, six were not serious candidates, two succeeded in gathering only around seventy thousand signatures (not enough to qualify), and two more withdrew from the race. Only the remaining six were successful in gaining formal nomination, including the two primary rivals, Walesa and Mazowiecki. Leaving aside the surprising nomination of Stanislaw Tyminski, the other three less popular candidates—Wlodzimierz Cimoszewicz, Roman Bartoszcze, and Leszek Moczulski—disproved the view that political parties were so weak that they would not be able to challenge the two separate Solidarity electoral machines working for Walesa and Mazowiecki.

Especially momentous was the nomination of Cimoszewicz, which represented the post-Communist, left-oriented electorate, because it showed that the Social-Democracy of the Republic of Poland (SdRP)—the successor of the dissolved PZPR—was still a force to be reckoned with. In the first round, Cimoszewicz overcame the symbolic 5 percent threshold of votes cast, although this represented only 5 percent of the eligible voters. This result, however, anticipated the success of the Democratic Left Alliance (SLD) in the parliamentary elections in 1991. The same can be said about Moczulski, leader of the then generally ignored KPN. Moczulski was seemingly the greatest loser in the presidential election, obtaining only 2.5 percent of the votes cast. But his participation in the presidential race encouraged KPN members to work for further success in the forthcoming parliamentary elections. Bartoszcze, the unsuccessful leader of the Polish Peasant Party (PSL), in spite of his weak campaign, proved that his party was an important actor on the Polish political scene.

Nevertheless, in 1990 Polish political parties were feeble and were only weakly anchored in society. Dozens of groups claimed the status of "party." Few, if any, were political parties in the usual sense. Significantly, few Poles trusted any political party following the failure of "real socialism." Antiparty feeling is characteristic of all the post-Communist societies throughout Central and Eastern Europe, as illustrated by the results of three 1990 sociological surveys I performed in August, November (just before the first round of presidential elections), and December (after the second round of presidential elections). Respondents were asked: "What political party would you vote for if the elections to the Sejm were today?" Antiparty sentiment, or at least indifference, was widespread and growing: In the December survey, half of the respondents (51 percent) had no opinion or favored no political party (see Table 4.3).

The most popular parties were the Solidarity Civic Committees, which were viewed by the general public as a nonparty civic movement. Support for the Civic Committees, however, rapidly decreased—from nearly 40 percent in August 1990 to 15 percent in December of that year.

TABLE 4.3 Support for Political Parties and Groups in Poland, 1990 (%)

	August	November	December
Solidarity Civic Committees	38.7	20.3	15.7
Polish Peasant Party	6.3	8.3	6.0
Center Alliance	—	6.0	8.0
Democratic Action	—	5.9	3.9
Polish Peasant Solidarity Party	4.2	3.6	3.4
Social-Democracy of the Republic of Poland	1.2	2.0	2.0
Confederation for an Independent Poland	2.6	2.8	1.2
Democratic Party	2.1	1.4	0.9
Christian-National Union	2.3	2.3	0.8
Polish Green Party	2.7	1.0	0.7
Freedom Party	—	0.5	0.6
Christian Democracy-Labor Party	0.9	0.6	0.5
Forum of Democratic Right	—	—	0.5
Union of Real Politics	0.9	0.9	0.4
Polish Socialist Party	0.9	0.5	0.2
National Party	0.1	0.6	0.2
Liberal-Democratic Congress	0.1	—	0.1
Polish Social-Democratic Union	0.2	0.2	—
Favor none of the parties	6.4	13.8	14.5
Difficult to answer	28.3	28.7	36.5

Note: These three surveys were conducted using representative nationwide random samples of approximately one thousand respondents each.

Support for each separate post-Solidarity political party—the Center Alliance, Democratic Action, the Democratic Union, and the Polish Peasant Solidarity Party—was also low (below 10 percent for each). Added together, however, the post-Solidarity parties and the Civic Committees still had the support of 34.9 percent of the respondents. If we compare this figure with the results of the 1989 parliamentary elections and those of the 1990 presidential election, it is obvious that Solidarity still had consistent support from more than one-third of the eligible Polish voters, whereas other new political parties had only slight support. The PSL and SdRP, two parties that inherited the legacy of the Polish People's Republic, could both have been easily eliminated from the Sejm under an electoral law providing a barrier of 5 percent (as was proposed).

   The outcomes of the surveys led me to the conclusion—formulated before the 1991 elections—that none of the political parties would obtain more than 10 percent of the total votes cast, which was nearly correct.[9] This illustrates that party politics and the balance of power in Parliament and in the country are deciding factors in the adoption of a given electoral system and ultimately determine the final results of elections.

Above all, the election results revealed that Solidarity no longer controlled the Polish electorate. Although taken together the two Solidarity candidates won 34.6 percent of the electorate at large (see Table 4.4), the spectacular defeat of Mazowiecki by a Polish emigrant from Canada, Stanislaw Tyminski, was a shock. His success in the first round of the 1989 presidential election is evidence of the strong opposition to both Solidarity and the post-Communists. Votes gained by Cimoszewicz, Bartoszcze, and Moczulski also portended the political fractionalization of the Polish electorate that manifested itself in the 1991 parliamentary elections.

The most important consequence of the presidential elections, however, was the fact that the forthcoming parliamentary elections would not take place under a majoritarian system. Because Poland again faced voter apathy and absenteeism in the presidential election (see Table 4.5), fear of such apathy led parliamentarians to reject electoral laws providing two-round ballots for either the Sejm or the Senate. In the five Polish elections between 1989 and 1990, the turnout ranged from 25 to 62 percent. The main reason for the introduction of PR (with the method of the largest remainder in regard to seat allocation by electoral district) was the fragmentation of the political scene, which was profoundly increased by the presidential campaign that led to sharp conflict within Solidarity. □

DESIGNING THE 1991 ELECTORAL SYSTEMS

Some crucial moments occurred in party politics in Poland between 1989 and 1991. Whatever limits were imposed by the roundtable's contract on the Sejm elections, as described previously, the vote of June 4, 1989, led to a landslide victory for Solidarity and a humiliating defeat for the PZPR. On June 6, the PZPR leadership conceded defeat and accepted the rules of parliamentary democracy. This was the beginning of the end for the hegemonic PZPR and its alliance with the ZSL and the SD. The extent of the defeat influenced relations between the PZPR and these parties by forcing radical changes in the party system, which had become visibly anachronistic.

After the 1989 elections, the regrouping and reaffiliation of Sejm deputies reflected deep political transformations occurring within what until then had been the government establishment. The decomposition of the PZPR was the key force in this realignment.

Simultaneously, in fall 1990, internal conflicts in the OKP were increasingly obvious. The OKP, created by Solidarity as a heterogeneous political protest movement struggling against both the old political system and the monopolistic power of the PZPR, lost its purpose when the old regime collapsed. With the disappearance of the PZPR from the political arena, the civic Solidarity movement—both in Parliament and in Poland generally—experienced disputes, splits, and internal divisions within the OKP. This

TABLE 4.4 Results of Poland's 1991 Sejm Election Compared to the 1990 Presidential Election

Political Coalition	1991 Parliamentary Elections			1990 Presidential Elections		
	Votes	Percentage of Votes Cast	Percentage of Eligible Electorate	Votes	Percentage of Votes cast	Percentage of Eligible Electorate
Walesa				6,569,889	40.0	23.86
Christian National Union	4,395,884	39.18	15.98			
Center Civic Alliance	1,007,890	8.98	3.66			
Liberal Democratic Congress	977,344	8.71	3.55			
Peasant Alliance	839,978	7.49	3.05			
Autonomous Independent Trade Unions "S"	613,626	5.47	2.23			
	566,553	5.05	2.06			
Christian Democracy	265,179	2.25	0.96			
Party of Christian Democrats	125,314	1.12	0.46			
Tyminski	52,735	0.47	0.19	3,797,605	23.1	13.49
Party X	52,735	0.47	0.19			
Mazowiecki	1,664,682	14.84	6.05	2,973,264	18.1	10.79
Democratic Union	1,382,051	12.32	5.02			
"Solidarity of Labor"	230,975	2.06	0.84			
Democratic Social Movement	51,656	0.46	0.19			
Cimoszewicz	1,344,820	11.99	4.89	1,514,025	9.2	5.50
Democratic Left Alliance	1,344,820	11.99	4.89			
Bartoszcze	1,033,885	9.22	3.76	1,176,175	7.2	4.27
Polish Peasant Party	1,033,885	9.22	3.76			
Moczulski	996,182	8.88	3.62	411,516	2.5	1.49
Confederation for an Independent Poland	996,182	8.88	3.62			

TABLE 4.5 Voter Turnouts in Poland, 1989–1991

Election	Percentage of Eligible Voters
Parliamentary Elections, June 1989	
First Round	62.32
Second Round	25.11
Local Elections, May 1990	42.47
Presidential Elections, 1990	
First Round (November)	60.63
Second Round (December)	53.40
Parliamentary Elections, October 1991	43.20

situation launched a second phase of advanced fragmentation within the Polish political arena that was produced by a combination of three factors: (1) splits within the old establishment, (2) attempts to recreate traditional parties, and (3) spontaneous mushrooming of new parties or quasi parties.

Only a few months prior to anticipated parliamentary elections, the Polish parliamentary scene was in disarray. As discussed previously, the 1990 presidential campaign—which was dominated by the struggle between the two prominent Solidarity figures, Walesa and Mazowiecki—produced the final split within Solidarity itself, and the creation of various new post-Solidarity political parties reinforced that fragmentation. This splintering proved to be a decisive factor in the final shape of the 1991 electoral law. The highly fragmented Sejm accepted a Hare version of PR (i.e., the method of the largest remainder in seat allocation) instead of the Sainte-Laguë or d'Hondt method (i.e., the highest average), and it rejected any legal thresholds. Thus, the many parties and groups would avoid being victimized by legal threshold requirements or by a seat allocation method that favored stronger parties. The one exception was the application of a 5 percent threshold to the allocation of 69 seats (i.e., 15 percent of the total 460 Sejm seats) to the parties' national lists. The Sainte-Laguë method was used for the seat allocation for national lists.

The other 391 seats were distributed among thirty-seven multimember districts according to their population size. Electoral districts ranged from seven to seventeen seats, and the districts included one to three provinces (*voivodeships*). The two most populous *voivodeships* were divided into two or three separate electoral districts.

The electoral law for the Senate was similar to the one adopted in 1989, with one important difference: An overall majority system with two ballots was replaced by a plurality system with a single ballot. The nomination of candidates was uncomplicated. Lists for electoral districts were created by a local electoral committee made up of at least three voters who could collect a minimum of five thousand voter signatures of support. Sixty-four local committees were established that registered their list of candidates for a single electoral district only.

Nationwide electoral committees set up by political parties or their coalitions, or by trade unions or other organizations, were able to nominate lists in more than one electoral district once they collected a minimum of five thousand voter signatures in at least five districts. Achieving this level of support gave these committees the right to nominate a list of candidates in all of the remaining districts without having to collect further signatures. In the end, however, only twenty-nine nationwide electoral committees were able to nominate their lists of candidates across all of Poland. Thus, they were (with one exception) also entitled to nominate national lists.

Initially, 65 nationwide committees were formed. Of these, 18 failed to collect the necessary signatures and thus lost the right to nominate a list; another 12 were able to register their lists in only two, three, or four electoral districts; and 6 nominated their list in only one district. Nearly three-quarters of all 111 electoral committees (both the national and local ones) failed to gain seats in the Sejm. In the October 1991 election, 66 committees obtained fewer than five thousand supporters. It could be said that Polish voters behaved rationally in regard to these fringe candidates—a fact that has been neglected in almost all analyses of the 1991 parliamentary elections. □

THE 1991 RESULTS: FRAGMENTATION IN BOTH HOUSES

The 1991 electoral law is often blamed for the fragmentation of the Sejm. It may appear as though this law created twenty-nine separate political parties that were able to place their candidates in Parliament, but this is inaccurate. Although deputies elected to the Sejm ran under twenty-nine differently labeled electoral committees, most of these were merely different names selected locally for tactical reasons. This was the case, for example, with two peasant parties allied with the KPN (see notes to Table 4.6). In addition, some committees were set up only to support the election of individual candidates, and they lacked any real political party: for example, the Democratic Social Movement, the Tatra Highlanders' Union, the Social-Democratic Union in Poznan, the Electoral Committee of Orthodoxies, the Trade Union "Solidarity '80," or the regional Union of Ziema Lubuska—all of which are examples of single-seat "parties." These six combined with the two deputies from the Silesian Autonomous Movement and one from the SD, created a total of nine "single-seat deputies."

Furthermore, 424 (or 92.2 percent) of the Sejm's deputies represented ten political parties or party coalitions or were registered by trade unions (the top ten groups in Table 4.6). Together with the seven deputies of the German Minority, they controlled 93.7 percent of all seats in the Sejm.

TABLE 4.6 1991 Sejm Elections: Votes Won and Seat Allocation by Political Grouping

Political Group	Votes	Seats	Seats (%)	Votes (%)	Percentage of Eligible Electorate
Democratic Union	1,382,051	62	13.48	12.32	5.02
Democratic Left Alliance	1,344,820	60	13.04	11.99	4.89
Confederation for an Independent Poland[a]	996,182	51	11.09	8.88	3.62
Polish Peasant Party[b]	1,033,885	50	10.87	9.22	3.76
National Christian Union	980,304	49	10.65	8.74	31.56
Center Civic Alliance	977,344	44	9.57	8.71	3.55
Liberal-Democratic Congress	839,978	37	8.04	7.49	3.05
Peasant Alliance	613,626	28	6.09	5.47	2.23
Autonomous Independent Trade Unions "Solidarity"	566,553	27	5.87	5.05	2.06
Polish Beer Lovers' Party	367,106	16	3.48	2.97	1.33
German Minority	132,059	7	1.52	1.17	0.48
Christian Democracy	265,179	5	1.09	2.25	0.96
Christian Democratic Party[c]	152,900	5	1.09	1.36	0.56
Solidarity of Labor	230,975	4	0.87	2.06	0.84
Union of Real Politics	253,024	3	0.65	2.25	.92
Party X	52,735	3	0.65	0.47	0.19
Others	336,803	9	1.96	3.00	1.22
Failed groups	693,078	—	—	6.18	2.52

[a] I added four deputies elected from lists of the Polish Western Union (Nationalists) and a female deputy elected in Krakow from the list labeled "Women Against the Difficulties of Life." These lists were blocked with the lists of the KPN for the allocation of seats both in the electoral district and in Poland as a whole. The five deputies initially joined the KPN's parliamentary faction in the Sejm. The total number of votes indicated in this table as votes cast for the KPN also includes all votes for lists blocked with the KPN.

[b] I added two two deputies elected in two electoral districts (Tarnow and Bydgoszcz), where the PSL did not nominate its own lists but supported candidates who were close to the PSL platform, although they were running for election under different labels. After the election, these two deputies joined the PSL parliamentary faction in the Sejm.

[c] One deputy was elected in Krakow from the separate list that was blocked with the Electoral Catholic Action. After the election, however, he declared himself unaffiliated with any parliamentary faction, but he eventually joined the Christian Democratic Party (PChD) faction in the Sejm. Thus I added the votes for his list to the total PChD votes.

A second complaint lodged against the electoral system is based on the false assumption that the Hare method favors the smallest parties at the expense of the stronger ones. The data in Table 4.6 prove this to be untrue. The representation in the Sejm of the first eleven political parties or groups, in percentage of total seats held, is higher than the percentage of votes they actually received. In this sense, the smaller parties are underrepresented.

A third argument against the electoral system is that in some cases it was possible to win a seat with less than 3 percent of the votes cast in the district. Undeniably, it would have been preferable if a 3 percent threshold had been established. Objections to the practical consequences of using the Hare method are exaggerated, however, especially in the case of smaller electoral districts—those with fewer than thirteen seats. In practice, in twenty-seven districts more than 4 percent of the votes cast were needed to gain a seat.

In reality, the political fragmentation of the Sejm following the October 1991 election resulted from the fragmentation of Polish society. No electoral system could have prevented such political rupture. This can be demonstrated by simulating (1) alternative methods of seat allocation under PR, (2) hypothetical thresholds, and (3) hybrid or mixed systems. I will not explore these possibilities in detail here, but some conclusions bear mentioning.

First, under all simulations (with one exception), elections would have resulted in at least ten parties (or "parties") in the Sejm. Minor groups or individual candidates would have lost out, but they constituted only 6 percent of the total seats. Second, none of the simulated outcomes would have altered the essential balance of power among the ten parties. The only exception might be the simulation applying a 10 percent threshold at the national level, which might have led to a two-party Sejm. Such a requirement, however, is untenable for several significant reasons.

Most important, this requirement would create an extreme distortion of election outcomes. Two political "parties"—the Democratic Union (UD) and the SLD—which together gained less than 25 percent of the votes cast and less than 10 percent of the eligible electorate, would win all of the Sejm's 460 seats. Furthermore, the spectrum of right-wing political groups would disappear from the Sejm, which, given today's Poland, would lead to political and social turmoil. Third, the post-Communist SLD was the party that was perhaps the most disadvantaged by the 1991 electoral law. Yet that law's fiercest critics, who are also ardent anti-Communists, have clearly overlooked this fact. Fourth, the primary beneficiaries of the 1991 law were candidates of the Polish Beer Lovers' Party, which gained nearly 3 percent of the votes cast. Under all other hypothetical scenarios, this party would have been eliminated altogether, or at the minimum its representation would have been drastically reduced.

(Despite its misleading name, this party represents the newly flowering business community.)

As mentioned earlier, the Senate was elected by the plurality system. It, too, was highly fragmented (see Table 4.7), a situation that was not prevented by the plurality rule in two-member electoral districts. The different outcome of the Senate election, compared with that of the Sejm, was caused by the extremely wide range of numbers of eligible voters in the different *voivodeships*. Two senators were elected in both the smallest *voivodeship* (Chelm) with 175,554 votes and the largest (Gdansk) with 1,039,242 votes.

It is worth mentioning that in the Sejm 1991 election, the post-Solidarity parties had their worst showing of any election since 1989. The UD, Center Civic Alliance, Liberal-Democratic Congress, Peasant Alliance, Christian Democratic Party, Solidarity of Labor, Democratic Social Movement, and Solidarity combined attracted only 22 percent of the eligible voters. In 1989, Solidarity candidates were supported by 36 percent of voters in the Senate elections and by 40 percent of eligible voters in the Sejm election. In a comparison with the presidential elections, the constituency of Tadeusz Mazowiecki was cut in half, and Lech Walesa lost more than a third of his supporters. The post-Communist constituency has been reduced somewhat. The only remarkable progress in the 1991 parliamentary elections was achieved by the KPN and its leader, Leszek Moczulski (see Table 4.4). ☐

CONCLUSION

The 1991 parliamentary elections changed the political landscape of Poland. It is true that the resultant Sejm and Senate were fragmented, but this fragmentation was not caused by an inappropriate electoral system. Critics of PR often neglect to note that the Sejm was elected under PR, whereas the Senate was elected according to the plurality rule. If, however, the Senate had been elected under a mixed system—forty-nine seats in single-member districts under plurality rule and the remaining fifty-one seats under PR—the Senate would be *less* fragmented than it turned out to be. This appears to be an argument in favor of PR, which, in a highly fragmented political arena, more effectively achieves some consolidation of political parties. A majoritarian electoral system can be justified only on the condition that the party system is well established in society and is properly institutionalized. But this is not the case in contemporary Poland, which is in the process of deep political and economic transformation.

The results of the 1993 parliamentary elections appear to contradict these conclusions. For the Sejm election, the electoral law was changed in the direction of much weaker proportionality. A 5 percent national threshold was imposed (8 percent for party alliances), and the minimum

TABLE 4.7 Political Composition of the Polish
Senate After the 1991 Elections

Political Group	Seats
Democratic Union	21
Solidarity	11
National Christian Union	9
Polish Peasant Party	9
Peasant Alliance	9
Center Alliance	7
Liberal-Democratic Congress	6
Democratic Left Alliance	4
Confederation for an Independent Poland	4
Christian Democratic Party	3
Others	17

strength required to participate in the sixty-nine nationwide bonus seats
was raised to 7 percent. Because so many parties were unable to pass the
5 percent threshold (and because one party coalition failed to pass the 8
percent threshold), the result of the election was more majoritarian than
proportional. Six parties were elected to the Sejm, and the two winning
parties—the Democratic Left Alliance and the Polish Peasant Party (the
two Communist successor parties)—won 65.9 percent of the seats with
just 35.8 percent of the vote; four other parties (and the German minority
organizations, which were exempted from the 5 percent threshold) won
34.1 percent of the seats with 29.7 percent of the vote; and parties that
together received 34.5 percent of the vote were completely excluded. The
two winning parties in the Sejm elections also won the plurality elections
to the one-hundred-member Senate with thirty-seven and thirty-six seats,
respectively. These results show that in spite of the great obstacles for
small parties, many voters still cast their votes for them, and as many as
six parties still succeeded in entering the Sejm. Moreover, the reduction in
the number of parties came at a very high cost: More than a third of the
voters (those who voted for the parties that failed to win seats) lost their
democratic representation.

Other important arguments favor the adoption of PR in East and
Central European countries undergoing democratic transitions to a
Western model of pluralistic democracy. In this region there are no possibilities of creating the classical two-party system. I leave aside the question of whether the two-party system, which appeared in Britain and the
United States under very specific historical circumstances, is the ideal
model for every country. The long-established experience of Western
Europe proves that another model of the multiparty system can also be
efficient and can work well to create stable coalition governments. The
two-party system in post-Communist countries could eventually lead to

an authoritarian system of government, which is one of the reasons various political groups in these countries are afraid to accept the electoral system based on plurality rule. They fear a possible return of a government by minority, which was the very essence of Communist power.

At the same time, the anti-Communist opposition that took power in these countries is very heterogeneous. Multidimensional political splits and socioeconomic cleavages are conducive to fragmentation of the political arena and a fractionalization of society. In some countries, like Poland or the former Czechoslovakia, this fragmentation is clearly visible; in other countries, like Bulgaria or Hungary, it has the potential to exist. And this factor will probably be decisive for the consolidation of electoral systems under PR rules at the expense of the ideal of government stability. ☐

NOTES

1. Maurice Duverger, *Political Parties: Their Organization and Activity in the Modern State*, trans. Barbara North and Robert North (New York: John Wiley and Sons, 1954), Maurice Duverger, *L'influence des systemes electoraux sur la vie politique* (Paris: Armand Colin, 1954). See also Enid Lakeman and James D. Lambert, *Voting in Democracies: A Study of Majority and Proportional Electoral Systems* (London: Faber and Faber, 1955); Douglas W. Rae, *The Political Consequences of Electoral Laws*, rev. ed. (New Haven: Yale University Press, 1971), pp. 148–176; William H. Riker, "The Two-Party System and Duverger's Law: An Essay on the History of Political Science," *American Political Science Review* 76 (1982): 753–766; Bernard Grofman and Arend Lijphart, eds., *Electoral Laws and Their Political Consequences* (New York: Agathon Press, 1986); Martin Harrop and William L. Miller, *Elections and Voters: A Comparative Introduction* (London: Macmillan Education, 1987); Dieter Nohlen, *Wahlrecht und Parteiensystem: Uber die politischen Auswirkungen von Wahlsystemen* (Opladen: Leske Verlag, 1989); Rein Taagepera and Matthew S. Shugart, *Seats and Votes: The Effects and Determinants of Electoral Systems* (New Haven: Yale University Press, 1989).

2. Taagepera and Shugart in *Seats and Votes*, as well as Harrop and Miller in *Elections and Voters*, have presented a concise panorama of theoretical discussions and controversies regarding virtues and weaknesses of both PR and majoritarian rule and their influence on party systems.

3. See Arend Lijphart, "Constitutional Choices for New Democracies," *Journal of Democracy* 2, no. 1 (Winter 1991): 73–84; Arend Lijphart, "Democratization and Constitutional Choices in Czecho-Slovakia, Hungary and Poland, 1989–1991," in György Szoboslai, ed., *Flying Blind: Emerging Democracies in East-Central Europe* (Budapest: Hungarian Political Science Association Yearbook, 1992), pp. 99–113; Arend Lijphart, "Double-Checking the Evidence," *Journal of Democracy* 2, no. 3 (Summer 1991): 42–48. Guy Lardeyret, "The Problem with PR," *Journal of Democracy* 2, no. 3 (Summer 1991): 30–35; Quentin L. Quade, "PR and Democratic Statecraft," *Journal of Democracy* 2, no. 3 (Summer 1991): 36–41.

4. Harry Eckstein, "The Impact of Electoral Systems on Representative Government," in Harry Eckstein and David Apter, eds., *Comparative Politics: A Reader* (New York: Free Press, 1963), pp. 247–254.

5. Taagepera and Shugart, *Seats and Votes*, p. 53.

6. For an explanation of the Hare method, see Arend Lijphart, "Proportional Representation," in Seymour Martin Lipset, ed., *The Encyclopedia of Democracy* (Washington, D.C.: Congressional Quarterly, 1995), pp. 1012–1013.

7. Staffan Berglund and Jan Ake Dellenbrant are right in saying that "a rapid process of democratization, when subjects are turned into citizens literally overnight, is conducive to the extreme kind of pluralism" and "the existence of many cleavages, which are more or less independent of one another, promotes the extreme kind of multipartyism, particularly if the parties are in the early stages of organization." See "The Evolution of Party Systems in Eastern Europe," *Journal of Communist Studies* 8, no. 1 (March 1992): 155.

8. Lijphart, "Proportional Representation," pp. 1012–1013.

9. In my chapter "Political Institutions in the Process of Transition a Post-Socialist Formation: Polish and Comparative Perspectives," in Walter D. Connor and Piotr Pioszajski, eds., *Escape from Socialism: The Polish Route* (Warsaw: IFiS Publishers, 1992), I wrote: "Taking into account the strong antiparty feeling (based on the populistic anti-elitist attitudes) that is widely and deeply rooted in the general public, it cannot be excluded in all post-Solidarity political parties would be rejected by the Polish voters. Several sociological surveys are proving that each of these parties would obtain no more than 10 percent of the cast vote. In conclusion it must be said that it would be difficult to predict a clear majority as a result of the forthcoming parliamentary elections. It is also very doubtful that these elections will lead to a stable new configuration of the party system in Poland" (p. 252).

CHAPTER FIVE

■

Electoral Engineering and Democratic Stability: The Legacy of Authoritarian Rule in Chile

Peter Siavelis and Arturo Valenzuela

LATIN AMERICA IS experiencing a severe crisis of representation. Public opinion polls reveal that citizens believe they have little genuine voice in the political process and are profoundly alienated from their leaders. Whereas presidents have often lost support in dramatic fashion, the distance between citizens and leaders appears greatest with respect to national and state legislatures, in which delegates are viewed as venal politicians with little interest or concern for their constituents. This gap between leaders and followers is as significant in countries that have strong parties, such as Venezuela and Uruguay, as it is in countries with notoriously weak and diffuse parties, such as Brazil and Ecuador.

Alienation of citizens from politics throughout the continent has been exacerbated by the inadequate working of electoral systems. Pointing to the lack of responsiveness and efficacy of Latin America's political institutions, politicians and academics have underscored the need for reform of the proportional electoral systems (operating in all of the countries of the region except for Chile and Mexico) in favor of the adoption of the Anglo-American, first-past-the-post, or other type of majority-plurality system.

However, dissatisfaction resulting from the perceived lackluster performance of political institutions should not be causally linked to proportional representation (PR) electoral systems; nor will a reform of these systems necessarily enhance the functioning of Latin American democracy. Evidence from the Chilean case, where the historical proportional representation system was replaced with a majoritarian system, suggests that the effects and consequences of this type of shift are not as clear-cut as the debate on electoral reform in Latin America has suggested. Reformers in newly democratizing nations, as well as those in polities with long-standing democratic traditions, should approach with caution the issue of the adoption of majoritarian electoral systems for three principal reasons.

First, the Chilean case confirms recent theoretical findings that emphasize that electoral systems are not the sole, nor necessarily the most important, determinant of the type of party system that exists in a given country.[1] The modified majoritarian system enacted by the Chilean military government was designed to transform the country's polarized multiparty system into a moderate two-party system. The electoral system, however, has not reduced the number of major parties. Rather, parties have developed elaborate political pacts to compete within the framework of two-party slates, pacts that intensify interparty conflicts rather than promote party unity.

Second, the adoption of a majoritarian system may exacerbate existing problems of governability and create new ones given the characteristics of local party systems. Proportional representation systems developed where they did for historical reasons. This was the electoral system of choice in multiparty contexts, in which parties that could aspire to gain only a plurality of the electorate required an electoral mechanism that would permit a relatively fair representation of sharply divergent political tendencies. Within the context of winner-take-all Latin American presidential systems, PR allowed opposition parties in multiparty systems access to the institutions of democracy in proportion to their electoral strength, and it assured that all major party sectors had a stake in supporting democratic institutions. These aspects of PR served as moderating forces within highly divided and heterogeneous societies.

In the Chilean case, PR developed precisely for these reasons. It allowed representation for parties across the political spectrum in the country's complex, well-entrenched, European-style party system—traditionally characterized by three broad political tendencies of the Right, Left, and Center.[2] Despite the efforts of military authorities to fundamentally transform this system, Chile continues to be characterized by a multiparty system, and a three-way division of the electorate. Given this reality, the new majoritarian electoral system has the capacity to exclude one of the three historical tendencies, as well as small nonaligned parties, from political representation and to produce volatility and instability in the composition of Congress.

Finally, real or perceived problems with proportional representation systems should not lead to their wholesale abandonment. There are different types of PR, many of which encompass the positive aspects ascribed by theorists to both proportional and majoritarian systems. Moderate proportional systems characterized by small district magnitudes, open-list ballots, and more genuine regionally based representation can facilitate the representation of all major political sectors while avoiding the hyperproportionality in the representation of extremely small parties, abrupt shifts in parliamentary composition, and alienation that result from nonregional representation. As the Chilean case demonstrates, in certain contexts PR systems may balance more efficaciously than majoritarian systems the often contradictory challenges of representation and democratic stability. □

THE CHILEAN ELECTORAL SYSTEM: DESIGN AND GOALS

The Chilean electoral system was designed by military reformers to achieve two goals. The first was the short-term goal of assuring overrepresentation for pro-government forces of the Right in the first congressional elections. The party configuration in Chile prior to the 1989 elections was characterized by two broad coalitions, each of which presented a presidential candidate and a slate of parliamentary candidates for the Chamber of Deputies and the Senate. The Center-Left coalition, Concertación por la Democracia, was composed of fourteen parties— including the centrist Partido Demócrata Cristiano (Christian Democratic Party) and Partido Radical (Radical Party) and the Center-Left Partido por la Democracia (Party for Democracy), as well as smaller parties and independents. The parties of the Center-Right alliance, Democracia y Progreso, included the Unión Demócrata Independiente (Independent Democratic Union) and the more moderate Renovación Nacional (National Renovation), as well as a few smaller parties and independents. Finally, a small group of left-oriented parties not allied with the Concertación joined forces to form the list of the Partido Amplio de Izquierda Socialista (Party of the United Socialist Left [PAIS]).[3] Military authorities sought to create an electoral formula that would give supporters of the Democracia y Progreso alliance a majority of seats in the legislature, with a level of support comparable to the vote received by General Augusto Pinochet in the October 1988 plebiscite—that is, about 40 percent.

The second and longer-term goal was to fundamentally transform the nature of the party system through electoral engineering aimed at the creation of a two-party system, which authorities considered a more stable alternative to the often polarized multiparty system that had characterized much of Chile's preauthoritarian history. To achieve these two goals, reformers rejected Chile's traditional proportional representation system in favor of a modified majoritarian electoral system with two-member congressional districts.

The electoral reforms undertaken prior to the 1989 elections thus dramatically transformed the electoral system. The 1925 Chilean constitution had established a proportional representation system to allocate seats in multimember districts following the d'Hondt formula (see Chapter 3, note 12), the most widely used PR system in Latin America and Europe. For the elections to the Chamber of Deputies, the country was divided into twenty-eight districts, with district magnitudes (number of seats per electoral district) ranging between 2.0 and 18.0 for a total of 150 deputies, and an average district magnitude of 5.36. Parties prepared slates that could include as many candidates as there were seats in each district. The voter chose an individual candidate from a particular party list. Seats were then distributed according to the d'Hondt formula.

According to the new law, parties or coalitions present lists that include a candidate for each of the two seats to be filled. The system takes into account the votes for both the total party list and the individual candidates. The first seat is awarded to the highest-polling candidate of the party or coalition list that receives a plurality of votes. However, the first-place party list must receive twice the number of votes as the second-place party list to win both seats in the district.[4] Consequently, the cutoff point a party must reach to obtain at least one seat becomes 33.4 percent of the votes of the two largest parties or coalitions, assuming there are two lists. Hence, the system tends to favor the second-largest list because, to obtain two seats, the largest party must receive twice the vote of the second-largest party, or 66.7 percent of the vote of the two largest parties or coalitions. Therefore, any electoral support the largest party may have over 33.4 percent of the two largest parties or coalitions is effectively wasted until its level of support approaches 66.7 percent. In other words, within the context of two-list competition, if the party lists of the largest and the second-largest parties earn 66 percent and 34 percent of the vote respectively, they will divide the district, with each receiving one seat, or 50 percent of the seat allocation for that district.

In the context of a two-coalition pattern, the degree of interparty competition is relatively low if support for the parties in a particular district is almost equally divided, since each can be assured of winning one seat. Competition becomes centered within districts where the largest party can expect to receive around 66 percent of the votes of the two largest parties, or where the second-largest party's support hovers around 33 percent. Of course, within the context of competition among more than two parties or coalitions, the competitive dynamic changes. With more than two-party lists, the threshold for the first-place party to win the second seat may be lower, because it needs to receive only twice the vote of its nearest competitor. If several smaller lists have similar levels of electoral support, the result will be fierce competition for the second seat or, in situations of greater party fragmentation, for both the first and second seats, creating a potentially volatile electoral outcome.

Examination of competition within an individual district clarifies how the counting system, coupled with district magnitudes of two, can lead to counterintuitive results. Table 5.1 shows the returns from the 1989 Senate election in Circunscripción 7 (the Seventh Senate District).[5] It reveals that each of the Concertación candidates individually received a higher number and a higher percentage of votes than did either of the Democracia y Progreso candidates. Nonetheless, this contest resulted in one seat being awarded to Zaldívar of the Concertación and one to Guzmán of Democracia y Progreso, because the total Concertación list vote did not equal twice the percentage of total votes received by the Democracia y Progreso list. The Concertación received 65.57 percent of the votes received by *the two highest polling lists*, while Democracia y Progreso received 34.43 percent. The returns from this district approached the critical threshold discussed previously, and Democracia y Progreso was awarded a seat in the Senate, despite the fact that its best-performing candidate came in third overall in both the number and percentage of votes received. Although this is an extreme example, it is indicative of a general trend that served to skew the national aggregate totals in the allocation of seats to the benefit of the Democracia y Progreso alliance. A prominent leader of the Concertación attributed the defeat of Senate candidate Ricardo Lagos to "the arithmetic of authoritarianism."[6] □

EMPIRICAL RESULTS AND POLITICAL CONSEQUENCES

The designers of the electoral system were moderately successful in achieving their goal to create overrepresentation of the Right. Military authorities assumed a worst-case scenario that provided for complete unity of purpose on the part of anti-Pinochet forces, which would at best give the opposition about 50 percent of the vote in congressional races. However, government authorities were convinced that the opposition

TABLE 5.1 1989 Senate Election Results for Circunscripción 7—
Metropolitan Santiago

	Total Votes	*Percentage*
Concertación		
Ricardo Lagos	399,721	30.6
Andrés Zaldívar	408,227	31.3
Total	807,948	61.9
Democracia y Progreso		
Jaime Guzmán	224,396	17.2
Miguel Otero	199,856	15.3
Total	424,252	32.5

alliance would fragment, resulting in multiple lists. The list of the Right would then become the largest, enabling it to easily double the votes of its closest competitor and give the Right not only half of all elected representatives but also a comfortable majority in Congress—even with only 40 percent of the vote.

For the parties of the Right the worst-case scenario came to pass, and their prescient planning bore the expected results. The fourteen parties of the opposition were able to create a common list and agree on a single presidential candidate, and although the Concertación garnered a majority of elected seats in Congress, Renovación Nacional—the largest party of the Right—won more seats than would have been expected given its national percentages.[7]

In regard to the goal of creating a two-party system, evidence suggests that military reformers were mistaken in relying on Maurice Duverger's thesis and similar notions concerning the relation between majoritarian electoral formulas and two-party systems.[8] Although results from the 1989 elections did demonstrate something of a bipolar dynamic—with moderate party competition between an alliance of the Center-Right and an alliance of the Center-Left—and survey data demonstrate a narrowing of the ideological scope of the Chilean electorate, a fundamental transformation has not occurred in the nature of party competition in the country.[9] This is the case for four principal reasons.

First, the unique characteristics and context of the first democratic election had a powerful influence on its results. During the initial phases of the transition process, deep divisions within the Chilean political system were overshadowed by the collective effort of opposition parties to end the authoritarian regime. The parties of the Concertación first came together to work collectively for a "NO" vote in the October 5, 1988, plebiscite. This unified front led to an opposition alliance in the 1989 elections.

This situation temporarily gave Chilean politics a plebiscitary nature. This dynamic, when coupled with the democratic opposition's recognition of the political exigencies of the structure of the electoral law, led to an incipient bipolar pattern of competition between opposition and progovernment forces. Because the overriding issue in the early phase of the transition was the nature of the political regime itself, the parties of the democratic opposition were able to subordinate their programmatic differences to the wider goal of safeguarding the democratic transition.

The need to maintain both a presidential and a parliamentary alliance, combined with the two-seat electoral formula, led Concertación parties to negotiate and allocate congressional candidacies among the coalition's diverse members, thereby muting the three-bloc dynamic of competition.[10] This fusion of the Center with a portion of the Left obviated the expression of an independent voice on the Left. For example, the Partido por la Democracia presented only six candidates for the Senate, and it would have presented one in every *circunscripción* if it and its coalition partners had formed an independent list on the Left with its own presidential candidate. In addition, the split between the small leftist PAIS list and the left-wing parties of the Concertación alliance further distorted the profile of the Left in the minds of the voters. Both of these factors tended to depreciate the presence and perceived strength of the Left, despite the fact that it remains an important and independent current within the political system—both programmatically and in respect to public opinion and popular support.

Second, the disaggregation of election returns into forces representing the Right, Center, and Left shows that strong undercurrents of the three historical ideological blocs remain. In each congressional district and each Senate district, voters were given the opportunity to choose between candidates of the Left and the Center within individual Concertación lists. The often large variations in support for the Left and that for the Center show that voters did indeed differentiate between the two in their choice of candidates. Although the size of the differential varies, in the 1989 elections the average variance was a substantial 11.4 percent of the total district vote for the Chamber of Deputies. Of the forty-five districts in which the Concertación presented a candidate of both the Center and the Left, the former was victorious in twenty-eight districts and the latter in seventeen.

What is more, if election returns from the 1989 elections for the Chamber of Deputies are disaggregated into forces representing the Right, Center, and Left without considering coalition labels, they garner 33 percent, 30 percent, and 23 percent of the vote, respectively.[11] Similarly, for the Senate, when each of the ideological blocs is considered separately, the three forces win 33 percent, 35 percent, and 22 percent of the vote, respectively.[12] These results correspond in general terms to the traditional support for each of the historical ideological pillars in past Chilean elections, as summarized in Table 5.2.

The historical three-way division of Chilean politics persists not only at the electoral level but also at the elite and policy levels. Political leaders in Chile continue to have strong political and personal ties with individual party organizations and subcultures, which serve as important referents of self-identification and political solidarity.

Third, a narrowing of the ideological scope of the Chilean electorate does not mean the historical blocs of the system have necessarily disappeared; there may simply be less ideological space between them. Despite the cautious and conciliatory pattern of interparty interaction within the Concertación, programmatic differences remain that will become increasingly visible with the emergence of more controversial issues such as poverty, divorce, and abortion, which strike at the core of individual party principles. More significantly, if future Concertación governments

TABLE 5.2 Percentage of Total Vote Received by Parties of the Right, Center, and Left in Chilean House of Deputies Elections, 1937–1973

| | Percentage of Total Vote | | | | | | | | | | 1937–1973 |
	1937	1941	1945	1949	1953	1957	1961	1965	1969	1973	Mean
Right (Conservative, Liberal, National after 1965)	42.0	31.2	43.7	42.0	25.3	33.0	30.4	12.5	20.0	21.3	30.1
Center (Radical, Falangist, Christian Democrat, Agrarian, Labor parties)	28.1	32.1	27.9	46.7	43.0	44.3	43.7	55.6	42.8	32.8	39.7
Left (Socialist, Communist)	15.4	33.9	23.1	9.4	14.2	10.7	22.1	22.7	28.1	34.9	21.5
Other	14.5	2.8	5.3	1.9	17.5	12.0	3.8	9.2	9.1	11.0	8.7

Source: Arturo Valenzuela, *The Breakdown of Democratic Regimes: Chile* (Baltimore: Johns Hopkins University Press, 1978), p. 6.

are less successful, pragmatic, and willing to negotiate than that of President Patricio Aylwin, the Left will have strong incentives to distance and disassociate itself from the Concertación alliance in an attempt to become the premier political force in the country. In sum, with a return to more openly competitive democratic politics, the pragmatism that currently characterizes relations within the Concertación coalition may be supplanted by a more traditional pattern of competition between the Center and the Left.

Finally, although the party system may be less ideological from the point of view of party programs, given the widespread agreement concerning the sanctity of private property and the validity of the market as the fundamental motor of the economy, clear differences between parties still exist. As was the case in the preauthoritarian period, in contemporary Chile four or five parties can be considered significant, with distinct organizations, followers, and programs: the Christian Democrats, the Party for Democracy, and the Socialist Party (of the Concertación alliance) and the Independent Democratic Union and the National Renovation Party (of the Democracia y Progreso alliance). These parties are not only relevant—in Giovanni Sartori's terms, as having coalition and blackmail potential—they were also successful in electing representatives to Congress in 1989.[13]

It is difficult to sustain the proposition that a simple change in electoral law can transform a party system as deeply institutionalized as that of Chile. It is fairly clear that in political systems with already consolidated party systems, it is extremely difficult, if not impossible, to alter the party system through the manipulation of electoral laws. Party systems acquire a dynamic of their own and at times can even overcome the very deep social divisions that led to the creation of the parties in the first place.[14] What is more, political parties seek to maintain the set of electoral laws that best serves their interests.[15] The modification of electoral systems tends to occur only during periods of severe crisis, but crises may or may not affect the party system depending on their strength and other secular transformations within society. □

THE UNANTICIPATED CONSEQUENCES OF ELECTORAL REFORM: REGIME INSTABILITY?

As we have seen, military reformers were mistaken in their assumption that a majoritarian electoral system would lead to the creation of a two-party system. But the electoral system's failure to transform the party system does not mean the electoral system will not affect the future of Chilean democracy or the operational dynamic of the party system.

Although an electoral system cannot mechanically create a more stable democratic system, it is clear that an inappropriate, ill-fitting electoral system can have a highly destabilizing effect on an already well-consolidated

party system. Indeed, we argue that given the current nature of party competition in Chile, the electoral system has the capacity to create problems of
democratic governability for two principal reasons.

First, the binomial system (two-member district) tends to produce a
great deal of electoral volatility, given the characteristics of Chile's consolidated multiparty system. Because the electoral system has the attributes
of a majority/plurality system—and an extremely sensitive one at that—
very small shifts in voting patterns can produce sweeping changes at the
legislative level.

Second, given this volatility, the law has the potential—and, indeed, the
tendency—to exclude entire ideological currents from legislative representation. Because of the electoral thresholds created by the binomial system, if
any one of Chile's three important ideological blocs falls below a certain
level of electoral support nationally, it can easily be barred from legislative
representation. The exclusion of any one of these important blocs could easily leave a president without a legislative majority and create other potentially problematic consequences for long-term democratic stability.

Thus, in the Chilean case, an electoral system specifically designed to
produce moderating drives and party-system integration has failed to do
so. In fact, it may produce more serious problems for long-term democratic governability. □

VOLATILITY AND EXCLUSION: SOME ELECTORAL TESTS

To assess the impact of the features of the electoral system outlined previously, and to explore the possible consequences of the reemergence of a
three-bloc pattern of competition, we performed a series of simulations of
electoral outcomes, given different patterns of party competition and vote
distribution.[16] Using returns from the 1989 election as a base, we factored in
small changes in the percentage of votes received by each party in individual
districts for both the alliance pattern in force during the 1989 election and a
hypothetical three-way race among coalitions of the Left, Center, and Right.

These simulations demonstrate both the exclusionary tendencies of
the new majoritarian system and the system's potential to produce a
marked degree of unpredictability, volatility, and instability in legislative
composition. However, the strength of each of these tendencies greatly
depends on the configuration of the party system and alliance
patterns.[17] □

Two-List Test

The two-list test assumes a coalitional configuration identical to that in
the 1989 election. From the baseline of the election results we shifted, district by district, 3 percent of the total district vote from the Democracia y
Progreso alliance to the Concertación and then allocated seats according

to the electoral formula. Next, we performed the same procedure using a 5 percent shift.

The choice of this simulation, with a gradual erosion of support for the Right, was based on two suppositions: (1) Public opinion survey data suggest that voter preferences are indeed shifting from the Right to the Center and Left; and (2) because the system was designed to benefit the Right in the short term, we wanted to demonstrate the ease with which the electoral formula could turn against this party sector. The last row of Table 5.3 simulates an election using public opinion data, proportionally distributing the result of the survey data within each individual district and computing the seat allocation.[18] The results, in terms of national percentages and the allocation of seats, are summarized in Table 5.3.

The table clearly shows the potential volatility and exclusionary tendencies of the electoral system even with the current pattern of party coalitions. If the data are analyzed in terms of the percentage of parliamentary seats that would change hands, given these rather modest shifts in voter preferences, the consequences of the electoral law for this configuration of party competition become clearer:

- With a simple 3 percent transfer of the total individual district vote to the Concertación from Democracia y Progreso, the Concertación

TABLE 5.3 Two-Alliance Pattern: Concertación and Democracia y Progreso[19]

	Alliances					
	Concertación		Renovación Nacional and Unión Demócrata Independiente		Other	
National Vote	Vote (%)	Seats	Vote (%)	Seats	Vote (%)	Seats
1989 Election	49.33	70	32.40	48	12.96	2
Simulation 1— 3 percent transfer[a]	52.33	82	29.40	35	12.96	3
Simulation 2— 5 percent transfer[b]	54.33	91	27.40	25	12.96	4
Public opinion survey data[c]	67.75	109	26.55	11	3.40	0

[a] 3 percent of the votes received by the Democracia y Progreso Alliance were transferred district by district to Concertación.

[b] Simulation 2: 5 percent of the votes received by the Democracia y Progreso Alliance were transferred district by district to Concertación.

[c] Simulated election employing survey data from the "Estudio de Opinión Pública," CEP-Adimark (June 1990).

gains twelve seats, representing a 17 percent increase in seats and a 10 percent shift of the total seats in the chamber.

- Alternatively, with a loss of 3 percent of the total district vote, the Democracia y Progreso alliance loses thirteen seats, or 27 percent of its total seat share, with a roughly corresponding shift in the percentage of total seats in the chamber.
- More dramatically, with a 5 percent shift in the total individual district vote, the Democracia y Progreso alliance loses 23 seats, a decrease of 48 percent in allocation to that coalition.

If public opinion survey data are considered, the Right loses an even greater number of seats. If the current pattern of coalitional competition persists—despite the design of the system to benefit the second-largest coalition—small shifts in voting preference that bring the second-most-powerful coalition below a certain threshold of support nationally translate easily into sweeping changes at the legislative level and can result in exclusion or severe underrepresentation of major parties or alliances. □

Three-List Test

Our second group of simulations builds on our premise that beneath the veneer of coalition politics, a three-bloc ideological division persists.[20] We sought to uncover the political consequences for the electoral system if a pattern of three-way coalitional competition reemerges. To simulate the results of an election with such a configuration, we began again with the 1989 election as our baseline for electoral opinion in the country. For this set of simulations, however, we disaggregated election returns into forces representing the Right, Center, and Left in each district and grouped the constituent parties of the Concertación into one of the latter two categories according to their ideological orientations. We then combined the vote totals for the leftist parties of the Concertación with those received by the smaller PAIS list and other parties of the Left and grouped individual parties of the Right with those of the Democracia y Progreso alliance. Next, following a procedure similar to that outlined earlier for the two-list test, we simulated a shift of 3 percent and then 5 percent in electoral returns. For this test, however, we evenly distributed the loss of the alliance of the Right between the Center alliance and the Left alliance. In other words, for the 3 percent simulation the Right lost 3 percent, and each of the other lists gained 1.5 percent of the total district vote. The same was done for the 5 percent simulation, with the Right losing 5 percent and each of the other alliances gaining 2.5 percent of the total district vote. Finally, we computed the seat allocations that would result if the party preferences expressed in public opinion survey data were translated into votes.

At this juncture it is important to note that these suppositions are extremely conservative. For the 1989 election, in the majority of districts the Center and the Left were each represented by only one candidate to stand for their respective sectors. Logically, in a situation with three lists, the Center and the Left would win more votes because each would be able to present two candidates, resulting in an increased *oferta electoral*. From a mathematical perspective, an increase in the number of candidates to two increases the chances that at least one candidate would be attractive to voters. More important, independent lists on the Center and the Left would strengthen the electoral bases of both by allowing each tendency to appeal to its core constituency and to attract those voters who had voted for other parties because they did not approve of either the Center's partnership with the Left or the Left's alliance with the Center. With a three-coalition dynamic, a list on the Left could win back voters who opted for other parties of the Left not aligned with the Concertación. Many voters on the Left had a distaste for an alliance with the Christian Democrats, based on the party's current social policies and its purported complicity in supporting the military coup. Similarly, the Center would benefit by winning back voters who found it difficult to vote for an alliance that included the Left and who opted for parties of the Right instead. Table 5.4 summarizes the results of the three-bloc simulation.[21]

Again, an analysis of percentage shifts in seats for a three-coalition pattern points to a volatility similar to that uncovered in the two-list tests, although with fewer negative consequences for the Right:

TABLE 5.4 Three-Alliance Pattern: Alliances of the Center, Right, and Left

National Vote	Center		Right		Left	
	Vote (%)	Seats	Vote (%)	Seats	Vote (%)	Seats
1989 election	31.15	44	33.31	55	23.12	21
Simulation 1— 3 percent transfer[a]	32.65	47	30.31	45	24.62	28
Simulation 2— 5 percent transfer[b]	33.65	50	28.31	37	25.62	33
Public opinion survey data[c]	46.97	75	22.87	10	26.87	35

[a]Using the elections of 1989 as a base, 3 percent of the votes received by the Right were transferred district by district to the Center and the Left, awarding 1.5 percent to each alliance.

[b]Using the elections of 1989 as a base, 5 percent of the votes received by the Right were transferred district by district to the Center and the Left, awarding 2.5 percent to each alliance.

[c]Simulated election employing survey data from the "Estudio de Opinión Pública," CEP-Adimark (June 1990).

- A 3 percent loss in total district vote for Democracia y Progreso produces an 18 percent loss in the number of parliamentary seats and a
  shift of 8.3 percent of the total seats. A 5 percent loss results in a 33
  percent loss in parliamentary seats and a 15 percent shift in total
  seats.
- On the Left, a 1.5 percent increase in total district vote results in a 33
  percent gain in parliamentary seats and a shift of 5.8 percent of the
  total seats. A 2.5 percent gain for the Left translates into a 57 percent
  gain in its share of legislative seats and a 10 percent shift in total
  seats.
- Data obtained from public opinion surveys would leave the Right
  with only ten seats.

What are the potential consequences of both this volatility and the exclusionary tendency of the electoral system for governability and long-term
democratic stability?

The answer to this question depends on many variables, the most
important of which are the structure of partisan alternatives (whether
there is a two-coalition pattern, a three-coalition pattern, or something
else), the distribution of votes across districts nationally, and the
sequence of presidential and legislative elections. The multiple options
that can result from the variability of each of these factors in the long
term prevent a definitive determination of the consequences of the tendencies exerted by the electoral system. Nonetheless, we can make some
generalizations on the basis of the most probable types of future political
configurations.

If a two-coalition pattern persists, the competitive dynamic that
operates will be similar to that which characterized the 1989 elections.
Assuming that the second-largest coalition is able to maintain approximately 33 percent of the vote across districts nationally, the results of the
election will be roughly similar. If the Concertación approaches a support level of 66 percent, the consequences for the Right could be disastrous.

This is the case because with the current two-coalition configuration,
the Democracia y Progreso alliance is much more vulnerable than the
Concertación to small shifts in electoral support because the base of
Concertación support is more secure. The shift of a few percent of the
popular vote will not bring the Concertación below the 33 percent threshold. If the coalition is not able to win the first seat, it will probably maintain sufficient support to win the second seat. This probability is vividly
demonstrated by the Concertación's consistent ability in the 1989 election
to take the first seat in each district. Fifty-five of the Concertación's seventy seats were first-seat victories, whereas only fifteen were second-seat
victories. The Democracia y Progreso alliance, for its part, was only able

to win the first seat in three of the sixty congressional districts. The bulk of its congressional victories (forty-five in the 1989 election) were second-seat victories. Because the alliance's level of support hovers in the 30 percent range, a small shift in the popular vote may put it below the threshold for second-seat victories. In essence, the current legislative power of the Right belies its precarious electoral position.

An analysis of the consequences of a three-way coalitional dynamic is more complex because of the increased combinations that are possible in the distribution of votes among the three coalitions across districts nationally. With a different pattern of vote distribution, the consequences of the system may vary. With certain vote distributions, the sensitivity of the electoral system to small shifts in votes increases, the results of which are problematic from a number of perspectives.

The electoral law stipulates that to win both seats in a district, the first-place coalition must double the vote of its closest competitor. Because a three-way race would disperse votes, however, it is unlikely that the strongest coalition would be able to garner enough votes to win both seats. Consequently, competition for the second seat would occur between the two remaining coalitions, with a lower threshold necessary to win the second seat.

This competitive dynamic can produce a number of outcomes. If the distribution of the vote across districts is relatively even and the second-place coalition can make a stronger showing in the majority of districts nationally, the third-place coalition could be barred from the legislature, despite the fact that it may have garnered a significant percentage of the popular vote.

A different distribution of votes across districts can create other results that are also fraught with potential difficulties. For example, if the second- and third-place coalitions are roughly equal in national strength, they could conceivably share in the allocation of second seats. It is also possible that each of the three coalitions could split the seats in approximate thirds if the national level of support for each of the alliances is about 30 percent.

An analysis of the potential results of a three-bloc pattern of competition provides additional evidence of the failure of the electoral system to achieve the purposes for which it was designed. Reformers believed the binomial system would provide an added measure of stability and predictability to the democratic system by ensuring presidents of more consistent majorities in Congress. Although this may be true within the context of the two-bloc pattern, the simulations clearly demonstrate that with other patterns of competition, the sensitivity of the system to small electoral changes can produce wildly fluctuating patterns of legislative representation. In the course of one election, the control of the Chamber of Deputies could shift from the Right to the Left, or vice versa, with only a small shift in the voting patterns of the electorate. This reality presents obvious difficulties for both the president and the continuity of government policy, especially if the shift occurs during a midterm election and the president's coalition is left without significant legislative representation. This is particularly important given the Chilean Congress's recent approval of a constitutional amendment to shorten the presidential term to six years. The reform means presidential and legislative elections will be held concurrently less often than would have been the case under the previous formula, in which presidential elections were to be held every eight years and legislative elections every four.[22]

In this sense, in the context of a three-bloc coalitional configuration, the electoral system loses many of the advantages it was designed and intended to have. On the one hand, proportionality is undermined because of its low threshold of exclusion. On the other, with a slightly different configuration of national vote distribution, the value of proportionality as a majority/plurality system—often lauded because of its ability to produce decisive legislative majorities—is undermined because of its low threshold for representation.

In the current system, because only two seats are available in each district, small nonaligned parties are barred from legislative participation. The translation of poor electoral performance into exclusion from the political system can turn electoral losers into antisystem oppositions. If parties are consistently precluded from the possibility of governing or participating in governing coalitions, why should their policy formulations have anything to do with reality? Parties can promise the moon without ever having to deliver.

An exclusionary electoral system can also affect the internal dynamics of smaller parties on the Right and the Left in ways that influence the stability of the political system as a whole. Moderate elements within these parties can fall prey to their more extremist colleagues, who have proof that participation in electoral politics has nothing to offer in regard to political influence and that extraparliamentary routes to power may be more appropriate and effective.

Sartori argues convincingly that a party opposition is more likely to behave responsibly if it has some expectation of governing or of participating in governing coalitions. In this sense, party systems have the capacity to integrate irresponsible oppositions into the realm of democratic politics. The mechanism Sartori identifies as best able to play this absorptive role is a proportional representation electoral system.[23] PR allows smaller parties the opportunity to participate, and participation fosters acceptance of the political system. The present electoral system does not provide incentives for absorption of semiresponsible oppositions into the political system; indeed, it creates a context that encourages their formation and long-term isolation.

Further, within the context of a three-bloc dynamic, the binomial electoral system has the capacity—given a particular configuration of national vote distribution—to heighten political tensions by squelching not only small nonaligned parties but entire ideological tendencies. The consistent exclusion from the political system of even larger mainstream parties threatens long-term stability, because it can encourage the development of a dynamic of irresponsibility similar to that described earlier in regard to small parties. Long-term stability depends on the ability of the electoral system to adequately reflect all major party preferences. Even larger, relatively moderate parties of the Right and the Left can fall prey to radicalizing tendencies if they are continually excluded from participation in the political system.

Finally, the system's intended moderating function is completely undermined by the volatility and uncertainty each of these features of the electoral system introduces. □

PROPORTIONAL REPRESENTATION AND
THE IMPORTANCE OF CONTEXTUAL VARIABLES

It follows that the Chilean political elites should consider a comprehensive restructuring of the Chilean electoral system. Although the reputation of proportional representation has been tainted by severe problems with democratic governability and party discipline in countries such as Brazil and Italy, there are multiple PR systems with distinct characteristics and operational dynamics. Indeed, a key element that helped to make Chile one of the most democratic and stable political systems in the world prior to 1973 was its proportional representation electoral system, which allowed for the institutional representation of all party sectors across the political spectrum and provided institutional outlets for the political parties that emerged with successive waves of suffrage expansion and social transformation. By giving numerous and diverse social sectors a stake in the democratic game, Chile experienced fewer complications during the process of democratic consolidation than did other Latin American countries.

In much of the academic and public discourse on electoral systems, PR is criticized for leading to party proliferation, parliamentary representation for extremist sectors, minority governments, lack of identification between electors and representatives, and general democratic instability. The tendency for PR to encourage these developments depends to a great extent on the characteristics of a country's political and party systems. A moderate PR system with small district magnitudes, open lists, and regionally based representation can avoid the problems purer PR systems are said to encourage or exacerbate.

District magnitude is a crucial variable in determining the operational results of any PR system. Systems with large district magnitudes are more permissive regarding the representation of small parties, which may lead to party proliferation. By adopting a system with district magnitudes in the range of four or five, the possibility of an outright victory for smaller or extremist parties may be eliminated, and the probability of minority governments may decrease. This assumption is problematic in a situation of extreme party fragmentation and, despite possible exceptions, generally holds if two, three, or four major parties exist. In situations of severe party fragmentation, however, majoritarian systems may fare little better in decreasing the possibility of minority government or the victory of small extremist parties.

This does not contradict our earlier contention concerning the importance of the participation of potentially extremist parties in encouraging system loyalty. Because a more flexible set of rewards exists in proportional systems, smaller parties can participate in coalitions, given that larger magnitudes provide an opportunity for coalitions to distribute candidacies to their various party members in each district or in several districts. Smaller parties cannot win parliamentary seats alone and will be encouraged to ally with larger ones, thereby fostering negotiations and the moderation of party programs. In this sense, with district magnitudes of four or five, the largest, most important parties will receive parliamentary representation in proportion to their strength, thus avoiding the exclusionary tendencies of majoritarian systems. At the same time, smaller parties will have an incentive to negotiate with larger ones to allow them to achieve parliamentary representation, an inducement that does not exist in winner-take-all legislative elections.

With regard to the relationship between voters and representatives, the negative consequences attributed to PR in the area of representation are counterbalanced by some of its other features. In particular, the influence of party leaders over the nomination process, which is peculiar to PR systems, enhances the strength and representative capability of political parties. This influence permits party leaders to demand continued loyalty from elected representatives in the legislature, which contributes to more disciplined and cohesive programmatic alternatives and more successful coalition strategies. In countries as different as Argentina, Chile, Colombia, Costa Rica, Uruguay, and Venezuela, disciplined parties have been important factors in the success of democratic experiments. Coherent and well-articulated parties are as important to democratic consolidation as is the establishment of legitimate mechanisms for political representation.

The challenge for democratic reformers is to consider changes in party and electoral laws that provide genuine representation for all major party sectors but that at the same time encourage party coherence. Proportional representation systems can be made more legitimate if leaders are required to appoint candidates from the localities they will represent. Parties can be made more coherent if elected representatives are barred from running for reelection if they lose their party's support or shift parties, a practice that has undermined party coherence in Brazil.

An open-list PR system, in which voters are permitted to vote for individual candidates on a list rather than voting for the list as a whole, would also encourage closer identification between voters and representatives. Candidates with the largest number of votes on particular lists are elected to the legislature, provided their list as a whole generates enough votes to warrant seats. Such a system was in place in Chile prior to the military coup of 1973, which contributed to the selection of legislators who had strong roots in local communities.

Open-list systems, however, can only be successful if the district magnitudes are small, with only a few (four or five) seats in each district. Brazil is an example of how the open-list system can be counterproductive in a country with very large district magnitudes. Voters in states like São Paulo are asked to pick candidates from lists that contain hundreds of names, a situation that undermines the capacity of the voter to know anything about his or her candidate or representative.

The least valid argument concerning the negative aspects of PR is that which deals with democratic stability. As the previous discussion and the long-standing PR systems of Northern Europe show, the relative stability of PR systems is contextual and depends on party system characteristics and the type of PR. It is important to underscore that PR can actually promote democratic stability and provide some additional benefits given characteristics of local party systems. The Chilean case is a prime example. First, PR or a modified PR system would be less likely to produce sweeping legislative change.[24] The change of a few percentage points in electoral preferences would be reflected in a proportional change at the legislative level, providing much more stability in legislative composition. Second, this type of system would not exclude powerful political forces from legislative representation, a situation that can have serious consequences for democratic stability, and would add the benefits of more accurate and genuine representation of all major party options within the electorate. ☐

CONCLUSION

The Chilean case presents some fundamental paradoxes in regard to both the long-term durability of democracy and the theoretical work on electoral systems. The ultimate paradox is that whereas the military government designed the electoral system to foster stability and moderation, its very design contains the seeds of instability. In its attempt to use electoral laws to transform the party system, the military government imposed a framework that encourages volatility and exclusion, with potentially destabilizing consequences. For these reasons the Chilean electoral system needs to be modified to better correspond to the nature of the party system and the political reality of the country.

A number of significant political sectors have always existed in Chile and will continue to exist in the future. No electoral system is capable of changing that reality, as has been demonstrated by the party system's rapid adjustment to the binomial system. But unlike the binomial system, a moderate proportional representation formula would guarantee the representation of all significant political sectors in proportion to the relative magnitude of their support, thereby enhancing the predictability and long-term stability of the political system. Such a formula would eliminate the volatility and exclusionary tendencies that are intrinsic characteristics of the binomial system; at the same time it would exercise controls on the access of small or extremist parties to parliamentary representation and decrease the likelihood that presidents would be left without legislative support.

From a theoretical perspective, the Chilean case clearly demonstrates that the debate on the desirability of electoral reform as a remedy to some of the difficulties plaguing Latin American—and other newer—democracies is much more complex than it appears on the surface. Those who advocate a shift to majoritarian electoral systems in Latin America and elsewhere should approach the issue of electoral reform with caution. Reformers must go beyond the purely theoretical relationships that have been established between electoral formulas and party systems to consider the sociopolitical and party systems contexts of their individual countries. Even in the most well-designed electoral system, sociopolitical and party system variables may be capable of generating unanticipated complications. In this sense, electoral reform may create more problems than it solves.

In addition, despite a certain disillusionment with proportional representation systems in both theory and practice, in certain sociopolitical and party system contexts PR may possess more of the moderating characteristics the literature commonly attributes to majoritarian electoral systems. The real question is which type of electoral system best balances the advantages and constraints of majoritarian and proportional representation systems, given the characteristics of distinct party systems and the societies in which they are embedded. □

NOTES

1. Some interesting contributions to this debate include Giovanni Sartori, "The Influence of Electoral Systems: Faulty Laws or Faulty Method?" in Bernard

Grofman and Arend Lijphart, eds., *Electoral Laws and Their Political Consequences* (New York: Agathon Press, 1986), pp. 43–68; Arend Lijphart, "The Political Consequences of Electoral Laws, 1945–1985," *American Political Science Review* 84, no. 2 87(June 1990): 482–496; and the dialogue among Guy Lardeyret, Quentin Quade, and Arend Lijphart in "PR vs. Plurality Elections," *Journal of Democracy* 2, no. 3 (Summer 1990): 30–48.

2. For a description of the preauthoritarian party system, see Federico Gil, *The Political System of Chile* (Boston: Houghton Mifflin, 1966); and Kalman H. Silvert, *Chile: Yesterday and Today* (New York: Holt, Rinehart, and Winston, 1965). For a more recent discussion, see Ronald McDonald and Mark Ruhl, *Party Politics and Elections in Latin America* (Boulder: Westview Press, 1989). For a discussion with particular reference to Chilean postauthoritarian party system continuity, see Timothy Scully and J. Samuel Valenzuela, "De la democracia a la democracia: Continuidad y variaciones en las preferencias del electorado y en el sistema de partidos en Chile," *Estudios Públicos* 51 (Winter 1993): 195–228.

3. In the congressional races, the Concertación garnered 49.3 percent of the vote, to 32.4 percent for Democracia y Progreso, in the chamber and 50.46 percent of the vote versus 43.04 percent, respectively, in the Senate. In the Chamber of Deputies, Democracia y Progreso elected forty-six members, the Concertación elected sixty-six, and the PAIS list elected eight. In the Senate, Democracia y Progreso garnered sixteen seats, the Concertación won twenty-two seats, and the PAIS list failed to elect any senators.

4. For one of the few studies on the effect of district magnitudes of two, see Rein Taagepera, "The Effect of District Magnitude and Properties of Two-Seat Districts," in Arend Lijphart and Bernard Grofman, eds., *Choosing an Electoral System* (New York: Praeger, 1984), pp. 91–101.

5. Servicio Electoral de Chile, "Resultados Plebiscitos y Elecciones, 1988–1989, p.12." Blank and null votes were not considered in calculating percentages. Totals do not equal 100 percent because of the participation of other party lists.

6. Heraldo Muñoz, quoted in *La Epoca* 16 (December 1989): 20.

7. For the proportionality indexes of all of the major parties participating in the 1989 election, see Arturo Valenzuela and Peter Siavelis, "Ley electoral y estabilidad democrática: Un ejercicio de simulación para el caso de Chile," *Estudios Públicos* 43 (Winter 1991): 27–87.

8. Because the Chilean electoral system is characterized by magnitudes of two, one could correctly argue that Duverger's argument in its purest form does not apply. Nonetheless, district magnitude has come to be recognized as one of the most important determining variables of both the proportionality and the functional dynamic of electoral systems. Lijphart and Grofman have demonstrated convincingly that the party system effects of low-magnitude PR systems are fairly similar to those exerted by purer majority/plurality systems. In this sense, rather than only majority/plurality and PR existing as distinct types, there is actually a continuum of electoral systems, depending on district magnitude and a number of other variables. Chile is closer to the majority/plurality end of that continuum. See Lijphart and Grofman, "Introduction," in *Choosing an Electoral System*, pp. 1–12. For Duverger's argument in its original form, see Maurice Duverger, *Political Parties*, trans. Barbara North and Robert North (New York: John Wiley and Sons, 1955).

9. The Chilean public is experiencing a convergence of ideological self-identification. Whether this is a permanent development or simply a response to the democratic transition process remains uncertain. For the data supporting this contention, as well as a discussion of its consequences, see Timothy Scully, *Rethinking the Center: Party Politics in Nineteenth and Twentieth Century Chile* (Stanford: Stanford University Press, 1992).

10. Arturo Fontaine, Harald Beyer, and Luis Paúl have argued convincingly that the special context and characteristics of the election had a strong impact on their outcome. See their article "Mapa de las corrientes políticas en las elecciones generales de 1989," *Estudios Públicos* 38 (Fall 1990): 99–128. For a more explicit discussion of the effect of the presidential campaign on the legislative elections, see Enrique Barros, "El nuevo orden de partidos: Algunas hipótesis," *Estudios Públicos* 38 (Fall 1990): 129–139.

11. These percentages were obtained by disaggregating the Concertación list into parties representing the Right and the Left in individual districts and grouping all parties of the Right together. The percentages received in each district were then averaged to arrive at a national average for each of the ideological groupings. Our ideological classifications for each of the parties presenting candidates in the election are summarized in note 20. For additional evidence supporting the existence of continuity in the ideological orientation of the Chilean electorate, see Scully and Valenzuela, "De la democracia."

12. *La Epoca* 16 (December 1989): 14–17.

13. For Sartori's definition of party relevance, see Giovanni Sartori, *Parties and Party Systems: A Framework for Analysis* (Cambridge: Cambridge University Press, 1976), pp. 121–125.

14. See Seymour Martin Lipset and Stein Rokkan, "Cleavage Structures, Party Systems and Voter Alignments: An Introduction," in Lipset and Rokkan, eds., *Party Systems and Voter Alignments* (New York: Free Press, 1967), pp. 1–50.

15. Arend Lijphart, *Democracies: Patterns of Majoritarian Consensus in Twenty-One Countries* (New Haven: Yale University Press, 1984), pp. 158.

16. These simulations, as well as much of the discussion that follows, were drawn from previous work by the authors that was published in Spanish. See Valenzuela and Siavelis, "Ley electoral y estabilidad democrática." District-by-district breakdowns of each of the electoral simulations also appear in that article.

17. For a more detailed and complete set of simulations of electoral outcomes for Chile that consider distinct coalitional configurations, electoral returns, and alliance patterns, see Peter Siavelis, "Nuevos argumentos y viejos supuestos: Simulaciones de sistemas electorales alternativos para las elecciones parlamentarias chilenas," *Estudios Públicos* 51 (Winter 1993): 229–267.

18. For both the two- and three-list tests, the public opinion election simulation was based on survey data from Centro de Estudios Públicos, Santiago, *Estudio de Opinión Público: Junio 1990*, Documento de Trabajo no. 136 (Santiago: Centro de Estudios Públicos, August 1990), p. 52. The survey asked, "De los siguientes partidos políticos que se presentan en esta tarjeta, ¿con cuál de ellos se identifica más o simpatiza más Ud.?" (Of the following parties listed on this card, with which one do you most identify or sympathize?) To test the probable results if this survey were indeed an election, parties were grouped into the appropriate coalitions, given the particular coalitional configuration being tested, and the national percentages for each party were summed in

accordance with their coalition membership. Total coalition percentages were then distributed across national districts individually in proportion to the vote received by each alliance in the 1989 election. We divided the percentage of nonidentifiers (22.1 percent in this case) among each of the coalitions. Seat allocations were then computed. One of the principal problems with this type of test is the large number of interviewees who did not respond or who identified themselves as independents. This exercise, however, supports our contentions concerning the potential uncertainty and volatility of the electoral system.

19. All electoral data used in both the two- and three-list tests are from *La Epoca* 16 (December 1989): 14–17. For both tests, the total vote may not equal 100 percent because of blank and spoiled votes and votes cast for parties classified as "other."

20. The process for performing this test was similar to that described earlier, as was the process for the simulation based on public opinion. Because we rearranged the parties of the Concertación into forces representing the Center and the Left, we classified parties into two categories. We also grouped nonaligned parties of the Right into one list. Only parties that presented candidates for the Chamber of Deputies were included. "Center" parties or alliances included Partido Demócrata Cristiano, Partido Radical, Partido Alianza del Centro, and Partido Social Democracia; the "Left" alliances were the Partido por la Democracia, Partido Comunista, Partido Amplio de Izquierda Socialista, Partido Socialista de Almeyda, Los Verdes, Partido Radical Socialista Democrático, Partido Humanista, Partido Democrático Nacional, and Izquierda Cristiana; and the "Right" parties were Unión Demócrata Independiente, Renovación Nacional, Partido Nacional, and all members of the Avanzada Nacional–Democracia Radical list. Parties classified as "other" included all regional parties. In addition, the Partido Socialista Chileno and the Paritido Liberal were classified as "other" because their names were deliberately chosen to mislead voters, so the true intentions of those opting for one of the two parties are not ascertainable. In addition, we made every effort to identify the political orientations of candidates who identified themselves as independents because of laws prohibiting certain parties or registration problems. In all cases we were able to identify the partisan orientations of candidates on the Concertación list.

21. A category "other" was not included here, because none of the nonaligned candidates was successful in winning a seat in the legislature.

22. For a discussion of the importance of the timing and sequencing of presidential elections, see Matthew Shugart and John Carey, *Presidents and Assemblies: Constitutional Design and Electoral Dynamics* (New York: Cambridge University Press, 1992), chapters 10–12.

23. Sartori, *Parties and Party Systems*, pp. 139, 141.

24. This argument is elaborated more fully in Siavelis, "Nuevos argumentos y viejos supuestos."

PART TWO

The Design of Executive-Legislative Relations

CHAPTER SIX

—■—

Executive-Legislative Relations in Crisis: Poland's Experience, 1989–1993

Jerzy J. Wiatr

POLAND'S DEMOCRATIC TRANSFORMATION frustrated the hopes of those who believed democracy would be established with relative ease and would provide a functional framework for socioeconomic transformation. Despite the deeply rooted democratic opposition to the Communist regime and the perseverance of the reformist current within the ruling Polish United Workers' Party (PZPR), the transition was difficult. Although Poland was indeed a successful pioneer during the extrication stage of the democratic transformation, it failed to produce a stable institutional and political framework for system transformation. Between the critical election of June 1989 and the 1993 election, Poland had six prime ministers and four cabinets—only one of which lasted longer than a year. The first president elected under the terms of the negotiated contract for the transition to electoral politics, General Wojciech Jaruzelski, was forced to resign long before the end of his term, and his successor, Solidarity leader Lech Walesa, found himself under severe attack from former supporters.[1] By the mid-1990s, the popularity of democratic institutions was low and was continuing to sink.[2]

Only 43 percent of eligible voters took part in the parliamentary election in October 1991. Widespread corruption tarnished the image of the new democratic institutions.[3] Indicators of social unrest—from strikes to angry demonstrations—multiplied. Growing symptoms of new authoritarianism appeared, including nasty appeals to xenophobia and anti-Semitism on the extreme Right and appeals to populist militancy on the extreme Left. The new election in September 1993, with a 52 percent electoral turnout, produced a strong shift to left-of-center parties and demonstrated the strength of the opposition to the policies of post–1989 governments. Although the young Polish democratic regime survived, and some modest elements of economic recovery began to emerge, the basic question remained: Why has Poland failed to create a solid institutional framework for democratic transformation and the orderly transition to a market economy?[4]

There are several explanations for this failure. Observers, particularly in the right wing of the Polish political scene, see Poland's failures as the results of the compromise agreement reached in April 1989 between the ruling party and the Solidarity-led opposition. The "contractual election" of June 1989 and the power sharing during the first year of transition are blamed for the inadequate transformation of the political and economic institutions, as well as for the alleged lack of consistency of democratic governments in pursuing the goals of system transformation. Paradoxically, some also believe one of the reasons for Poland's political turbulence is precisely the opposite: The terms of the roundtable agreement were not observed, and Solidarity, once in power, abandoned the policy of national accord and temporary power sharing with the reformist elements of the ancien régime.

In some commentaries, the Polish malaise is presented as an example of déjà vu—as the old pattern of fragmented, personalized politics of the pre-Communist past reemerging in the new era. The argument that Polish politics in the 1990s can best be understood from the perspective of a political culture analysis has certain advantages but cannot close the door to interpretations based on current factors.

Of these, one deserves special attention. Poland is the only country in Eastern Europe where prior to the collapse of the Communist regime both a massive opposition movement and that movement's charismatic leader, Lech Walesa, played a significant role. The paradox of post-Communist transformation may be that whereas such factors pushed Poland to the front line of the wave of democratic change, they also made the institutionalization of the democratic regime more difficult. Without ignoring the historical role of the cultural and psychological characteristics of the nation, I will concentrate here on the analysis of institutional changes in Poland, particularly from the perspective of executive-legislative relations. Furthermore, I will compare the Polish experience with that of Hungary, trying to find the reasons these two countries—which are so similar in many respects—have followed different patterns in their institutional transformations. □

PARLIAMENTARISM, PRESIDENTIALISM, OR SOMETHING ELSE?

Institutional change is not deterministic.[5] Although many factors (economic, cultural, geopolitical, and ethnic, among others) may make some choices more likely than others, institutional arrangements ultimately depend on a relatively small number of people—political decisionmakers and key opinion makers. In the context of extrication from the Communist regimes, three patterns have emerged in regard to both the composition of these elites and their modus operandi. First, as occurred in Hungary, the Communist Party—prior to its departure from power—worked out a new constitution through negotiated agreement with the opposition.[6] Second, as happened in Czechoslovakia after the election of the Federal Assembly in June 1990, no constitutional change took place prior to the collapse of the regime, which occurred rapidly and without prolonged negotiations between the government and the opposition. Consequently, the new Parliament, elected after the collapse of the old regime, was charged with adopting a new constitution.[7] Third, no comprehensive constitutional reform was undertaken either before or immediately after the extrication from the Communist regime; instead, gradual and partial changes were introduced in the old constitution. This was the case in Poland.

Elsewhere, I have discussed the reasons the Polish process of constitutional reform followed the third pattern.[8] Neither the then-ruling PZPR nor Solidarity was prepared for comprehensive constitutional reform when the two agreed to enter the roundtable negotiations in early 1989. For too long, the PZPR had considered any negotiated power sharing with the opposition to be unacceptable, and it abandoned that position only on the eve of the negotiations. Solidarity (as well as other opposition groups) did not anticipate the change of the regime and, therefore, concentrated on more limited goals of partial liberalization. Consequently, amendments to the 1952 constitution resulted from ad hoc compromises achieved during the roundtable negotiations. A good illustration is the way in which the completely new idea of a bicameral Parliament, with a weak but fully democratically elected Senate, was introduced (and accepted) in the middle of the negotiations to persuade Solidarity to accept both the contractual preordained results of the election to the Sejm (the Polish lower house) and the establishment of a strong presidency.[9]

The system established by the roundtable agreement was a mixture of parliamentarism and presidentialism. Although its strongly parliamentary nature—as declared in the 1952 constitution—was preserved, new powers entrusted to the president of the Republic made the Polish system look more like the French Fifth Republic. The president was allowed to dissolve Parliament (if it failed either to create the cabinet or to adopt the budget within three months or whenever it "prevented the president from performing his constitutional duties"). He or she had the exclusive power to nominate the prime minister and had veto power (with the Sejm being able to overrule the presidential veto by a two-thirds majority). The reality of the system, however, was different from the letter of the Polish constitution. President Wojciech Jaruzelski was elected by both houses of the National Assembly by a one-vote majority, and from the outset he lacked a sufficiently strong political base. As a result of the reorientation

of the former allies of the PZPR—the Peasant and Democratic parties—
which chose a new alliance with Solidarity, and because of the PZPR's
self-dissolution in January 1990, President Jaruzelski's power became
progressively weaker. The Polish system temporarily became more parliamentary in reality than it was on paper.

In the second half of 1990, political pressure on President Jaruzelski—
launched by the supporters of Lech Walesa—resulted in Jaruzelski's initiative to amend the constitution's provisions for the election of the
president to allow for an election by popular vote. A presidential election
followed soon after the adoption of the amendment. Jaruzelski did not
run for reelection, and Lech Walesa won overwhelmingly (but only in the
runoff, after Prime Minister Tadeusz Mazowiecki had been defeated for
second place by a little-known émigré businessman, Stanislaw Tyminski).

After Walesa's election in December 1990, the system reversed itself
and became more presidential. Mazowiecki resigned, and the president
nominated one of his supporters, the previously little-known parliamentarian Jan Krzysztof Bielecki, as the new prime minister. The Sejm, conscious
of its lack of legitimacy vis-à-vis the democratically elected president, readily approved Bielecki's nomination. Until the next parliamentary election
in October 1991, President Walesa clearly had the upper hand.

The 1991 election produced a highly fragmented Sejm (and an
equally fragmented Senate) with twenty-nine parties represented, some
by only one parliamentarian. The degree of fragmentation in the Polish
Sejm can best be seen in comparative perspective. Percentages of seats
won by all but the smallest parties in the lower houses of East European
Parliaments elected during the 1990–1992 period are listed in Table 6.1.[10]

President Walesa did not officially support any political party and had
no permanent base in the Parliament. Immediately after the election he
made an unsuccessful effort to build a centrist coalition under the leadership of the then largest parliamentary party, the Democratic Union (Tadeusz
Mazowiecki's party, created after his defeat in the 1990 presidential election). When the attempt failed, Walesa accepted as his new prime minister
the candidate of the right-of-center parties, a well-known Solidarity lawyer
Jan Olszewski. Olszewski's cabinet quickly developed a clearly antipresi-
dential position, particularly regarding control over the armed forces.[11]

President Walesa won this round of conflict—although not without
difficulty—largely because of the support of political parties of the opposition, including the Left. Minister of Defense Jan Parys was dismissed on
May 15, 1992, after several weeks of forced "vacation." Olszewski's cabinet fell on June 5, 1992, self-destroyed by its ill-advised campaign to dis-
credit many key politicians—including Walesa—by alleging that they
secretly collaborated with the security police of the old regime. Briefly
enjoying for a short time the support of the parliamentary majority,
President Walesa nominated another new prime minister, Waldemar

TABLE 6.1 Seats Won by Different Parties in the Lower Houses of
Eastern European Parliaments, 1990–1992 (in percentages of total seats)

Poland	Romania	Hungary	Czech Republic	Slovakia	Bulgaria	Albania
13.48	34.31	42.49	48.49	47.06	45.83	65.71
13.04	24.05	23.83	19.19	19.61	44.17	27.14
11.09	12.61	11.40	10.10	11.76	10.00	5.00
10.87	8.80	8.55	8.08	11.76	1.43	
10.00	7.92	5.44	7.07	9.80	0.71	
9.56	4.68	5.44	7.07			
8.04	3.81	0.26				
6.09						
5.87						
3.48						
1.52						
1.09						
1.09						
0.87						
0.65						
0.65						

Note: Columns may not total 100 percent because some minor parties are omitted.
Source: The Economist Newspaper Group, Inc., 1993. Reprinted with permission, further reproduction prohibited.

Pawlak, the leader of the Polish Peasant Party. Pawlak won a vote of confidence but after a month of intense negotiations failed to build a coalition.

After his resignation, the Parliament approved as prime minister Hanna Suchocka, one of the parliamentarians of the Democratic Union. Her cabinet was based on a fragile coalition of seven parties (from the Democratic Union to the rightist Christian National Alliance). Relations between the president and the cabinet appeared congenial, and in at least one case—the crucial vote on the 1993 budget—the president's forceful support saved Suchocka's cabinet from defeat. In early 1993, the cabinet lost some of its original supporters, mostly because of the defection of a number of representatives of Solidarity who had been deeply frustrated by the economic performance of the government. This weakened the cabinet, whose very existence depended on divisions within the opposition. Although numerically strong, the opposition was unable to present an alternative to Suchocka's cabinet because of deep divisions between the right-wing and left-wing parties. On the Right, the cabinet was opposed by the populist-nationalist Confederacy of Independent Poland, Jan Olszewski's Movement for the Republic, the Center Alliance, and two minor groups—a total of 94 members of the Sejm (out of 460). On the Left, the opposition consisted of the Democratic Left Alliance, the Polish Peasant Party, and the

Labor Union—altogether, 114 members of the Sejm. Because of the divisions within some of the coalition parties, as well as the presence of independents, the forces of both the coalition and the opposition were more or less equally balanced, but the two opposition blocs could not agree on any common program that would constitute an alternative to the Suchocka cabinet.

The fragmentation of Parliament and the difficulty of building the two-thirds majority needed to adopt a new constitution led to a provisional solution. On October 17, 1992, the Constitutional Act (colloquially called the Little Constitution) came into force. Under its terms, the 1952 constitution lost validity, except for those articles that were temporarily retained pending the adoption of the new constitution. Relations between the legislative and executive powers were reshaped in such a way that the cabinet was strengthened at the expense of the president. Most important were the provisions of Articles 57 to 60, which regulate the way in which new prime ministers are appointed. Unlike the previous rules, the Sejm can elect its own candidate—after rejecting the candidate of the president (who has the right to initiate the procedure). In case of a deadlock, in which no candidate wins the necessary majority, the president can either dissolve Parliament or appoint a cabinet whose duration is not to exceed six months. If during this period the cabinet fails to win the parliamentary vote of confidence, the president dissolves Parliament (Article 62).

The president's power to dissolve Parliament was further defined in a more precise and narrow way. He or she can do so in the case of a no-confidence vote if a new prime minister is not elected (Article 66). According to Article 21, if, after three months following its submission by the cabinet, the budget has not been accepted by Parliament, the president has the right to call a new election.

The question of parliamentarism versus presidentialism remains one of the unresolved issues of Polish politics. In April 1993, President Walesa submitted his draft of a new constitution, based on substantial strengthening of presidential powers. An alternative proposal, submitted by the Democratic Left Alliance, opts for a consistently parliamentary system of government. There are various middle-of-the-road proposals as well. Western analyses of the relative advantages of both systems in conditions of democratic transformation can be helpful and have been referred to in Polish political dialogue (for instance, in my speech on constitutional reform in the Sejm).[12] There is also a strong tendency, however, to ignore foreign experience and to seek new solutions in a theoretical vacuum. Presidentialism may find support among the general public, which is frustrated with the poor performance of the cabinets and is increasingly willing to accept the concentration of power in the hands of a strong leader. On the other hand, Lech Walesa's diminished popularity makes the adoption of the presidential system less likely, at least for the time being.

In late May 1993, Parliament adopted the no-confidence motion against Suchocka's cabinet. The initiative came from the Solidarity parliamentary caucus and was supported by all opposition parties from both the Left and the Right. Since Parliament had failed to name its candidate for prime minister, President Walesa refused to accept Suchocka's resignation and dissolved Parliament (acting on Article 66 of the Little Constitution). The election on September 19, 1993, produced a radical change in the composition of both houses of Parliament. Because of the 5 percent threshold adopted in the new electoral law for the Sejm election, the number of parliamentary parties was reduced to only six (plus four members of Parliament elected on the lists of German minorities). Moreover, there was a strong shift to the left as a result of growing frustration with the socioeconomic record of the cabinets dominated by the post-Solidarity parties.

The Democratic Left Alliance won 20.41 percent of the votes and received 171 seats, becoming the largest party group in the Sejm. The only other parties that qualified were the Polish Peasant Party, with 15.40 percent of the votes (132 seats); the Democratic Union, with 10.59 percent of the votes (74 seats); the Labor Union, with 7.28 percent of the votes (41 seats); the Confederacy of Independent Poland, with 5.77 percent of the votes (22 seats); and the newly formed, pro-presidential Non-Party Bloc for Support of Reforms, with 5.41 percent of the votes (16 seats). In the Senate, the Democratic Left won 37 seats, and the Polish Peasant Party won 36 seats (out of 100) allocated by a plurality system in forty-nine provinces. The elimination of all extreme right-wing parties from the lower house of the Polish Parliament, as well as the strong position of the two main parliamentary forces, produced the situation in which a stable parliamentary majority was possible as long as the Democratic Left Alliance and the Polish Peasant Party cooperated.

The electoral victory of the Center-Left coalition strengthened the Parliament vis-à-vis the president but did not prevent open conflicts. In February 1995, President Walesa made an unsuccessful attempt to dissolve the Parliament (a move that, according to all legal authorities, lacked constitutional justification). Confronted with almost unanimous opposition from the Parliament, as well as with negative domestic public opinion and unfavorable reactions from foreign governments, Walesa gave up his attempt. The governing coalition of the Democratic Left and the Polish Peasant Party regrouped and, after dismissing Prime Minister Waldemar Pawlak (of the Peasant Party), elected a new cabinet under the former speaker of the Sejm, social-democrat Jozef Oleksy. □

LEARNING FROM HUNGARY

Hungary, unlike Poland, has had a reasonably well-functioning system of parliamentarism, which was established during the negotiated extrication in 1989 and consolidated by the parliamentary election in March–April 1990. The unicameral Hungarian Parliament was elected in 1990 on the basis of a mixed electoral system (with 176 seats allocated on a majority basis in one-seat constituencies and the remaining 210 seats distributed by a proportional system with a 4 percent threshold). The result was a moderately fragmented Parliament in which the three largest parties won 300 (out of 386) seats. The largest party—the Hungarian Democratic Forum—received 42.49 percent of all seats (164), and the second-largest party—Union of Free Democrats—received 23.83 percent of the seats (92).[13] The coalition of three parties—the Hungarian Democratic Forum, the Smallholders Party, and the Christian-Democratic People's Party—had a solid majority (229 seats at the beginning); and the cabinet of Joseph Antall and, following Antall's death, of Peter Boross was the most stable cabinet in any post-communist country. Parliamentary elections in May 1994 ended the rule of the right-of-center coalition and gave an absolute majority to the Hungarian Socialist Party, whose chair, Gyula Horn, became prime minister. The transfer of power to the former (post-Communist) opposition went smoothly and confirmed that the parliamentary system of government works well in Hungary.

The Hungarian constitution (Articles 29–32) defines the position of the president of the republic in a way that is consistent with the parliamentary character of the Hungarian system. Elected by Parliament for a four-year term, the president has little real power. He or she can, however, act as a moderating force, something President Árpád Göncz has been doing with remarkable skill (for instance, refusing to use the army to end a taxi and truck drivers' strike in 1990 or to dismiss directors of state radio and television, as demanded by the prime minister).[14] Both Poland and Hungary have suffered economic crises (recession, high unemployment, declining standards of living), yet Poles have reason to envy Hungarians for their success in establishing a well-functioning parliamentary system.

There are a number of explanations for this difference. Neither the political cultures—with interesting similarities between Poland and Hungary—nor the socioeconomic situations will suffice, however. The explanation should be sought in the way in which the "negotiated revolution" has taken place, in the behavior of the main actors (on the part of both the former regime and the former opposition), in the legal framework chosen in the first stage of the democratic transformation, and in the role of the leader.[15]

Background of the Regime-Opposition Negotiations

Although both countries entered the crucial stage of negotiated extrication from the Communist regime in 1989 (Poland convened its roundtable discussions barely four months before Hungary did), the background of these events was different in Poland than it was in Hungary. Long before 1989,

Poland had given rise to the massive Solidarity movement—the strongest democratic opposition ever to emerge in a Communist state. When it entered negotiations in February 1989, the Polish opposition was stronger than that in Hungary at a similar stage. The opposition's strength allowed it to be the pioneer of the democratization process in the entire Soviet bloc, but it also forced upon it a high degree of moderation. Only after the Polish agreement had been reached and after Solidarity's overwhelming victory in June 1989 did the impossible become possible. Prior to that, the round-table discussions in Poland negotiated not the abolition but the transformation of the Communist system, based on a principle of negotiated power sharing. The Hungarians, who came later, were in a better position to negotiate the institutional framework needed for extrication from the Communist system and for the establishment of a democratic republic.

The Role of the Partners

In Poland, the ruling party was deeply divided among conservative hard-liners, reformers, and centrists. The reformers never held a dominant position and were weakened considerably by the martial law of 1981–1983. Three factors led the Polish United Workers' Party to open negotiations: (1) the failure of the post-martial-law regime to solve the economic crisis and regain public support; (2) the memory of the 1981 confrontation, with its heavy risks for national security, and the resolve of the political leadership to avoid repeating such a situation; and (3) the favorable international climate created by Gorbachev's reforms in the USSR and his assurances that the Soviet Union would not intervene even if Poland were to move ahead with deeper democratic change. Motivated by these factors, General Jaruzelski, with the support of his key aides in the government and in the party's Central Committee, decided to open negotiations with Solidarity. This decision was forced on an unwilling majority of the party's Central Committee.

In Hungary, the reformers were much stronger within the ruling party. Following János Kádár's death in June 1989, they were able not only to capture complete control of the party but also to change its name (to the Hungarian Socialist Party) and its program, forcing the hard-liners to leave the party and establish their own group (under the old name of the Hungarian Socialist Workers' Party). Consequently, the reformers were willing and able to negotiate the orderly transition to parliamentary democracy rather than having to settle for a fragile contract of power sharing as occurred in Poland.

Not only were the partners on the side of the ruling parties in different positions in these two countries but so were their interlocutors from the opposition. The Hungarian opposition, which was a relatively recent phenomenon, was considerably weaker than the Polish one. After the

Soviet intervention in 1956 and brutal persecutions during the late 1950s, the Hungarian opposition gathered strength slowly and thus came to be a significant political actor much later than its Polish equivalent. Its true beginning is usually traced to the meeting of 160 intellectuals in Lakitelek in September 1987, at which demands for a multiparty system were officially voiced. In 1988, several political associations were formed under a newly liberalized law on association. Opposition political parties began to emerge prior to the beginning of the roundtable talks: the Hungarian Democratic Forum in September 1987 (at the Lakitelek meeting), the Union of Young Democrats in March 1988, the Smallholders Party in November 1988 (at a meeting in Szetendre), the Union of Free Democrats in November 1988, and the Christian-Democratic People's Party in March 1989. The Hungarian opposition thus entered the negotiations with at least an embryonic party structure.

At this stage the Polish opposition was divided between Solidarity, which played a crucial role, and other groups, of which the oldest and strongest was the Confederacy of Independent Poland (founded in the underground in 1979). Solidarity entered the negotiations as a movement rather than a party. For a period of time it tried to maintain its nonpartisan character, acting as an umbrella organization for all democratic forces in the country. In reality, however, several individuals and groups of the opposition were either excluded from the roundtable talks or excluded themselves voluntarily, citing their complete rejection of any compromise with the Communists. This is one of the main reasons for deep divisions and animosities within the Polish political class today and is one of the sources of the fragility of the roundtable agreements.

The Nature of the Legal Frameworks

In both countries, the roundtable talks resulted in several changes in the legal order. In Hungary, these changes were carefully planned and shaped in a way that was conducive to the establishment of viable parliamentarism: a strong Parliament and cabinet, a (almost) symbolic president, and a mixed system of representation. These changes contributed to the success of the parliamentary design. In Poland, however, the institutional changes were introduced in a piecemeal fashion, more because of considerations of political expediency than from a blueprint of the new system. Because of the tremendous uncertainty, neither side was able to come forward with a consistent model for the new system.

The Role of the Leader

Although certain individuals played significant roles in the Hungarian transformation, the process itself cannot be identified with any single person—unlike the Polish political scene in the 1980s, which was dominated by Lech Walesa. His powerful personality and political ambitions significantly influenced the process of transformation. In the first stage of extrication, Lech Walesa was not only able to persuade the ruling elite to open negotiations, but he also brought to the roundtable a truly representative group of opposition leaders. He was also instrumental in persuading Solidarity to accept the compromise. Later, it was Walesa who began the process of moving beyond the roundtable agreement, particularly by building the Solidarity-dominated government coalition in August 1989. Finally, not satisfied with the situation after most of the Communist regimes in the region had collapsed, Walesa raised the banner of "acceleration" of political change—with the objective, at least in part, being his election to the presidency. As president, Walesa was uncomfortable with a role as the head of state who had limited power (even though his power was much greater than that enjoyed by his Hungarian counterpart). Walesa's constant maneuvering for greater power contributed significantly to the instability of the Polish political system. □

SUMMARY

Whatever the reasons for Poland's inability to establish a stable constitutional system, it can learn much from the Hungarian political experience. Having been the first country to depart from the Communist regime, Poland can benefit from the experience of the country that in 1989 had all of the advantages of the latecomer. □

NOTES

1. For observations about the early stages of the campaign, see Louisa Vinton, "Olszewski's Ouster Leaves Poland Polarized," RFE-RL [Radio Free Europe/Radio Liberty] *Research Report* 1, no. 25 (June 19, 1992). On January 22, 1993, leaders of the anti-Walesa opposition organized a street demonstration in Warsaw demanding the president's resignation. The demonstration was followed by similar events in various parts of the country. Accusations against Walesa and his entourage were also presented in interviews published in Jacek Kurski and Piotr Semka, eds., *Lewy Czerwcowy* (Warsaw: Editions Spotkania, 1992).

2. Surveys demonstrate the decline of approval for all institutions of state power. According to the Center of Social Opinion Research (CBOS, research report, June 1992), approval for the president fell from 46 percent in October 1991 to 36 percent in May 1992, approval for the cabinet fell from 39 to 32 percent, approval for the Sejm declined from 34 to 30 percent, and approval for the Senate fell from 36 to 29 percent. The Catholic Church, in the first survey on this issue, registered declining approval as well—from 64 to 48 percent in the same period of time. Even the highly popular Armed Forces fell from a 75 percent to a 68 percent approval rate (from October 1991 to May 1992). In another study, Ewa Karpowicz

found that Poles evaluated the performance of the Sejm elected in 1989 as considerably better than that of the one elected in 1991 (Ewa Karpowicz, "Sejm X Kadencji i Sejm i Kadencji w opinii spolexcczenstwa," Biuro Studiow i Analiz, Kancelaria Sejmu, June 1992).

3. See Charles T. Powers, "Corruption Replaces Socialism as Roadblock to Business in Poland," *Los Angeles Times*, August 2, 1992.

4. See data provided by *The Economist* (March 13, 1993): 3–32, in its survey of Eastern Europe.

5. On this issue I share the methodological position of Adam Przeworski, "Some Problems in the Study of the Transition to Democracy," in Guillermo O'Donnell, Philippe C. Schmitter, and Laurence Whitehead, eds., *Transitions from Authoritarian Rule: Comparative Perspectives* (Baltimore: Johns Hopkins University Press, 1986), pp. 47–63.

6. Györgi Szoboszlai, "Political Transition and Constitutional Change," in Szoboszlai, ed., *Democracy and Political Transformation: Theories and East-Central European Realities* (Budapest: Hungarian Political Science Association, 1991), pp. 195–212. Technically, the Constitutional Act of October 18, 1989, is the extensively amended text of the 1949 constitution. The Preamble clearly states that this is a provisional act, valid only "until the ratification of the new Constitution of our country." However, the text has been amended so substantially (about four-fifths of the original text has been changed), and it fits the political needs of Hungary so well, that the transition has taken place under the rules established by it.

7. Jana Reschová, "Parliament and Constitutional Change (The Czechoslovak Experience)," paper presented at the International Conference on Europeanization of the Central European Political System, Budapest, Hungary, November 26–28, 1992.

8. Jerzy J. Wiatr, "Constitutional Change and Contractual Democracy in Poland, 1989–1990," paper presented at the Conference on Constitutionalism and the Transition to Democracy in Eastern Europe, Pécs, Hungary, June 18–20, 1990, organized by the American Council of Learned Societies and the Department of Sociology of Law, Eötvös Lorand University, Budapest. The German text was published in *Freibeuter* (Berlin) 45 (1990): 36–46, under the title, "Verfassungsanderungen and kontrachtliche Demokratie in Polen, 1980–1990."

9. See the comments on this issue by David M. Olson and Lawrence D. Longley, "Conclusions: Cameral Change, Politics, and Processes in Three Nations and Beyond," in Olson and Longley, eds., *Two into One: The Politics and Processes of National Legislative Cameral Change* (Boulder: Westview Press, 1991), pp. 222–223.

10. *The Economist* (March 13, 1993): 4.

11. See Jerzy J. Wiatr, "The Political Role of the Military in a New Democracy: Poland," in Constantine P. Danopoulos and Cynthia Watson, eds., *Political Role of the Military: An International Handbook* (Westport, Conn.: Greenwood Publishing Group, forthcoming).

12. See in particular Juan J. Linz, "The Perils of Presidentialism," *Journal of Democracy* (Winter 1990): 51–69; Juan J. Linz, "The Virtues of Parliamentarism,"

Journal of Democracy (Fall 1990): 84–91; Arend Lijphart, "Constitutional Choices for New Democracies," *Journal of Democracy* (Winter 1991): 72–84; and Arend Lijphart, "The Virtues of Parliamentarism—But Which Kind of Parliamentarism?" in H. E. Chehabi and Alfred Stepan, eds., *Politics, Society, and Democracy: Comparative Studies* (Boulder: Westview Press, 1995), pp. 363–373. For the author's speech, see the proceedings of the Twelfth Session of the Sejm (April 2, 1992), pp. 31–32 (in Polish).

13. Andras Korosenyi, "Wegierskie wybory parlamentarne—rok 1990," in Jacek Raciborski, ed., *Wybory i narodziny demokracji w krajach Europy Strodkowej i Wschodniej* (Warsaw: Institute of Sociology, University of Warsaw, 1991), pp. 56–73.

14. Ernest Beck, "Hungarian President Seeks to Reconcile His Nation's Troubled Past, Uncertain Future," *Wall Street Journal—Europe* (April 19, 1993).

15. László Bruszt, "1989: The Negotiated Revolution of Hungary," in Szoboszlai, *Democracy and Political Transformation,* pp. 213–225.

CHAPTER SEVEN

———————— ■ ————————

Parliamentarism in the Making: Crisis and Political Transformation in Hungary

György Szoboszlai

Since the publication of Juan Linz's article "The Perils of Presidentialism," many scholars have regarded parliamentarism as the superior form of democratic government in multicultural, multiethnic, and socially divided societies—especially when these societies are undergoing transformation.[1] Parliamentarism tends to be more consensual and flexible than presidentialism.[2] Arend Lijphart considers the majoritarian tendencies of presidentialism to be especially harmful in divided societies, and he has acknowledged that rigidity and immobilism are the most serious general weaknesses of presidentialism. He has argued that "in the many democracies where a natural consensus is lacking, a consensual instead of a majoritarian form of democracy is needed."[3] This would mean that in democratizing societies, in which a less pluralistic and noncompetitive type of political system is replaced by a pluralistic one, constitution drafters should opt for a basically parliamentary model of democracy. But this option avoids only the rigidity and inflexible majoritarianism of presidential systems. If a presidential system is combined with a two-party system, it can still produce a high degree of stability, but "the combination of presidentialism and multipartism makes stable democracy difficult to sustain," as Scott Mainwaring has shown.[4]

Depending on the electoral rules, however, parliamentarism can also be very rigid and majoritarian, even in a multiparty framework. The governmental system—presidential or parliamentary—is only one component of the constitutional framework that determines the institutional character of a polity. Therefore, it is necessary to distinguish among different types of parliamentarism.[5] Linz has argued that a parliamentary system combined with proportional representation (PR) is a better option than either majoritarian parliamentarism or majoritarian presidentialism.[6] Lijphart—refining this proposal—has advised the drafters of new democratic constitutions to choose a parliamentary system with moderate PR to maximize governability.[7]

In this chapter I analyze the Hungarian constitutional transformation by asking what kind of parliamentarism has emerged since democratization, which factors were the most decisive, and how this institutional development took place. I try to demonstrate that (1) only pure parliamentarism can result in a consensus system, whereas the strong position of the prime minister in Hungary makes the system similar to the combination of presidentialism and multipartism; (2) in unstable democracies, the role of stabilizing factors is important, and this function can best be served by the separation of powers and the creation of autonomous domains in the constitutional structure; and (3) to foster participatory democracy and civic political culture, parliamentarism has to be combined with decentralization and plebiscitary elements. □

THE BIRTH OF MULTIPARTY PARLIAMENTARISM

It is important to note that the Hungarian constitutional transformation took place prior to the establishment of the parliamentary system; that is, parliamentarism was more a result of than a framework for the transition from state socialism to pluralism. Dramatic changes occurred during 1988 and 1989, when the old centralized model was peacefully dismantled in two main political arenas—one within the existing institutional setting of the old state-socialist Parliament and government (the ruling "one-party" system) and the other in the politicized civic movements that constituted an informal political space for new and reestablished political parties.

Peacefulness and gradualism are the most notable characteristics of this nonviolent, nonrevolutionary systemic transformation. Its nonrevolutionary nature has a twofold implication. On the one hand, the old and the emerging new party elites played an accentuated role in defining the course of social and political transformation; on the other hand, the role of civic nonpolitical organizations was less important, and participatory elements were not decisive. The majority of the society remained politically passive—with the exception of a referendum in November 1989 on four political issues.[8] (Only one of the issues was politically decisive—namely, the timing of the election of the president. The liberals wanted to block the holding of a presidential election by popular vote prior to the parliamentary elections.) Otherwise, most of the society belonged—and still belongs—to the category of onlookers. People behaved as passive observers; they did not take to the streets, demonstrate, or take part in strikes.

Another important exception to political passivity was the reburial of Imre Nagy—Hungary's prime minister during the 1956 uprising who was executed under pressure from the Soviet rulers—as a demonstration against the Soviets. The March 1989 demonstration—on the anniversary of the 1848 revolution—also showed open popular dissatisfaction with the political regime. But these events were special occasions of mass mobilization, signaling the wishes of the politically more active groups, which were located mainly in the capital. It was evident that the situation was ripe for radical change, but because this fact was widely accepted, additional mass actions were not necessary. The key actors in the political transition were the incumbent and the newly self-activated elite groups.

The May 1988 national conference of the ruling Hungarian Socialist Workers' Party (HSWP) was the signal for true political change. János Kádár, the person identified with the stability of the old regime, was removed.[9] Overt political pluralization started immediately.[10] Pluralization had already begun covertly as early as the 1970s, following the introduction of a semidecentralized economic management system and a flexible and pragmatic, although paternalistic, governing style. This was important because it created a general atmosphere of openness and legitimized the market-oriented, pragmatic business spirit. During the transition this informal pluralization proved to be decisive, because a well-developed multiparty system was created only a few months during 1989—just prior to the first multiparty general election in spring 1990.

But as mentioned earlier, the political transformation in Hungary preceded the arrival of a fully developed parliamentarism. The key elements of the legal-constitutional transition were completed by the end of 1989, when a new legal framework for the mixed economy and a new constitutional framework for institutionalized political pluralism had been created.

Economic Transformation

The first preconditions were created in the sphere of economic legality. The Business Associations Act, passed in 1988, paved the way for the legal transformation of state-owned public enterprises. As a result—and thanks to a financial regulation that rewarded legal transformation of the "state enterprise" form into limited liability and shareholding companies—the transformation of state-owned enterprises began on a large scale. At the same time, the personal income tax and the value-added tax system were introduced to dismantle state subsidies and open the gates to private enterprise. The 1989 Enterprise Transformation Act lifted barriers to selling shares of legally transformed state-owned enterprises, inviting in foreign capital as well as the Hungarian domestic business community.[11] As a result, a spontaneous privatization process had already started, that was debated and criticized by some leftists and, with even more vehemence, by some conservatives (mainly populists and Christian Democrats).

Constitutional Transformation

A dual political structure has existed in Hungary since 1956. (Before the uprising, a clear Stalinist regime existed in which the ruling party coercively controlled both public and private life, and unofficial political life was very restricted.) In this duality of a formally constitutional state and an informally ruling state party, political power was granted to the ruling party elite through practical control of the state apparatus and through the international system, in which the military and political dominance of the Soviet Union over Eastern Europe was acknowledged. Political power was also based on a hidden social compromise, in which the political elite accepted a philosophy of possible social reform, and civil society passively accepted the noncompetitive polity as a constraint derived from international factors.[12]

This hidden compromise became irrelevant only after the collapse of Soviet hegemony. In the 1960s and 1970s, the state-socialist political leadership tried to find a third way to balance international and internal pressures under the ever-increasing influence of different intellectual movements among the social scientists and the mid-level bureaucracy.[13] Following the introduction of a cautious economic reform program in 1968, the leadership announced a political reform program as well. It quickly became clear that the reforms were meant to be technical rather than structural. The constitutional reform of 1972 did not resolve the contradiction between the Hungarian Parliament's formally superior power and the real superiority of the Presidential Council. According to the constitution, all power originated from Parliament. Nevertheless, the Presidential Council, a smaller body unofficially controlled by the ruling party, enjoyed regulatory freedom that permitted it to ignore and overshadow Parliament. Only very cautious steps were taken in reforming this system until the electoral reform in 1983.[14]

In the second half of the 1980s, however, structural constitutional reform became inevitable. It took place in the Parliament that was elected in 1985 and was based on an electoral reform enacted in 1983, that had introduced competitive elements into the electoral law by making multiple nominations compulsory in each of the 352 individual electoral districts.[15] This Parliament was more responsive socially than previous ones dating as far back as the 1960s; it was open to civically expressed needs for reform, and the informal power of the ruling party became more limited. Abruptly, duality surfaced from political obscurity: The power of the incumbent elite was not institutionally legitimized by open political competition, and its weakening facilitated the emergence of para-constitutional civic movements, which rapidly became organized.

In the democratization of the constitutional system, it was enough to remove the basic structural limits to pure parliamentarism and to enact a few new laws. The logic of this process is revealed by the most important modifications:

- Acts 10 and 11 of 1987 to defend the scope of authority of Parliament and to restore the constitutional principle of the rule of law.[16]
- Act 1 of 1989 amending the Constitution, which ordered the establishment of a genuine constitutional court and limited the term of office of the executive to link it to the term of Parliament (formerly, there was no time limit). This amendment obliged Parliament to reformulate the procedural rules, and as a result these rules were adjusted to the requirements of pure parliamentarism. The house rules were amended to create procedural mechanisms for a multiparty Parliament, faction formation, voting procedures, agenda setting, and so forth (Parliament Decision no. 8/1989).
- Act 2 of 1989 on the freedom of association; this liberal regulation affirmed the inalienable right of citizens to establish civic movements and political parties.
- Act 3 of 1989 on the freedom of assembly, which liberalized the right to political opposition.
- Act 7 of 1989 to regulate the right to strike within the framework of a democratic polity.
- Act 8 of 1989 on the institution of a no-confidence vote to make government responsible to Parliament. According to the new regulation, the government could also ask for a vote of confidence, linking it to the acceptance of a specific act.
- Act 17 of 1989 on the plebiscite and referendum.
- Act 31 of 1989 on the general modification of the Constitution, which reinstituted the parliamentary framework.
- Act 33 of 1989 on the functioning and financing of parties, which created the basic legal framework of a pluralistic party system.
- Act 34 of 1989 on the election of members of Parliament (MPs), which lifted the barriers to free party competition.

The basic provisions of the new constitutional framework were worked out at a roundtable conference held from June to September 1989. By this time, most of the important legal modifications had already been enacted. Tripartite negotiations were held to conclude an agreement on the most important features of the constitutional reform and on the basic procedural laws for political transformation to multiparty parliamentarism.[17] Two important subjects surfaced in the roundtable discussion: (1) the relationship between the legislature and the executive and (2) the electoral system. □

CHOOSING PARLIAMENTARISM AS THE BASIC FORM OF GOVERNMENT

During the political transition process, at no time was the choice between parliamentarism and a presidential form of government seriously raised by any of the key actors—the members of the ruling elite and the experts or activists from the opposition movements. One explanation for this phenomenon is historical tradition. Hungary was among the first countries in Europe to institute parliamentarism. From the time of the passage of Act 3 in 1848, through the stream of bourgeois revolutions, and up to the 1949 state-socialist constitution, the country had a parliamentary governmental structure in which, "at least legally, the government was responsible to parliament."[18]

The failure of the 1848 revolution blocked the development of modern parliamentarism, and the 1867 Austro-Hungarian Compromise allowed only limited parliamentarism because of undemocratic electoral regulations.[19] Nevertheless, pure parliamentary traditions were developed historically during the decades of capitalist modernization between 1867 and 1918. In the interwar period, the regime also maintained this formal framework, but it was too conservative to introduce democratic electoral rules. After World War II, this abridgment of democracy was removed when a modern PR system was adopted, and it was fairly evident to the political actors that their choice could be nothing other than a modern parliamentary system. This development was represented by Act 1 in 1946 concerning the republican parliamentary structure, whereby the executive functions were divided between the government—which was politically responsible to the Parliament—and a weak president. This arrangement proved to be short-lived; the state-socialist transformation retained only the empty structure of formal parliamentarism.

During the roundtable talks in summer 1989, the main dividing line was between the HSWP and the opposition roundtable. The ruling party hoped to preserve as much of its power as possible by assigning executive functions to the government and a semistrong president. The direct election of the first president was also meant to be helpful in this respect. The conservative parties and most of the other members of the opposition accepted this solution, but the two dominant liberal parties—the Alliance of Free Democrats (AFD) and the League of Young Democrats (LYD)— were unwilling to accept a presidential election prior to the parliamentary elections. This was in part a matter of principle and in part a question of political tactics. The liberals wanted a pure parliamentary arrangement in which the president would mainly play a symbolic or ceremonial role that expressed national unity. His or her functions could be enhanced only in crisis situations, as a mediator among parliamentary political forces.

After refusing to sign the roundtable agreement, the liberals launched a nationwide campaign to hold a referendum on the question of—among other things—the timing of the presidential election. The Hungarian Democratic Forum (HDF)—then a center-right populist party— announced a boycott of the referendum. This move assured the victory of the liberals' proposal, if only by a narrow margin. This result decided the form of government in Hungary: The weak-presidency model could no longer be challenged in elite circles.

This constitutional model—which was stabilized by the end of 1989, the year of political transformation—instituted a system of power sharing that gave Parliament a relatively strong position. The government was politically responsible to Parliament, and the ministers were also individually accountable to it. The president was to be elected by Parliament, and most of his or her decisions required ministerial approval. The pre-eminent role of Parliament reflected the opposition's cautiousness resulting from fear of the influence of the old elite in the public and private bureaucracies.

Parliament's power was limited, however, by the Constitutional Court, which was a special body designed to defend the stability of the newly created democratic system against dictatorial inclinations. The court was to be set up in three stages by three different Parliaments, an arrangement that also reflected the constitutional designers' attempt to achieve balance.[20]

The judiciary can be classified as the fourth important autonomous component of the constitutional setting defined in the basic law. Its autonomy is guaranteed by its institutional and procedural separation; the president of the Supreme Court is elected by Parliament. This principle of autonomy has been only slightly reduced by the enactment of the court organization system. According to Act 67 of 1991, the presidents of the county courts are appointed by the minister of justice based on the opinion of the council of county judges. This power of the executive offends the autonomy of the judiciary. Indeed, on several occasions the minister of justice has disregarded the opinion of the judges' forum concerning particular appointments.

I must also draw attention to the structural position of the state prosecution. Dating back to the last decades of the nineteenth century, this function was built into the executive branch. Direct executive control of the state prosecution system formally ended as recently as in 1953, although informally the system remained under direct party control at the highest level. During the 1989 roundtable talks, the opposition forces agreed to reestablish executive guidance, but the HSWP insisted on maintaining the prosecutors' independence. Retaining the old form in the new pluralistic setting again reflected the desire for legal-constitutional guarantees of constitutional stability.

The structural position of the public prosecution was not questioned by opposition parties during the roundtable talks, since they all favored placing it under executive control. After the 1990 election, the political situation changed greatly, and the "old opposition" split over this issue as well. The mainstream liberals feared a strong interventionist state and opposed direct executive control over public prosecution on practical grounds, claiming the conservative government would use this power for political purposes. Although the government coalition wanted to change the constitutional position on prosecution and argued that in West European parliamentary systems public prosecution is normally under government control, it lacked the required two-thirds majority to modify the constitution. The socialists opposed the change on theoretical grounds. They wanted to maintain a structure in which the separation of basic organs increased the chances that the idea of checks and balances could function. In the 1994 election, the socialists gained an absolute majority in the Parliament, but it is unlikely that they will support placing of public prosecution under executive control.[21] □

THE EFFECTS OF THE ELECTORAL SYSTEM

Of the three basic components of a political system—the form of government (parliamentary versus presidential or mixtures thereof), the electoral system, and the party system—the consequences of the structural features of the electoral system are the most easily observable and measurable. The choice of the electoral system affects the development of the party system and, in turn, the political composition of the legislature. In Hungary, the parliamentary option was supplemented by a mixed majoritarian-PR electoral system as a result of the roundtable political negotiations. The unicameral national representative body is elected for four years by means of a single-member-district system combined with a territorial PR system and with PR on the national level (the latter applied only for the sake of a higher degree of proportionality).

The system is highly selective in both phases of the electoral process. In the first phase, when candidates are nominated and party lists are established, the selection is carried out by setting up different legal requirements. For instance, the individual candidates have to be backed openly by at least 750 local citizens and must establish a county or territorial party list, and a certain number of valid individual candidates must run in a given county and in the capital. To be able to run on a national-level list (intended to compensate for the so-called lost votes in the first round of the individual district competition and in the regional-list competition), a party is supposed to have at least seven territorial lists.[22] As a consequence of the selectiveness of these rules, in the 1990 general elections only twelve parties could compete for at least fifty-eight compensation seats; the actual number reached ninety as a result of the disproportionality of the territorial system—that is, thirty-two seats originally assigned to the regional level were shifted to the compensation group.

In the 1994 election, fifteen parties competed to receive national list seats, but only six obtained at least 5 percent of the vote and became eligible for compensation—the same six parties that had received parliamentary seats in the previous election. The compensation package was increased again by twenty-seven additional seats for the 1994 elections.

A second type of selection is carried out after the balloting is over, based on the nationally aggregated results of regional list competition. A 5 percent threshold excludes parties falling below this minimum from the national-level competition. In 1990, half of the parties with nationwide representation were penalized by the slightly lower 4 percent threshold, which was not changed until 1993. In 1994, the higher threshold resulted in a similar outcome.[23]

As a result of this twofold selectivity, the Hungarian mixed system is markedly disproportional. This characteristic of the parliamentary electoral system is caused mainly by the inherently majoritarian nature of the elections in single-member districts, although these seats represent less than half (45.6 percent) of the seats, and also by the disproportionality of the territorial lists.

The majoritarian tendencies of the electoral system had far-reaching political consequences in the first multiparty elections. The leading conservative party, the HDF, obtained 42.5 percent of the seats in spite of the fact that it had received only 23.7 percent of the nationally aggregated territorial list votes.[24] If a fully proportional electoral system had been applied, the 1990–1994 three-party coalition government would have won only 43 percent of the seats.[25] Instead, the coalition obtained a comfortable 58.3 percent majority. This majority was insufficient to amend the Hungarian constitution but was strong enough to run the country for four years during a crucial period of sociopolitical transformation, privatization, and recapitalization.[26]

In summary, the mixed majoritarian-PR system helps coalition formation and increases the degree of governability, but it makes the political system less consensual by excluding minor parties from parliamentary representation. In 1990, 15 percent of active voters remained unrepresented as a result of the 4 percent threshold. The increase of the threshold to 5 percent blocked nine parties that together gained 12.6 percent of the regional list votes in 1994. These voters are now unrepresented. The peculiarity of the Hungarian system can be illustrated by the fact that the voters can split their preferences by choosing two different parties; they can cast one vote for a party's candidate in the single-member district (or for an independent candidate), and the other vote can be cast for a different party's regional list. The figures show a high degree of correlation of the two preferences, however, at least as measured by nationally aggregated data. □

POLITICAL CONSEQUENCES OF THE MAY 1990 CONSTITUTIONAL REFORM

The constitutional reform in 1989 resulted in a parliamentary system of government in which the unicameral legislature enjoyed a very strong political position and the executive was almost powerless. The Hungarian constitution defined numerous basic issues on which the legislature had to adopt so-called constitutional acts that required a two-thirds majority vote. This arrangement could have paralyzed the government or would have necessitated the formation of a grand coalition. Immediately following the election but before the formation of the new government, however, the HDF, the leading conservative party, and the AFD, the largest liberal party, concluded a pact to eliminate most of these issues—mainly having to do with the political compromise between democratic socialism and market capitalism—from the constitution. The central goals were to provide stable government and to establish the executive's political responsibility to the legislature. The reform did not result in a general constitutional change, but it did basically alter the philosophy of governance. The temporary nature of the constitution was maintained, but unlike the 1992 Polish constitution, it represents a complete and workable state structure on which a lasting system of governance can be built.[27]

The pact introduced a strong executive by means of two important sets of modifications. First, the notion of a "constitutional act" was eliminated, and the issues formerly requiring an extraordinary majority vote were downgraded to a simple majority requirement. This gave the government much greater maneuvering room. Second, the pact makers strengthened the position of the prime minister by introducing the constructive vote of no-confidence, following the model of the German constitution.[28] This new institution reversed the relative powers of Parliament and the government by giving the Hungarian prime minister powers similar to those of a strong president (Kanzlerdemokratie). The prime minister is nominated by the indirectly elected president of the republic and is elected by Parliament by an absolute majority. In practice, this means the leader of the party with the most seats automatically becomes the prime minister, provided he or she has a comfortable major-ity in the Assembly or can form a workable coalition government. Assuming the continuation of the present Hungarian party system, the main components of which appear to be frozen, it is not unrealistic to expect that a center-right or a center-left majority coalition is easily realiz-able in different but equally viable settings.[29] This paradigm was rein-forced after the electoral defeat of the center-right conservative government in 1994, when a center-left coalition was formed by the socialists and the Free Democrats.

Under these circumstances, a strong prime minister is less dependent on Parliament and can monopolize strategic state functions by using the ministerial departments, the evergrowing cabinet office, and the extra-ministerial bureaucracy. Furthermore, the prime minister nominates the members of the government, based on coalition negotiations if needed. The president's countersignature is purely formal. According to the con-stitution, the Parliament has no means to control this procedure, and the prime minister introduces his or her government after first being elected. The minister is responsible to, but not removable by, Parliament; in other words, a vote of confidence cannot be initiated against him or her. The MPs have the right to put questions to the minister, and they can submit interpellations, but neither of these actions has any direct political conse-quences. Thus, even if the minister's reply is not accepted by Parliament, this does not lead to his or her resignation or removal.

According to the pact, the role of the Hungarian president has been slightly enhanced without being basically changed. Árpád Göncz, a prominent writer and member of the largest opposition party, the AFD, was given the post of president, but this was only a part of the political give-and-take designed for a unique constitutional situation. The AFD intended to use the position to counterbalance the enhanced prime minis-terial power, but the government majority—composed of three parties—stuck to the principles of classical Westminster-type parliamentarism in which executive power is not divided between the president (the monarch) and cabinet members (the king's advisers). The role of the pres-ident, however, is much more important than that of a neutral head of state. The so-called transitory constitution that emerged from the 1989 reform gives the president some counterbalancing authority vis-à-vis the Parliament and the government. Before his election the president belonged to the camp of Free Democrats, and their political tactics regard-ing pragmatic policymaking were influenced by this fact. It was under-standable that they did not support the summer 1990 referendum, which was initiated to gain support for the election of the president by popular vote.

The first conflict between the prime minister and the president emerged when the president refused to sign the bill on property compensation, because the coalition—fully in line with the electoral program of the Independent Smallholders' Party (ISP)—accepted the idea of land reprivatization. This was an important political issue that deeply affected the social relations of the rural population. The president initiated a constitutional court review of the bill, and essential parts of it were declared unconstitutional. This case showed that the president could counterbalance the parliamentary majority and the government fully in harmony with his constitutional powers. The extreme right harshly attacked the president, but nobody questioned the legality of his move.

In the second conflict, the prime minister questioned the president's constitutional role when the president refused to approve the prime minister's nomination of vice presidents for public radio and television. This time, the government and a parliamentary committee turned to the Constitutional Court, asking for an interpretation of the president's function and authority in relation to the executive.[30] The court interpreted the president's role in line with the classical parliamentary division of roles, and it declared that, in general, the president cannot refuse a nomination or other initiation if the person holding the right of countersignature makes the proposal (except in a very extreme situation when executive action would seriously endanger the democratic operation of the state).[31]

According to some experts, this decision by the Constitutional Court was political. The constitution does not specify the president's role, but the court is not allowed to contradict the intentions of the constitution drafters—the Parliament. Some judges of the court referred to the so-called invisible constitution, which would mean a coherent parliamentary system in which the logic of different functions defines the limits of roles in clashes of authority. Some references were made to the parliamentary traditions and to the analogy of other countries' constitutional practice. The court decision reinforced the original political intention not to have even a moderately strong president and to keep him or her out of the executive branch of government. □

CONCLUSION

The organic development of political institutions, which had started well before the emergence of a multiparty system, led logically to a pure parliamentary framework. Two factors explain why parliamentarism stabilized during the constitutional transformation. One explanation is the new elite's fear of an activist or a strong charismatic political leader who, by informal or unconstitutional means, could build up a paternalistic political regime that would not be subject to democratic control. This would not only slow down or reverse democratic development but could also threaten economic transformation by preserving a strong state with a bureaucratic apparatus inclined to retake control of the economy.

Hungary has a tradition of a strong state that goes back to the second half of the nineteenth century, since the paternalistic state was a central instrument of both the capitalization and conservation of the political power of the established social classes. In this second historical wave of capitalistic modernization, the state can be stripped of its undue weight. The parliamentary form of government provides more guarantees for this than does a strong presidential system.

The other important factor is the role of political elites in the transformation. The elite nature of the changes is embedded in the logic of dismantling the old regime. The foremost characteristics of the Hungarian transition are its gradual and peaceful nature and its elitist-reformist character, which dates back to the late 1960s. This stands in sharp contrast to Poland, where a mass movement—Solidarity—played a key role, and to the former Czechoslovakia, where the reformist movements were crushed by military and police forces. In Poland the opposition elite gained all of the important constitutional positions, whereas in Hungary the old and the new elites had to compromise on an institutionally balanced parliamentary framework.

The elite wanted, and still wants, to exclude the wider public from policymaking—paradoxically because the new elite does not yet have a strong social and economic base. Although it preserved most of its economic and expert positions, the old elite has lost its social legitimacy, which has greatly weakened its political influence. Parliamentarism gives the elite a chance to redistribute wealth and political influence with in a formally and fully democratic framework without interference by marginalized and dissatisfied social groups. At the same time, the system is genuinely legitimate, and the political cycles reproduce elite power—even under permanent conflict- and crisis-ridden circumstances.

Government stability is secured by the constructive no-confidence vote and by the lack of a possible rival executive branch—the presidential bureaucracy. According to the normal logic of this parliamentary arrangement, the president, the prime minister, and the speaker of Parliament belong to the governing coalition. The situation between 1990 and 1994 was exceptional, because it was the result of a political pact between the main government party and the main opposition party. The price that had to be paid for the constructive vote of no-confidence (which greatly strengthened the prime minister) was the control of the presidency. Since the 1994 elections, the governing coalition has controlled a two-thirds majority in Parliament, and the two parties alone can choose a president. It is highly probable that the new president will belong to one of these parties.

This distribution of the most important public offices concentrates power in the governing party or parties, and the popular control over this kind of parliamentary rule is practically nonexistent. The political and legal professional elite is very hostile toward plebiscitary movements and initiatives. In a famous case, the Constitutional Court declared that indirect, representative democracy is superior to direct democracy, and it is unconstitutional to modify the constitution by referenda (Decision no. 2/1993 of the Constitutional Court). In my judgment there were no valid constitutional grounds to take such a decision.

Political parties play an extremely powerful role in this model. The strong position of the government cannot be balanced by the opposition, because the parliamentary front lines are rigid, and there is no spirit of compromise. (This can be explained in part by the "social distances" and the deep social cleavages political parties represent. The confrontational style of the governing parties' elite is also worth mentioning.) The party elites have not yet realized that they should be interested collectively in maintaining a consensus model to preserve an economically and socially effective governance; otherwise, the elites themselves may threaten the legitimacy of parliamentary democracy.

The opposition parties can use publicity only as a means of indirect control over issues decided by simple majority, which is why control over the mass media became a very sensitive issue in the second half of the 1990–1994 parliamentary cycle. The government majority tried to directly influence public television and radio in the hope that this would help the governing parties during the electoral campaign. This turned out to be a miscalculation—which does not mean, however, that the mass media is unimportant in party competition.

But the Hungarian constitution has a built-in stabilizing mechanism: a powerful veto on the side of the opposition. On a number of issues, more than a simple majority is needed. (The present coalition government formally has the required extra majority, but on some controversial issues the support of MPs can become unstable even in this situation, when the coalition controls 72 percent of the seats.)

This arrangement is criticized by constitutional lawyers because of the political responsibility of the majority, which is curtailed by the qualified majority requirement. The two-thirds majority rule does limit the government parties and also makes amendment of the constitution difficult. The logic of parliamentary government would require a drastic reduction in the number of issues that would fall into this category.

There are three important means by which to limit the parliamentary majority and the council of ministers it supports. A para-constitutional means can be the strikingly high inclination of the MPs within the dominant governing party or parties to rebel. Between 1990 and 1994, interpellations often came from the governing majority, and it was not uncommon for the majority to vote against its ministers. This phenomenon seemed to indicate true parliamentary control, but it was simply the expression of cleavages within the coalition or even within a government party or between the coalition parties. This rebellion factor has been weakened during the second parliamentary cycle by a change in the house rules. Under the new regulations, MPs who abandon an established parliamentary faction are punished.

The second important counterbalancing factor is the independent position of the local self-government system. In Hungary, local governments enjoy—to an unprecedented degree by international standards—a constitutionally guaranteed political and legal freedom vis-à-vis the central government. Many criticize this liberal arrangement, and the government has tried to diminish the independence of local authorities, but these efforts have not been successful overall. The regional level has been stripped of its independent functions and, therefore, cannot be used to counterbalance the central government's power. Most of the larger local bodies are controlled by opposition political parties—mainly liberals—which further reinforces the counterbalancing nature of local power.

Finally, I must underline the importance of the Constitutional Court. In Hungary's parliamentary system, the Constitutional Court is the most independent organ. The president has no real veto power and is not authorized to effectively control the Parliament, even in a deadlock situation. The right of dissolution is designed for extreme situations, a presidential refusal to sign a bill can be overruled by a simple majority, the president is not authorized to order a referendum, and he or she is elected by Parliament—just to mention the most important limitations. Characteristically, the most important presidential power is that he or she can submit a bill to the court instead of signing it. This arrangement reflects the original intentions of the designers of the constitution, who wanted to avoid the duplication of the executive branch but at the same time were very much in favor of strong constitutional control. The court has been very active so far, but it has been activist in the narrow meaning of the word. On the one hand, the court is a watchful guardian of the positive constitutional stipulations; on the other hand, the majority of the court has accepted the concept of the "invisible constitution." This means the court goes beyond the explicit text of the constitution, arguing that it must examine the value system behind it. The functioning of the court to date has proved to be an effective barrier to legislation in every case in which Parliament was inclined to give up the principles of the rule of law to serve prime political objectives. In such instances, the court has annulled bills that have already passed, referring to its responsibility to maintain legal stability and to the fact that the Council of Europe has recognized the principle of the rule of law.

The present parliamentary system appears to be durable. The fundamental systemic change of historical importance is over, and further state building can be carried out within the existing framework. Stein Rokkan's hypothesis concerning the possible "freezing" of initial constitutional choices seems to be confirmed.[32] The democratic nature of the form of government could be increased further, but the political capacity for such a move is lower than expected or needed. Therefore, the existing executive-legislative unity and the lack of active control over the executive and legislature are likely to endure. The parliamentary parties intend to stabilize their position either by increasing the selectivity of the electoral system (which is backed by the conservative parties) or by reducing the size of Parliament (which is supported by the liberals). In these circumstances, the consensus capacity of Parliament needs to be improved, a goal that could be realized by eliminating the constructive vote of no-confidence and making the presidency a bit stronger without adopting a true semi-presidential system. A parliamentary deadlock can be counterbalanced only by an active external control.[33] Such a control can be instituted—in addition to the existing means—by modifying the president's role, reinforcing the autonomy of civil and civic society, and introducing plebiscitary elements beyond pure parliamentary rule. Thus, the spirit of the rule of law could be more effectively disseminated, and the basis for legitimacy could be enlarged.

At present, these proposals are only expressions of thinking in terms of value-based theoretical models. If I had to predict the constitutional future, I would say that only after a trial-and-error type of development, in which the Constitutional Court will play a crucial role, will a balanced structure of semiparliamentarism be achieved. □

NOTES

1. Juan J. Linz, "The Perils of Presidentialism," *Journal of Democracy* 1, no. 1 (Winter 1990): 51–69.

2. With regard to immobilism, see Juan J. Linz and Arturo Valenzuela, eds., *The Failure of Presidential Democracy* (Baltimore: Johns Hopkins University Press, 1994). For a discussion of majoritarianism, see Arend Lijphart, "Presidentialism and Majoritarian Democracy: Theoretical Observations," in György Szoboszlai, ed., *Democracy and Political Transformation: Theories and East-Central European Realities* (Budapest: Hungarian Political Science Association, 1991), pp. 75–93.

3. Lijphart, "Presidentialism and Majoritarian Democracy," p. 76.

4. See Scott Mainwaring, "Presidentialism, Multipartism, and Democracy: The Difficult Combination," in György Szoboszlai, ed., *Flying Blind: Emerging Democracies in East-Central Europe* (Budapest: Hungarian Political Science Association, 1992), p. 59.

5. Para-constitutional factors (that is, the political culture, degree of civic individualism, spirit of association and social solidarity, and so forth) can be even more decisive for a well-balanced political system. In this analysis, however, I do not deal with these dimensions.

6. See Juan J. Linz, "The Virtues of Parliamentarism," *Journal of Democracy* 1, no. 4 (Fall 1990): 84–91.

7. He concludes: "If forced—or begged—to give advice, it seems to me that the evidence does point in the direction of moderate PR as the safer choice. It appears to give an at least slightly better governing ability without having to pay a heavy price in terms of minority representation. To sum up, Linz's recommendation of the parliamentary-PR option is fully justified, and, since the acceptance of this advice inevitably means that a further choice must be made, the combination of parliamentarism and moderate PR appears to be the wisest recommendation." Arend Lijphart, "The Virtues of Parliamentarism: But Which Kind of Parliamentarism?" in H. E. Chehabi and Alfred Stepan, eds., *Politics, Society, and Democracy: Comparative Studies* (Boulder: Westview Press, 1995), p. 373.

8. I analyzed this event elsewhere: György Szoboszlai, "Constitutional Transformation in Hungary," in Szoboszlai, ed., *Flying Blind*, p. 325.

9. János Kádár, the general secretary of the HSWP, had held the political position continuously since he took power with the help of Soviet invaders on November 4, 1956.

10. By this time the political elite had split into groups that were organized informally along ideological lines. The historical, cultural, and political cleavages were strong enough to offer a formal framework for institutional pluralization. A well-developed multiparty system emerged long before the general elections. For a detailed analysis, see Robert M. Jenkins, "Movements into Parties: The Historical Transformation of the Hungarian Opposition," East-Central European Working Paper no. 25 (Cambridge: Minda de Gunzberg Center for European Studies, Harvard University, 1992).

11. During the period 1990–1992, Hungary attracted more than half of the foreign investments made in the entire East European region. Compared to the size of the country, this proportion is striking and can be explained by the timely and liberal privatization laws.

12. This situation was ironically depicted by the characterization of Hungary as the "most cheerful barrack in the camp."

13. I have shown in another chapter that the political transformation was backed by the most influential faction of the ruling state-socialist party. György Szoboszlai, "Political Transition and Constitutional Changes," in Szoboszlai, ed., *Democracy and Political Transformation*, pp. 195–213.

14. Instead of true judicial constitutional control, the Constitutional Law Council was established in 1982 as a controlling organ. It was not granted the right to annul unconstitutional laws; it could declare invalid only governmental or subgovernmental regulations. This was a cautious step toward the real practice of the rule of law. The original constitutional reform in 1972 upheld the model of state and a single party and went even further in making this arrangement explicit. The limits to true pluralization were expressed in the new formulation of the legal role of the ruling party. This constitutional regulation stipulated that "the leading force of the society is the Marxist-Leninist Party of the working class." Although this was a pure ideological declaration that lacked any further institutional consequences in the constitution, it was evident that within the framework of reform state socialism, pluralism was not meant to be legally institutionalized. This was the farthest front line of political compromise.

15. The 1983 electoral reform was very significant and influenced the later developments in the political transformation process. For example, the Parliament elected in 1985 was more fragmented than it would have been without the pluralizing reform.

16. Act 10 had far-reaching importance by annulling the right of the Presidential Council to modify the acts of Parliament. This modification meant the political leadership was not able to use the council as an alternative decisionmaking organ, and the ruling party had to submit all important matters to Parliament. Politically, the risk was not yet too high, given that around 70 percent of the MPs were members of the ruling HSWP. With the disintegration of the old regime, however, this move turned out to be decisive.

17. Participants were the HSWP, the Opposition Roundtable (integrating various opposition movements and parties), and trade unions and civic organizations. See László Bruszt, "1989: The Negotiated Revolution of Hungary," in Szoboszlai, ed., *Democracy and Political Transformation*, pp. 213–226.

18. Péter Schmidt, "The Constitutional Contradictions of Hungarian Parliamentarism," in Sándor Kurtán, Peter Sándor, and László Vass, eds., *Magyarország Politikai Évkönyve 1992* (*Political Yearbook of Hungary 1992*) (Budapest: Economix Rt., 1993), p. 47.

19. See Kálmán Kulcsár, "A 'jog uralma' és a magyar alkotmánybíráskodás" (The Rule of Law and the Activity of the Hungarian Constitutional Court), *Politikatudományi Szemle* 1 (1993): 5–39.

20. The first five members were chosen by the old Parliament in 1989, and the second five were selected by the new one in 1990. Contrary to the original plan, the third group of five members was not chosen by the Parliament elected in 1994. The court has challenged the election of the last quota, arguing that the enlargement would bureaucratize its functioning. The judges who initiated the reduction also held the opinion that the responsibility of the court was too broadly defined and made its constitutional role disproportional. As a result, the legal framework was changed in 1994. According to the new rules of the constitution, the court consists of eleven members. After one judge resigns, two seats are to be filled.

21. In 1993, the governing conservative coalition wanted to place the prosecutors' office under the control of the government instead of Parliament. The socialists opposed the idea in principle, and the liberal opposition considered this move untimely. Without a two-thirds majority, constitutional modification could not occur, so parliamentary control seems to be a stable arrangement.

22. The selectivity of this system can be shown by the following figures (based on the results of the first multiparty elections after the political transformation): From among sixty-five registered political parties, twenty-eight were able to validly nominate at least one individual candidate, nineteen were successful in running territorial lists (in the capital, Budapest, and in nineteen counties), and only twelve parties were able to present a national-level list. The remaining six parties were unable to nominate even one candidate.

23. The nationally aggregated number of list votes cast for the thirteen regionally represented parties was 777,777 in 1990, which constituted 15.8

percent of all the regional list votes. In 1994, thirteen (somewhat different) parties that fell under the 5 percent threshold gathered 683,892 votes, 12.7 percent of all the regional list votes.

24. The HDF received 26 percent of the individual district votes, but its aggregated number fell under that of the regional list votes (1,186,376 versus 1,214,328).

25. After the general elections, the HDF refused to form a broad coalition with the second-largest party—the AFD—and instead formed a coalition government with the Independent Smallholders' Party and the Christian Democratic People's Party, based on ideological unity.

26. To amend the constitution, a two-thirds majority is required. In the previous parliamentary cycle, the government majority was insufficient: The cooperation of at least three parties was needed to amend the constitution, including that of the dominant opposition party, the AFD. After the 1994 election, the two parties of the government coalition—the Hungarian Socialist Party and the AFD—which held 72 percent of the seats, obtained a so-called constitution-making majority and passed important bills that modified the basic law. In 1995, however, the six parties in Parliament agreed to prepare the new constitution with the cooperation of the government and the opposition. According to the agreement, the consent of at least five parties is required to accept a new version or institution.

27. The Preamble of the revised constitution declares that the text will be valid until the new constitution is accepted "to promote a peaceful political transition to a law-based state [rule of law] that realizes the multiparty system, a parliamentary democracy and a social market economy."

28. This constitutional formula is also used in other new democracies that have undergone a deep political transformation to liberal democracy. Spain, Portugal, and other newly democratized countries have accepted this constitutional solution to stabilize the executive vis-à-vis the legislature.

29. At present, there are six parliamentary parties: the Hungarian Socialist Party, the AFD, HDF, the Independent Smallholders' Party (ISP), the Christian Democratic People's Party, and the LYD—all the same parties that gained representation after the transition. Before the 1994 election, the ISP had split into several factions, but the strong mainstream ISP—the legal successor—has easily taken the dominant position. The results of the two elections show that the newly established multiparty system has proved to be stable. The very nature of the existing electoral system involves the possibility of great swings and surprises. The majoritarian component of the mixed system gives the winner a representation that is well over the list results; this difference was 18 percent in 1990 and 21 percent in 1994. Moreover, the preballoting selectivity of the rules favors the insiders. The small and the newly formed parties are disadvantaged, and the 5 percent threshold makes their chances especially difficult.

30. The court had to interpret these issues: The president (1) is the chief commander of the army; (2) appoints and dismisses ministerial undersecretaries at the suggestion of the minister when the proposal is made through the prime minister; (3) appoints and dismisses, at the suggestion of bodies provided by separate act, the vice presidents of the National Bank of Hungary and university professors; (4) appoints and dismisses rectors of universities; (5) appoints and

promotes generals; and (6) confirms the president of the Academy of Sciences. These personal decisions are taken only in conformity with the executive; in the wording of the constitution, these measures and provisions "shall be countersigned by the Prime Minister or the responsible minister" (section 30/A, subsection 2).

31. The decision was based on the constitutional definition of the president's role: "The President of the Republic is the head of state of Hungary; he or she embodies the unity of the nation and watches over the democratic operation of the mechanism of the State" (section 29, subsection 1).

32. See Arend Lijphart, "Democratization and Constitutional Choices in Czechoslovakia, Hungary, and Poland, 1989–1991," in Szoboszlai, ed., *Flying Blind*, p. 99.

33. If the president had real veto power, Parliament would be forced to reach compromises to avoid the president's intervention. The 1992 Polish constitution stipulated a highly balanced relationship between the Parliament and the president. The more straightforward Hungarian constitution is much less sophisticated in this regard, mainly because it was designed before the first Parliament was functioning. The passive control of the Constitutional Court is ineffective because of the lack of constitutional sanction (that is, the court can declare that Parliament acted unconstitutionally by not accepting a bill, and the court can define a deadline by which to remedy the omission, but nothing happens if this decision is not respected). An effective presidential veto could bridge this constitutional gap. Naturally, the enhancement of the president's role should also be associated with his or her direct election on a nationwide basis. On the latest Polish constitution, see Stanislaw Gebethner, "The System of Government of the Republic of Poland According to the Constitutional Act of October 17, 1992," unpublished manuscript, 1992.

CHAPTER EIGHT

■

Changing the Balance of Power in a Hegemonic Party System: The Case of Mexico

Juan Molinar Horcasitas

MEXICAN POLITICS HAS been dominated by one party and noncompetitive elections since 1929, but the Mexican political system has never been a strictly single-party system.[1] This, concisely, is one of the mysteries of Mexican politics. How can a hegemonic party exist for seven decades without the situation evolving into single-party politics? On the other hand, how has it been possible that a political system with multiparty elections, at least at the national level, has not evolved into competitive elections? Both puzzles are two sides of the same coin—a coin that has stood on its edge for seventy years. In this chapter I focus on one institutional aspect of the process that has enabled this stability: the different electoral systems that—through a permanent process of adaptation—have supported that singular piece of equilibrium, the hegemonic party system. □

THE HISTORY OF MEXICO'S HEGEMONIC PARTY SYSTEM

The endurance of Mexico's hegemonic party system results from a constant process of electoral reform that has steered a delicate course between the Scylla of internal factionalism and the Charybdis of the depletion of a loyal opposition. The debates between party leaders over reforms are crossed by two main cleavages: the issue of democratization and the preference of political party leaders for consensual or majoritarian institutions. Some reforms move in the direction of political liberalization, whereas others increase authoritarian control; some introduce consensual features in the design of the political system, and others reinforce majoritarian features.

From 1929 to 1963, the aim was to control the factionalism of the official party and to suppress the electoral organization of dissent. The second phase, from 1963 to 1986, attempted to incorporate a weakened opposition into the legislative branch. The third phase, from 1986 to the present, has zigzagged between the two extremes, introducing some reforms that move toward a more consensual system along with others that are more majoritarian in character.

The remote predecessor of the Partido Revolucionario Institucional (PRI) was founded in 1929, made up of a coalition of dozens of local and national-level parties and political machines run by the former leaders of the Mexican Revolution (1910–1917). Before 1929, "competitive elections"—that is, elections between two or more candidates—were restricted to large cities. At the aggregate level, Congress had pluralistic features, because it was the meeting place of a vast and complex network of local and regional bosses. Congress was not a model of democratic stability, but it was the only institution in which a number of parties could be formed and carry out national politics.

Political control of Congress was substantially transformed in 1929 with the creation of the Partido Nacional Revolucionario (PNR). Since this party was joined by almost all of Mexico's preexisting parties and political bosses, it established a state party system that monopolized power. The creation of the PNR did not dramatically alter the noncompetitive nature of elections at the local level, but it substantially modified the aggregate outcome. The PNR was created as an instrument of coordination among revolutionary leaders, factions, and cliques. It was created to ease the internal struggles for central authority: to rule and to regulate the circulation of rulers, not to compete. If factionalism had not been controlled, the hegemonic party system would have perished in a division into two or more parties. And if the monopoly of the official party had become too harsh, a strict single-party system would have evolved in the absence of opposition. The two extremes are polar: Political actions required to solve one problem usually exacerbate the other. The ruling elite has to solve these problems simultaneously, for they are always present, although they have varied in intensity over time.

Between 1929 and 1938, the PNR built its organization and gradually but relentlessly centralized power. During the formative years of the hegemonic party system, factionalism was the ruling elite's main problem. Political discipline was imposed through several means. Disputes over elections for congressional seats were settled by the Electoral Colleges, which were formed by the incoming members of each house. Decisions were taken by a majority of votes and did not have to follow judicial procedure. Thus, opposition candidates, or even undisciplined

PNR members, could be deprived of their seats by majority decision. Executive orders imposed compulsory contributions by bureaucrats to the official party. Later, Congress banned immediate reelection for all federal, state, and municipal elected offices, giving more leverage to the central officers of the party vis-à-vis the local bosses.[2] The PNR authorities dissolved all of the political parties that had joined the PNR coalition and still remained active. By that point, state legislatures began to reform their own electoral laws and those of their municipalities, moving in the direction of municipal councils elected at large (by plurality through closed party lists in districts congruent with municipalities) so the winning party would control all council seats.

These measures shared the common purpose of discouraging factionalism by giving all seats to the winning party. They rapidly transformed Mexico's political landscape, reinforcing the centralized control of the vast network of local and regional political leaderships. Thus, dissenters could only discipline themselves and wait for future opportunities within the official party or leave politics. The centralization of power and discouragement of political contestation were so successful that by the 1937 election almost all of the PNR candidates for deputyships and Senate seats ran unopposed, and Mexico was on the verge of becoming strictly a single-party system. A year later, the PNR was reorganized as the Partido de la Revolución Mexicana, but by the 1940 presidential election it faced a serious schism.[3]

After the 1940 presidential election, which divided the "revolutionary family," the government increased the centralization of the political process. Management and oversight of elections were transferred from municipal and state authorities to federal agencies, especially to the Interior Ministry (Secretaría de Gobernación), whose head is appointed by the president. After a few years, Gobernación gained control of the electoral processes, including those that were not at the federal level.[4]

Nevertheless, the presidential nominations in 1946 and 1952 still triggered important defections from the official party. Although officially the defectors tallied only around 20 percent of the vote (because the official party rigged the elections), they presented a serious threat to the stability of the official party, which by 1946 carried its current name, Partido Revolucionario Institucional. The scattered evidence that exists suggests that the PRI was facing a cumulative process of minority coalition building, whereby the defectors in one election and their constituencies would support other defectors in subsequent elections by means of nominations. To prevent this, the government raised the costs of entry to the electoral arena, so potential defectors from the PRI knew they would not be allowed to form a party to back their candidacy in any federal election. Under the new rules, only parties that were registered at the Secretaría de Gobernación were authorized to take part in elections.

Thus, the PRI steered away from factionalism and came face-to-face with the problem of the depletion of its external and loyal opposition parties as a result of noncompetitive electoral practices. Avoiding this peril, particularly between 1946 and 1973, was perhaps more complex than coping with factionalism.

Historically, the relevant actor in this story has been the Partido Acción Nacional (PAN), founded in 1939. Initially, the PAN pursued a strategy of inducing a division within the official party.[5] When the reforms of the 1950s ended that option, the PAN confronted a strategic choice that has subsequently been reevaluated by its leaders: to assume the role of a loyal opposition in a noncompetitive system, aspiring to reform it gradually, or to assume the role of an antisystem opposition in an authoritarian regime. The decision has not been easy. The PAN is basically an urban party, and its leaders knew that in the absence of a major split within the PRI they had very few chances of winning a presidential election, because the PRI resorted to electoral fraud—especially in the countryside, where neither the PAN nor other parties nominated candidates against the PRI. In this way, competitive elections in urban areas were balanced in the aggregate by fraudulent landslides in rural areas. Malapportionment and gerrymandering added up to produce very few opposition seats in the Chamber of Deputies. Although the PAN's electoral support doubled between 1946 and 1958—from 5 to 10 percent—the system of plurality elections in single-member districts punished the party heavily.[6]

It would be fair to say that the stability of the Mexican electoral system between the mid-1950s and the mid-1970s depended on the renewal of the PAN commitment to its status as a loyal opposition. To ensure this, the government reacted to each new PAN demand or challenge with a "big-stick-and-small-carrot" policy.

The big stick was always applied by means of a "good cop, bad cop" game that was played whenever a new reform was introduced: "We would love to offer you a better deal, but those hard-liners won't allow us to do it. And you know how rough they are. So take the package or else." Further, the PRI promoted and supported a number of small "opposition" parties, which served not only as "pinch-hitter parties" in the case of a PAN defection but also as dependable allies when the government needed to control the agencies overseeing the elections. The PAN leadership was well aware of the role of these parties, but a threat of defection from elections would cause the PAN to lose credibility if the other parties would not join.[7]

The small carrots took two forms: a relaxation of the total control of the PRI over the elections and a modification of the electoral formulas for the Chamber of Deputies.[8] The electoral formulas have been revised relentlessly since 1963. From then until 1986, the PRI imposed formulas that ameliorated the negative effects of the first-past-the-post system (FPTP) on small parties. These electoral formulas were designed to satisfy two apparently contradictory objectives. They guaranteed that candidates of the PRI could win almost all of the seats (the so-called *carro completo*, or clean sweep), yet at the same time they did not deprive the opposition parties of the minimal representation required to keep them alive. □

MEXICO'S ELECTORAL REFORMS

In contrast with other countries, until recently Mexico's electoral formulas have been based on two principles: differentiation and segmentation. These principles are gross departures from the notion of one person, one vote. Differentiation refers to the existence of two sets of rules governing the translation of votes into seats. One set of rules applies to certain parties and the other only to the remaining parties. Segmentation refers to the division in the allocation of seats in the Chamber of Deputies. Any party is entitled to seats in the FPTP segment of the chamber, although in practice the PRI wins all of these seats, and only small parties are entitled to the remaining seats. Two different versions of these principles were established. Between 1963 and 1976, a party-seats system, called *diputados de partido*, was enforced. Subsequently, a system that vaguely resembles the West German method of additional member seats was established.

The *diputados de partido* formula was basically a correction of the FPTP system by means of complementary seats that assured small parties of minimum levels of representation. A party was considered small if it won fewer than twenty seats in the single-member plurality districts. Small parties were guaranteed one seat for each 0.5 percent of the vote. If the party did not win its total number of seats with pluralities in the single-member districts, the system would allocate as many seats as necessary to the party to allow it to reach its total. For instance, suppose a party wins 10 percent of the national vote and four seats in single-member districts. It will then be entitled to a total of twenty seats (or twenty times the quota of 0.5 percent). The total includes the four seats the party won in single-member districts plus sixteen complementary seats from the *diputados de partido* system. A minimum threshold of 2.5 percent of the total vote and a maximum allocation of twenty party seats was established, and the party seats were filled by defeated candidates in single-member districts. This formula was used for three elections (1964, 1967, and 1970). In the 1973 and 1976 elections, the party-seats system was slightly modified: The threshold was reduced to 1.5 percent, and the maximum number of party seats was increased to twenty-five.[9]

Through these electoral mechanisms, the Mexican regime was able to incorporate increasing numbers of opposition members into the Chamber of Deputies without inflicting defeat on the official party. That monopoly helped to enforce discipline within the PRI and also allowed the opposition to gain a few seats in the chamber regardless of what the PRI did in the FPTP districts. Thus, the party-seats method "liberated" the PRI from any constraint the goal of allowing a minimal opposition representation imposed on its fraudulent practices.[10]

Although the party-seats method divided the PAN leadership, after a long process of political soul-searching it decided to maintain its commitment to electoral participation. One possible reason for this decision was the leaders' recognition that the government would try to sustain the facade of fair elections with or without the PAN. Allocation of party seats to the parastatal parties in 1964, 1967, and 1970—even when they failed to pass the threshold established by the constitution—was just one of the signals in that direction.

In spite of this, the hegemonic party system experienced difficulties during the early 1970s, culminating in a major crisis in 1976. An increase in radical political activities in labor unions, universities, and other arenas—including a brief period of urban and guerrilla warfare that was suffocated through the usual methods of *guerra sucia* (dirty war)—provoked serious problems in the early 1970s. The electoral arena and the party system were unable to cope with this rise in radicalism. The Mexican party system was no longer a credible alternative for many dissatisfied people, because it was widely recognized that elections were rigged. The government also denied illegal parties, such as the Communists, access to the electoral arena. Thus, because of government obstruction or opposition disdain, the electoral arena was losing relevance. The hegemonic system was tilting toward an implosion into strict single-party politics.

In this already difficult context, the PAN was caught in a political deadlock that ended in its default in the 1976 presidential election. By the time the PAN decided not to nominate a presidential candidate, the two other opposition parties with legal registration at that time—the so-called parastatal parties—had already endorsed the PRI candidate, who then had to run unopposed. So the strategy of supporting an artificial opposition backfired when the PRI needed a "credible" opponent to pinch-hit for the PAN. Parastatal parties could not provide that option because the PRI had supported them for other purposes. The situation was even more paradoxical because several parties could have played the credible-opposition role perfectly, but they were banned by the entry-barrier law designed as a disincentive to potential PRI defectors.[11] Freed from the threat of factionalism, the regime found itself grappling with the depletion of its credible opposition.

By the late 1970s, the PRI feared the perils of antisystem opposition more than it did its own factionalism. After all, the PRI presidential nominations of 1958, 1964, 1970, and 1976 had produced no any major defection from the PRI. This sequence of successful and disciplined transfers of power may have led the PRI leadership to evaluate the electoral outcomes as a product of institutionalization of party discipline that was independent of the institutional disincentives against factionalism. Therefore, subsequent reforms were aimed at expanding the party system. This increased the strategic value of the parastatal parties and induced the government to provide them with institutional mechanisms to facilitate their survival, such as electoral formulas favoring smaller opposition parties and a near deregulation allowing those parties to form coalitions with the PRI under certain conditions.

At first glance, the electoral system introduced in 1979 resembles the German mixed system of an additional-member parliament. But a careful observation of the Mexican system belies this. The system in force in 1979, 1982, and 1985 provided a four hundred-member Chamber of Deputies; of that total, three hundred members were elected by plurality in single-member districts. All of the registered parties were eligible to win these seats. The remaining one hundred seats, which were distributed in a variable number of multimember districts, were reserved for exclusive allocation to minority parties.[12] Candidates for these seats were nominated by parties in closed and blocked ballots. A party was considered minority if the number of pluralities it won in single-member districts was below sixty. If the opposition parties were to win ninety or more single-member seats, the number of additional seats would be reduced from one hundred to fifty. The minority party seats were allocated by electoral formulas chosen by the Federal Electoral Commission (Comisión Federal Electoral, CFE). One of the formulas was biased against the larger of the minority parties; the other had an equally strong bias against the smaller minority party. Since the parastatal parties that provided the government and the PRI with the necessary votes to control the CFE were the smaller ones, the formula selected for the 1979, 1982, and 1985 elections was the one biased in favor of the smaller minority parties.

As in the German model, each elector cast two votes: one for the single-member districts and one for the list seats. But since presumably the PRI was not going to participate in the distribution of list seats (because they were reserved for minority parties), this aspect of the system gave the PRI the possibility of choosing its own preferred opposition. In Mexico, the majority party could instruct its constituents to vote for a given minority party in the list seats, thereby enabling the majority constituents to choose both the government and its major opposition. The PRI never actually invoked this power, but its mere existence irritated most of the opposition leaders.[13]

The 1979 electoral reform proved to be very successful. By expanding the party system, it infused new life into Mexican elections. Indeed, the 1979 reform provided the minimal institutional basis to make possible a relatively peaceful political transition through the difficult economic times in the 1980s. Even though opposition parties tended toward radicalization, the system survived.

In summary, the PRI avoided losing its loyal opposition as a consequence of a long chain of gradual concessions to the "external" opposition combined with an expansion of the party system and the development of segmented and biased electoral formulas. Yet electoral pressures from the opposition were growing so strong that the government again leaned toward more restrictive laws. Thus, in 1986 the PRI reformed party rules to obstruct the growing electoral opposition and also changed the electoral formula for the Congress, introducing a so-called *cláusula de gobernabilidad* (governability clause).[14] The new laws took effect in the 1988 election. □

THE GOVERNABILITY CLAUSE

In 1988 the system tested a new set of rules that included the governability clause, a feature that provided for the plurality party to be allotted a majority of seats in the Chamber of Deputies. The chamber was enlarged to 500 seats, 300 of which were elected by plurality in single-member districts and 200 by list proportional representation. The law provided two set of rules, one applicable to the winning party—the party receiving the most seats in single-member districts and the other to the rest of the parties. The allocation of seats to the winning party ensured that it would always have a majority in the Chamber of Deputies, regardless of the level of votes received (thus the name "governability clause", implying that majority control of the Chamber of Deputies is a necessary condition of governability). If the winning party vote was lower than 51 percent, it would receive 251 seats (out of 500 total); if the vote was between 51 and 70 percent, the winning party would obtain the same number of seats as its percentage of the vote (using the Hare quota, in which the total number of votes is divided by the total number of seats); at 70 percent or above, the winning party would receive 70 percent—and no more than 70 percent—of the chamber's seats, or 350 representatives.

The allocation of seats was made using the West German method: The number of list seats is equal to the total seats minus the plurality seats. The remaining seats are allocated among the rest of the parties. In this case, the rule consisted of a two-step, modified largest-remainder method. In the first step, up to two seats were allocated for each party in each of the five multimember districts, using as the quota the number of votes divided by two times the number of seats. That is, the first two seats in each district were allocated using half the Hare quota. These "cheap seats" were strongly biased in favor of the smaller parties.

The rationale was to guarantee majority control of the Chamber of Deputies. In 1986 lawmakers clearly believed the PRI would win the election but probably with less than 50 percent of the vote, which explains why the main opposition parties—especially the PAN—voted against the reform.[15] And indeed that was the case, although the official tally gave a bare majority to the PRI, which in the 1988 elections was confronting the strongest opposition performance in Mexican history. □

ELECTORAL ENGINEERING AFTER 1988

Since that time Mexican politics has been marked by the schism suffered by the PRI in that election. By the end of the de la Madrid government (1982–1988), the Corriente Democrática (Democratic Current), the left wing of the PRI, had become increasingly critical of the government's policies. This faction claimed the government had been captured by a group of technocrats and conservatives who were establishing policies that were out of step with the PRI program. Working within the PRI, the Corriente Democrática had little success in its drive for reforms and failed to win the nomination as PRI presidential candidate.[16]

After the selection of Carlos Salinas as the party's candidate, a small but well-known group of PRI members defected. They were led by Cuauhtémoc Cárdenas, governor of Michoacán between 1980 and 1986 and son of Lázaro Cárdenas—a prominent revolutionary, former leader of the official party, and president of Mexico between 1934 and 1940. Lázaro Cárdenas is the paramount symbol of Mexican nationalism and was the main figure in the left wing during the Mexican Revolution. Another defector was Porfirio Muñoz Ledo, who had been a strong contender for the PRI presidential nomination in 1975 before losing the nomination to José López Portillo. Muñoz Ledo had also held the positions of Mexico's ambassador to the United Nations (during the de la Madrid government), secretary of labor, secretary of education, and president of the PRI party (during the Echeverría and López Portillo administrations).

Cárdenas and Muñoz Ledo were followed by a handful of left-wing PRI members. They hoped to attract support from other sectors of the party and their constituencies. The defection of such a prominent group was a major event in PRI history, but the real novelty was that the government found itself unable to stop the nomination of Cárdenas as the presidential candidate (nor could it stop the nomination of many of his followers as candidates for seats in the Chamber of Deputies and the Senate). The PRI was helpless, because the institutional features the government had established to cope with the problems of potential antisystem opposition were the very conditions that allowed Cárdenas and his followers to circumvent barriers to their nomination.

Cárdenas used the parastatal parties—nurtured and protected for many years to insulate the PRI from the pressures of other political parties—as his instruments. This was possible for two reasons. First, the parastatal parties began to rebel when the 1986 and 1988 electoral reforms sent strong signals that the government had changed its position toward them. The CFE, for instance, was reformed in such a way that the previously key votes of the parastatal parties became superfluous. The new law, in fact, gave the PRI a majority of votes in the CFE and in all of the other agencies of electoral management and oversight. This and other aspects of the electoral reform were strongly contested by the opposition. Apparently, the government read the PAN electoral growth as a threat, making it unwise for the PRI to divert political resources in support of its former allies.

The second reason Cárdenas was able to use the parastatal parties was the nomination of Salinas as the PRI candidate. Salinas, and the policies he had established during his post as minister of the economy, had been the target of continual attacks by the leadership of the opposition parties. Salinas and his team reciprocated this animosity. After his nomination, Salinas broke with tradition and announced that he was *not* seeking the support of any other party.[17] There is also evidence that during the opening months of the campaign, Salinas and his team focused their attention on the PAN and simply underestimated Cárdenas. Within a few weeks, the three parties that had customarily formed alliances with the PRI had nominated Cárdenas for president and had nominated many members of the Corriente Democrática for seats in the Senate and the Chamber of Deputies.

Members of the Corriente Democrática knew the government could easily forbid electoral participation by any defector party, but they also recognized that it could not—without risking the legitimacy of the entire election—prohibit a nomination made by all three parastatal parties. Legitimacy was a prime concern of the government, because opposition parties were beginning to act together in a variety of arenas regardless of ideological differences. This threatening strategy, launched under the umbrella of a "defense of the vote pact," had the same institutional incentives that had triggered the rebellion by the small parties: Because the reform in the composition of the Electoral Commission gave a majority of votes to the PRI, all other parties lost any incentive to vote with the PRI. Moreover, this reform reduced to zero the costs of voting in favor of the initiatives of any other opposition party. Opposition votes in the CFE had become useless, and voting against the PRI had no cost. Thus, very soon all of the opposition parties, regardless of their ideological differences, were voting in a bloc against almost any PRI position.

Ultimately, the PRI won the election, but it could not avoid the consequences of the defections. The *cardenistas*, who had abandoned the PRI in

1988 and merged with a vast number of political organizations on the left and the center-left, not only forged a sizable constituency that hurt PRI bases of support while leaving untouched the PAN constituencies but also formed a party, the Partido de la Revolución Democrática (PRD). The government could obstruct and harass this new party but could not ban it, because the PRD had used the registry of the Mexican Socialist Party, which could not be banned by the government without enormous costs.[18] By its act of secession from the PRI, the new party, headed by Cárdenas, set the conditions for a breakdown of the official party monopoly. By its mere existence, the PRD offered a low-cost defection alternative to many dissidents in the PRI, thus posing a permanent threat to PRI stability. This, in turn, has introduced pressure for the creation of new policies to regulate elections more strictly and has influenced the PRI's relationships with all opposition parties.

This pressure is especially threatening to a heterodox PRI government whose policies are outside the mainstream of the PRI political spectrum. Given the Salinas administration's distance from the historical PRIísta median, internal dissidence was inevitable. In the ongoing dilemma between the dual threats of secession and antisystem opposition, it is not surprising that the PRI leadership more greatly fears the former. Consequently, in 1991 the PRI reformed the electoral law to reinforce the governability clause.

The 1991 electoral formula is a modification of the 1988 formula. The size of the assembly, its division into plurality seats and list seats in five multimember districts, and the rules to be applied to the minority parties remain the same. The changes affect the rule for the allocation of total seats allotted to the winning party. The new law establishes that if the winning party receives less than 35 percent of the vote, it will get a proportional share in the chamber (the Hare quota and larger remainders), but if it reaches 35 percent of the vote, it receives 251 seats—a chamber majority. In addition, for each percentage point above the 35 percent mark but under 60 percent, the winning party will get two additional seats; if the winning party receives between 60 and 70 percent of the votes, it will get a proportional share of seats (using the Hare quota). Finally, if the winning party receives 70 percent or more of the votes, its number of seats remains fixed at 350—the equivalent of 70 percent of the chamber.

It is easy to understand why the PRI introduced this reform (granting that legislators assumed the PRI would be the plurality party). The puzzle lies in why the PAN voted for it, since the formula is detrimental to the runner-up in the legislative elections (and PAN leaders expected their party to be the runner-up). My explanation is that the PAN and the PRI traded votes: The PAN would accept reform measures in exchange for other measures that would benefit it.

The next major reform, in 1992, was aimed at oversight procedures and monitoring of elections. This means that recently the electoral rules in Mexico have been unstable. Indeed, the three federal elections in 1985, 1988, and 1991 each took place under different rules; moreover, the rules established in 1986 for the 1988 election were reformed even before their first test. The 1992 electoral rules were designed to regulate the 1994 elections, but they underwent a major reform a few months before the elections took place.

Unlike its two predecessors, the current electoral formula does not include a governability clause. Although simplified, it is not unbiased; it also tends to manufacture majorities through the systematic overrepresentation of the plurality party. The new formula is not differentiated or segmented—the rules for the allocation of seats are the same for all parties, and all parties can win seats in both the single-member and the multimember districts.

This is the simplest formula since the one that was in force in 1963. The Chamber of Deputies is currently formed by five hundred members. Three hundred are elected by plurality rule in single-member districts; the other two hundred are list seats elected by proportional representation (the Hare quota, largest remainder) in five multimember districts of forty seats each.

No minimum threshold is required to win a seat in single-member districts; the minimum threshold needed to receive proportional representation seats is 1.5 percent of the national vote. There is no governability clause, but there are maximum thresholds, or ceilings, of representation that vary according to the level of the party's electoral support.

If a party receives 63 percent or more of the votes, it gets exactly 315 seats, or 63 percent of the chamber.[19] If a party receives between 60 and 63 percent of the votes, its total share of the chamber will be exactly equal to its share of votes.[20] Finally, if a party gets less than 60 percent of the votes, it cannot receive more than 300 seats, or 60 percent of the chamber.[21]

With the new formula the winning party would be better off in some scenarios and worse off in others. To compare the old and new formulas, the new formula was applied to obtain the total number of seats the winning party would receive at thirty-five different levels of electoral support (from a minimum of 35 percent to a maximum of 70 percent), based on estimates of the number of plurality seats the party would win at each level of electoral support. Fifteen different scenarios were estimated for each level of support (which yielded 1,225 alternative scenarios). These estimations used actual electoral data (from the 1988 and 1991 elections) and imputed different "swings" to the main opposition parties, the PAN and the PRD.[22]

Under the new formula, the winning party would be worse off if it were to receive between 63 and 70 percent of the vote, because the new ceiling is lower (63 percent versus 70 percent), and it would also suffer in the range between 35 and 40 percent. However, the difference between the old and new formulas would be nonexistent between 60 and 63 percent of the vote, because the two formulas yield the same proportion of seats in the chamber (i.e., exhibit perfect proportionality) for any percentage within that span.

In contrast, the winning party would be better off with the new formula in most of the remaining scenarios, although to different degrees. For instance, the new formula is favorable to the winning party in all scenarios between 50 and 60 percent of the vote. In this range, the new formula collapses around the level of 60 percent of the seats, which is consistently higher than the proportion of seats the old formula yields for those levels of electoral support. Similarly, the winning party would be better off in most scenarios between 45 and 49 percent of the vote. In that range, it would be worse off only in extreme cases in which the split between the winning party and the runner-up is very slim (below 3 percent). Finally, the winning party would be better off in two out of three scenarios between 40 and 45 percent of the vote. In that range, the winning party would lose whenever the split between the winning party and the runner-up is 5 points or less.

In summary, the evaluation of the trade-off for the winning party in the new electoral formula compared with the previous one is somewhat inconclusive, because the new one contains a high degree of uncertainty. Yet the comparison between the electoral formulas used in 1988 and 1991 and the new 1992 formula does indicate that the winning party receives an advantage under many (but not all) electoral scenarios. Table 8.1 compares the number of seats the winning party would have received in 1988 and 1991 under the three different electoral formulas.

The evidence shown in Table 8.1, as well as the more extensive comparison among formulas discussed earlier, is intriguing, because both the 1991 and 1992 formulas required the approval of at least one opposition party. And as shown, in most scenarios the winning party has a greater advantage in comparison to minority parties. The PRD, the leftist minority, voted against both reforms, whereas the PAN, the conservative majority, voted for them. □

TRADE-OFFS IN WINNING SUPPORT FOR
THE NEW ELECTORAL RULES

The 1991 and 1992 electoral reforms were the most complicated pieces of electoral legislation the PRI had ever faced. For the first time, it had to seek the support of another party to pass the law, because approval

TABLE 8.1 Hypothetical Outcomes of the 1988 and 1991 Chamber of Deputies Elections Under Different Electoral Formulas

	Number of Seats Received by the Partido Revolucionario Institutional		
Election Data	1988 Formula	1991 Formula	1992 Formula
1988 (263 pluralities) 52 percent of vote	260	284	300
1991 (290 pluralities) 64 percent of vote	320	320	315

required a constitutional amendment, which, in turn, required a two-thirds vote of the Congress—and bipartisan collaboration, because the PRI alone did not have a two-thirds majority.[23] To pass the reforms, the PRI was forced to make a deal with either the PAN or the PRD.

Thus, in 1991 the PRI granted many of the PAN's demands regarding the organization and oversight of the electoral process, including the establishment of an electoral court with increased authority, in exchange for an electoral formula that benefited the winning party.[24] In return, the PAN voted in favor of the restrictive regulation of electoral alliances—especially the one allowing joint candidates, which the *cardenistas* used so successfully in 1988. The PAN also accepted a formula for the Chamber of Deputies that was even more favorable to the winning party, as long as its share of votes exceeded 35 percent.

In the 1992 electoral reforms, the PRI made additional concessions aimed at "cleaner elections." It accepted a lower cap on the maximum number of seats the winning party could hold and allowed a system of proportional representation in the Senate that guaranteed more seats to minority parties. These concessions were made in exchange for a stronger endorsement of the electoral system by the PAN and an electoral formula that would manufacture larger majorities for the winning party under the most likely electoral scenarios. □

REVERSING SELF-CERTIFICATION

Between 1917 and 1988, the Mexican constitution, based on the U.S. model, stipulated that the newly elected members of the Chamber of Deputies were the final judges of their own elections and that the chamber was the adjudicator of the outcome of the presidential election.[25] This system of *autocalificación* (self-certification) is vulnerable either to abuse by the majority party (if it commands a sizable majority in the chamber) or to the instability of majority cycles and a lack of decisiveness (if the largest party in the chamber holds only a plurality or, under certain conditions, even a slim majority).

For many years, the opposition parties on both the Left and the Right complained that the PRI systematically abused the system by disregarding evidence of fraud to impose its will in the settlement of electoral disputes. The majoritarian system is replicated in each of Mexico's thirty-one states (for state legislative and gubernatorial elections), and opposition parties complained that the PRI abused the system at that level, too. On several occasions the opposition introduced initiatives to abolish *autocalificación*, pressing for a judicial system in which the authority to settle disputes would be vested either in the Supreme Court or in a specialized electoral court.[26]

It is easy to see why opposition parties have disliked the majoritarian system of self-certification. Since the founding of the ruling party in 1929, the PRI has received supermajorities in the Chamber of Deputies (varying from 72 percent to 100 percent of the seats). In the numerous cases of contested elections, those majorities have always allowed a settlement in favor of the PRI. Between 1929 and 1988, the PRI never accepted the loss of a single governorship, in spite of many allegations of fraud. Opposition parties had only two options—to accept the decision of the majority party (which was almost always negative toward the opposition parties) or to boycott the entire electoral process. Opposition parties resorted to boycotts on several occasions and to rebellions in a few cases, but the PRI stuck firmly to the majoritarian system of judging the elections and passed laws imposing severe penalties against electoral boycotts. Rebellions were handled with a more direct approach.

In 1989 the PRI leaders suddenly changed course and relinquished the system of self-certification. Just as the opposition (including the Left, but especially the conservative PAN) had unsuccessfully proposed, the PRI introduced a constitutional amendment to transfer the authority to adjudicate elections from the Chamber of Deputies to a special electoral court.[27] Yet I argue that this change of preference for institutions did not result from persuasive arguments by the opposition but it was triggered by the change in the PRI's electoral fortunes, with a consequent lowering of its expectations. In short, the PRI preferred a political and majoritarian institution (self-certification) when it commanded strong majorities, and it chose a judicial institution when its majority shrank, as occurred in 1988. The opposition parties claimed the official results (49 percent of the votes for the PRI, 30 percent for the Left, and 19 percent for the PAN) were overtly fraudulent, but they had to accept them since their only options were a boycott or a rebellion—both of which were too costly.

As a result, 52 percent of the seats in the Chamber of Deputies went to the PRI, 28 percent to a leftist coalition that incorporated PRI defectors, and 20 percent to the conservative PAN. Although the PRI maintained a hefty lead over the second-largest party, the bitterness of the election encouraged both opposition parties to coordinate action against the PRI.[28] If the leftist coalition and the PAN had formed an anti-PRI bloc in the 1988–1991 chamber, they would have reduced the gap between the majority party and the runner-up from a comfortable spread of 24 percent to a narrow gap of only 4 percent (that is, 52 percent versus 48 percent). For a party that had just faced a major schism, this would have been dangerous. In any case, by the end of 1988 most political actors (including the leaders of the three main parties) anticipated that the upcoming elections were going to be even more competitive. The days of comfortable PRI supermajorities were over.

The point here is that weakened control of the Chamber of Deputies, and the PRI's pessimistic predictions regarding the upcoming elections, produced a change in the institutional design of the process of judging elections that was preferred by the majority party. The PRI understood that the majoritarian system it had exploited so successfully might turn against it if the party failed to receive the majority of seats in the chamber or even if it just passed that threshold. Thus, the remaining question is, why did one of the opposition parties vote for two electoral formulas that were apparently inconsistent with its preferences?

After 1988, opposition parties maintained a preference for a judicial system rather than the status quo. On the day of President Salinas's inauguration, the opposition parties formally reiterated their request for reform of the process. Since the PRI had already altered its preference from the majoritarian system to a judicial one, by 1989 the electoral court option was unanimously preferred. Hence, all parties anticipated a reform leading to the establishment of judicial institutions.

Despite its 1988 losses, the PRI still firmly controlled the legislative process, including setting the agenda and voting rules. Thus, it could introduce a bill that included reforms sought by the opposition together with a change in the electoral formula that was detrimental to opposition parties. Its control of the agenda and strong party discipline allowed the PRI to prevent the separation of issues. This was important, because the reform was a constitutional amendment that required the support of two-thirds of the Chamber of Deputies (334 votes out of 500). The PRI had only 52 percent of the vote (260 seats).

As the majority party in the chamber, the PRI had enormous advantages. The chamber organizes its legislative tasks through a system of standing committees that have veto power on every piece of legislation under their authority, and PRI leaders chair and control almost all of the committees.[29] There is no formal committee on rules, and the rules that govern agendas, debates, and voting procedures are so vague that the majority leader makes most of the decisions about of them.[30] In spite of this, the agenda is "forward moving": Once a bill is introduced to the floor, it is initially voted "in general." The bill is then separated into articles, and amendments are offered on the floor. This system ostensibly allows for a separation of issues, but in practice the majority leader may prevent separability, because at the end of the process the amended version of the bill must be voted on again.[31]

In the case of the 1989 electoral reform, the majority leader made clear his decision to vote jointly on the reform of both the electoral process and the electoral formula, which complicated the passage of the bill. The status quo formula was biased in favor of the majority party, but the new formula had an even stronger bias and was immediately denounced by both the Left and the PAN.

In spite of opposition threats to vote against the bill, the PRI leadership insisted on tying the creation of the electoral court to the reform of the electoral formula—a risky move. The PRI needed so many votes from each side that it was futile to attempt to pass the bill without the support of defectors. Assuming that all members of the PRI voted with the leadership, the PRI still needed 74 votes. Despite instability in the leftist coalition (138 votes), the PRI could obtain at most 40 votes from defectors. The PAN had 101 votes, so the prospects of obtaining a sufficiently great number of defectors from the Right was even slimmer. In fact, the PAN leadership faced an overt rebellion of forty of its backbenchers when it announced that the party had decided to support the PRI bill.[32] A few months later, some of these backbenchers formed an internal dissident group called Foro Doctrinario (or Doctrinaire Forum), claiming party leadership had abandoned the ideological guidelines of the PAN. The group counted the support of the electoral reforms as one instance of such "deviation." Eventually, most members of the Foro, including a former presidential candidate and the party president, split from the PAN to attempt to form their own party.[33]

During most of 1989, the PRI leadership negotiated with PAN leaders and, to a lesser extent, with the leftist coalition; at the eleventh hour it appeared that no agreement would be reached, because the PRI stuck firmly to linking the judicial reform with the approval of its preferred electoral formula.[34] Ultimately, the Left voted against the bill (as expected), but the PAN—to everyone's great surprise—voted in favor, providing the two-thirds majority needed to pass the bill. The PAN vote was so unexpected that the leadership faced an open rebellion of a dozen or so of its backbenchers. The most plausible explanation for the PAN vote is that the PAN received a crucial concession with regard to state elections—in particular, the government's first official recognition of a PAN victory in a gubernatorial race (in Baja California).

The political process that created the electoral law reform for the 1994 elections resembled its predecessor. The PAN would fare more poorly with the new electoral formula under most scenarios, yet it again supported the bill in the Chamber of Deputies. As in the previous round, the PAN vote can be explained by vote trading. This time the trade was more visible, and the position of the PAN leaders regarding the new formula was more ambiguous. Most PAN leaders preferred the old formula to the new one; a few saw certain advantages in the reform. Diego Fernández de Cevallos, the leader of the PAN parliamentary group, for instance, thought the new formula would less serve the interests of the smallest parties than the previous one had (which is a correct assumption). PANistas generally saw this as favorable, because small parties could be used for coalition building by the PRI—a strategy that would diminish the bargaining leverage of the PAN.[35]

PANistas do not always object to the manufacturing of majorities by means of the electoral formula, especially in cases where the winning party is near the majority threshold. Fernández de Cevallos, for instance, has defended the governability clause, basing his comments on a preference for majoritarian rather than proportional electoral systems. He has also argued, however, for an electoral formula that would facilitate the peaceful extrication of the PRI's political monopoly—probably by means of a formula extending some safeguards to the leaders of the old regime.[36] The new electoral formula is likely to manufacture majorities for the winning party if its plurality rises above 45 percent of the vote. But the formula is unlikely to manufacture a majority for pluralities below 40 percent; it would do so in only half of the scenarios in the range of electoral support between 40 and 45 percent.

In short, whereas the changes in the 1988 formula that were implemented in 1991 were favorable to the winning party in all scenarios, the new reform was in the interest of the winning party but, in certain cases, could also benefit the runner-up. This meant the "cost" of the trading could be lower. In fact, regarding the 1991 reform, one could ask why the PAN yielded so much; for the new reform, the question was why the PAN gained so much.[37]

A review of the "laundry list" the PAN made public at the beginning of the negotiations reveals that the new law satisfied those demands, albeit not completely.[38] Initially, the PAN leaders demanded a strengthening of the judicial settlement of electoral disputes (the law met most of that demand),[39] the introduction of some form of proportional representation in the Senate,[40] and modification of the constitutional qualifications for the office of President of the Republic.[41]

The new law also included some reforms regarding the agenda of the president, presumably designed to deter conflicts during the general election. These measures included new regulation of political money, including public subsidies, private donations, and limitations on spending; regulation of the role of the mass media in electoral campaigns; and reform of the process of appointment of electoral authorities. All of these measures were deemed insufficient by the PAN leaders, but they regarded them as a first step in a battle that will be continued in the next round of reforms.[42] □

CONCLUSION

Mexico's mixed pattern of reform reflects a process of political adaptation by the government, which "reacts" to short-term pressures from the opposition. It also reveals that the Mexican political elite is divided on the issues of political and—especially—electoral reform. Lorenzo Meyer, a distinguished Mexican scholar and an influential political columnist, has captured this tension in a telling metaphor:

> The Mexican political system and its authoritarian presidentialism—like a huge army that is in retreat, yet undefeated—have concentrated their best elements in the rear guard. It continues the fight. Its withdrawal is slow and orderly, but it retreats, since it is clear that it no longer owns the future. The system yields ground to a democratic future, but it does so little by little, controlling the timing and the conditions of the transition.
>
> The authoritarian regime is, indeed, in retreat, but no one knows where it is heading or when its demise will occur. What is important is avoiding the final battle. The immediate objective of Mexico authoritarianism is to protract the march and hold the army together, for the individual salvation of the PRI chiefs depends upon it.[43] □

NOTES

1. Federal elections are held every six years for the president and every three years for the Senate and the Chamber of Deputies. Each of the thirty-one state governors is elected every six years, and state chambers of deputies as well as city councils are chosen every three years. Federal, state, and local calendars are independent; thus, an election is underway somewhere in the country at almost any given time. Some states have synchronized their state and municipal elections with the federal ones, so that citizens are asked to vote just once every three years. In states that have not taken that measure, citizens are called upon to vote once a year.

2. See Jeffrey Weldon, "Congress, Political Machines, and the Maximato: The No-Reelection Reforms of 1933," paper presented at the Latin American Studies Association Eighteenth International Congress, Atlanta, Georgia, March 10–12, 1994.

3. The new party added to its territorial organization a corporatist structure integrated by four "sectors": peasants, workers, the military, and the *sector popular* (urban middle and lower classes). See Luis Javier Garrido, *El partido de la revolución institucionalizada* (Mexico City: Siglo XXI, 1982).

4. By the 1950s, for instance, all Mexican states had transferred their offices of registry from municipal agencies to a federal agency under the control of the Secretaría de Gobernación. See Juan Molinar Horcasitas, *El tiempo de la legitimidad* (Mexico City: Cal y Arena, 1991).

5. The PAN, for instance, failed to present a presidential candidate from its own ranks in 1940 and again in 1946. It chose instead to seek alliances and supported potential or actual defectors from the PRI (Luis Cabrera, Juan Almazán, Ezequiel Padilla).

6. Between 1946 and 1958, the PAN's best electoral performance rendered it only 6 seats in a chamber of 161 members.

7. These parties, primarily the Partido Popular Socialista and the Partido Auténtico de la Revolución Mexicana—both of which were created by defections from the official party—were indeed so dependable that many analysts and even average citizens referred to the PRI as the "state party" and to the others as the "parastatal parties."

8. One of the pro-PAN reforms was the gradual transfer of authority from the Ministry of Gobernación to the Comisión Federal Electoral (CFE), a collegiate body that initially was heavily dominated by the PRI and the government. Yet, because of opposition pressures, the balance of votes in the CFE gradually tipped in favor of the opposition. In 1946 the PRI had four out of five votes in the commission; in 1951, it had four of six, in 1973 four of seven, and by 1979 only four of eleven. Although several of the minority parties survived only as long as they played the "loyal opposition" role, greater involvement by the opposition in the electoral organization became critical in the future.

9. This party-seats system could produce some odd results. For example, after its introduction, the number of pluralities won by the PAN in single-member districts sank in spite of the growth in its proportion of votes. This anomaly peaked in 1976, when the PRI won all the single-member-district seats and gave the opposition only forty-one party seats.

10. Other unexpected consequences included a case in which four candidates from Mexico City competed for a seat. Although the PRI candidate won the plurality seat, his three "defeated" opponents each won a party seat. Nobody lost!

11. The Communist Party and other parties, which were founded by former leaders of the 1968 political movement who had recently been released from jail, were not allowed to nominate candidates, because only those parties that were registered with the Secretaría de Gobernación for more than one year prior to the election could do so legally. Some of these organizations were still trying to prove that they met the strict legal requirements set by Gobernación. In some cases, Gobernación had already denied them registry.

12. The number of multimember districts could vary from two to five, and thus the district magnitude varied as well.

13. During the 1985 election, however, the boss of the oil workers' union, who was affiliated with the PRI, asked the union members to cast their single-member ballots for the PRI and their list ballots for the Partido Socialista de los Trabajadores—one of the parties that later nominated Cárdenas as the presidential candidate.

14. In Mexican electoral parlance, governability clause means a legal and explicit provision for manufacturing majorities in the Chamber of Deputies.

15. The reform passed because the PRI had enough seats to reform the constitution without having to seek the support of seats held by other parties.

16. The PRI leadership did not allow Cárdenas to register even as a pre-candidate. The PRI nomination went to Carlos Salinas de Gortari, the candidate the Corriente Democrática feared the most. This triggered a major defection from the PRI by supporters of Cárdenas.

17. In fact, two of the three parastatal parties endorsed the PRI presidential candidate in the 1958, 1964, 1970, and 1976 elections.

18. The Mexican Socialist Party had little electoral support, but as a product of the fusion of most of Mexico's leftist organizations, its political relevance was substantial. The CFE harassed the PRD by refusing it permission to use the colors of the Mexican flag—green, white, and red—even though the PRI uses them. Using minor arguments, the CFE also delayed granting the PRD its registry. The PRD leadership reacted with great irritation and animosity.

19. Therefore, if a party wins 63 percent or more of the vote, the number of list seats it receives is equal to 315 minus the number of plurality seats it won.

20. Therefore, the number of list seats equals its proportional share in the chamber minus the number of plurality seats it won.

21. Therefore, the number of list seats equals three hundred minus the number of plurality seats it won.

22. This simulation was designed by Arturo Sánchez Gutiérrez and me.

23. The two-thirds threshold in the Chamber of Deputies is equal to 330 seats (out of 500). In 1991 the PRI had only 260 seats; in 1993 it had 319, still short by 11 seats. In 1994 the PRI would have been able to gather enough votes by seeking only the votes of the *smallest* parties instead of pursuing an alliance with the PAN or the PRD, but the PRI leadership preferred to avoid the overt opposition of these two large parties.

24. The new electoral court rulings could be reversed only by a two-thirds vote of the Chamber of Deputies (in other words, the PAN had a veto in this regard). The new Electoral Commission was integrated in a more balanced way. The 1993 reform moved even further in the direction of judicial settlement of contested elections.

25. The Mexican constitution follows the pattern established by the U.S. constitution: It employs federalism, separation of powers, municipal government, judicial review, and even the official name of the country, *Estados Unidos Mexicanos*. However, the Mexican constitution permits only an emasculated intervention by the judicial branch in electoral matters. The Supreme Court can hear cases on contested elections, but its findings are only opinions the chamber may disregard by majority vote. This provision has been modified on several occasions since 1917, and each reform has limited even further the domain of cases the court can hear.

26. The opposition was, in fact, advocating a comprehensive overhaul of the electoral system, including most aspects of electoral administration and ultimately the process for settling electoral disputes. Minority parties from the Left and the Right proposed different reforms, but they all preferred an electoral court over *autocalificación* and the process of electoral administration.

27. I say "suddenly" because only two years before, in 1986, the PRI passed a bill that strengthened the majoritarian nature of the self-certification process and

rejected amendments offered by the opposition that would have led to the creation of a judicial institution to settle electoral disputes. See *Reforma constitucional y Código Federal Electoral: Renovación política,* Vol. 6 (Mexico City: Secretaría de Gobernación, 1987).

28. For instance, during the inauguration of President Salinas, the parliamentary leaders from both parties affirmed that the PRI victory was fraudulent and that Carlos Salinas was not a legitimate president.

29. During the 1988–1991 legislature, the PRI leadership allowed the PAN to chair certain committees, albeit only those that did not deal with policy matters. This was the first time PANistas had been allowed to chair committees, and it decreased the ratio of PRI to non-PRI members of committees (while maintaining strong PRI majorities in all cases). During the 1991–1994 legislature, the PAN finally presided over a policy committee, the Committee on Justice, which was dealing with reforms of the penal code.

30. The lack of a comprehensive set of rules and precedents seems to be the expected consequence of one-party hegemony that has lasted more than six decades.

31. This agenda, and the strongly enforced party discipline found in the congressional parties in Mexico (where most divisions are straight party votes), also means there is little need for closed rules. PRI members rarely offer amendments, and amendments from the opposition are easily voted down unless the majority leader finds them appealing.

32. This rebellion did not end after the vote. Many of the insubordinate backbenchers extended their opposition to their party leadership, and they have made that vote a cause célèbre. This group ultimately defected to form its own party.

33. By the end of 1993 they had failed to obtain the legal registry as a party, and results at the polls—reflecting their alliances with the parties of the Left—were disappointing.

34. To order to take effect for the 1991 elections, the new law had to pass by early 1990 at the latest.

35. This and the assessments that follow of the positions of the PAN leaders are based on several personal interviews with Carlos Castillo Peraza, party president; Diego Fernández de Cevallos, parliamentarian leader, Felipe Calderón, secretary general; and Fernando Estrada, federal deputy.

36. The position of the PAN leaders is more divided. Secretary General Felipe Calderón, for instance, prefers proportional representation and opposes legal provisions for the manufacturing of majorities.

37. Of course, this assessment of the payoff to the PAN is disputable, and it is possible to see the PAN as the great loser in this round of reforms. In this case, the support of the PAN can be explained either by a gross miscalculation by its leaders or by the existence of other deals included in a secret agenda.

38. The PAN presented these demands on June 28 in a public document endorsed by the PAN and PRD leaders.

39. The reforms consisted of the exclusion of the Chamber of Deputies from the settlement of disputes over the election of its own members, the simplification of the procedural requisites to contest elections before the Electoral Tribunal, and the modification of the process for the appointment of electoral judges to allow

greater leverage by opposition parties in the Chamber of Deputies (see Articles 268–269, 327–328, 342–343).

40. On this issue, the reform dictated the following formula: Each state will elect four senators concurrently, each party will present a closed list of three candidates, the winning party will have all three of its candidates elected, and the top candidate on the list of the runner-up party will be elected. Consequently, opposition parties will receive a minimum of 25 percent of the Senate seats (see Article 60 of the General Constitution and Article 11 of the Electoral Code).

41. The constitution originally required that the president be a Mexican citizen (by birth, not naturalization) and that his or her father *and* mother also be Mexican citizens by birth. The new reform required the president to be a Mexican citizen (by birth, not naturalization), with the further requirement that *either* the father or the mother be a Mexican citizen *or* have resided in the country for twenty-five years (see Article 82, General Constitution).

42. Interview with Diego Fernández de Cevallos, congressional leader of the PAN (September 24, 1993).

43. Lorenzo Meyer, "Retirada sin dejar de pelear. El futuro ya no le pertenece al sistema," *Excelsior* (July 1, 1993), front page.

CHAPTER NINE

———————— ■ ————————

Hyperpresidentialism and Constitutional Reform in Argentina

Carlos Santiago Nino

ATTEMPTS AT CONSTITUTIONAL reform in Argentina, initiated in 1986 during the administration of Raúl Alfonsín, launched a debate that continues in the 1990s. Argentina is not alone in this process. Throughout Latin America, institutional reform appears critical to the consolidation of democracy. Debates have taken place over possible modifications of the constitutions of Chile, Brazil, Colombia, Paraguay, and Bolivia, and some constitutional amendments have been adopted.

In regard to innovations in the political system, however, constitutional reforms in Latin America have not produced dramatic results. Although these reforms have created protections for civil and political rights and have ensured the independence of the judiciary and other checks on political power, significant breakthroughs have not occurred in the organization of political power itself. This is surprising given the extent of discussions among academics (which have trickled into active political circles) about the deficiencies of current institutional arrangements. The presidency has received the most attention, but myriad proposals have also been made for reforming the electoral system. These have focused mainly on the legislative bodies, their formation and functioning (e.g., bicameralism), features of the party system (e.g., the financing of party activities), mechanisms of decentralization, and so forth. □

FALLACIES IMPEDING ARGENTINA'S
CONSTITUTIONAL REFORM

Lack of innovation in institutional design is the result of a combination of factors. First, Latin American political actors are curiously conservative regarding existing political institutions despite the fact that these institutions have been remarkably discontinuous throughout history; hence there are, in reality, very few long-standing institutional traditions. Moreover, during Argentina's intervals of military rule, politicians who sought to regain power when democracy was reestablished based their strategies on the rules that were in force prior to the coup instead of aiming for new and improved democratic rules. Finally, I believe a cognitive confusion is produced by the acceptance of informal fallacies inhibiting reform.

The three of these fallacies relate to Argentina's constitutional reform. The first I call the "fallacy of undue abstraction." Argentine politicians claim that agreement about constitutional reform exists among political actors and the population at large. This consensus is largely illusory, however, since it results from an excessively abstract discussion of reform. The Peronist Party has wanted to reform the constitution mainly to allow for the reelection of the incumbent president. The opposition Radical Party, which views reelection as a reinforcement of the presidentialist system, has proposed reforms that would attenuate or even abandon presidentialism. The Peronists, nevertheless, allege that widespread support exists for constitutional reform, citing polls that show that 70 percent of the population favors it. However, the meaning of "reform" to the general public may be a far cry from specific issues, such as the relative merits of the presidentialist system. In fact, each side sees the other's proposal as the worst possible outcome, which means the only true "consensus" is to have no meaningful constitutional reform.

The second informal fallacy that disrupts a lucid discussion of constitutional reform is the assumption that political systems—parliamentarism, presidentialism, or mixed systems—are "sealed packages" that must be either adopted or rejected in toto. Each of these systems, in reality, consists of mechanisms that can be adopted independently. The impression that one must adopt political systems in an all-or-nothing fashion discourages significant, albeit less far-reaching, innovations.

A third fallacy of "partial valuation" is accepted by many political scientists and by the politicians they influence. It consists of judging systems of government exclusively on the basis of some values—mainly stability and efficiency—while disregarding others on which the former depend. For example, the efficiency of a political system depends on its capacity for satisfying some other values that must be specified, and stability is a value only insofar as it is predicated on a system that is valued on grounds other than stability itself. The central value of a political system is its moral legitimacy—that is, its capacity for producing decisions that are morally justified and binding on those who are subject to them. Assuming that the system whose value is at stake is a democratic one, that value cannot be specified without articulating a normative conception of democracy. This conception must determine which features of the democratic system are central and which are peripheral, which, in turn, enables a determination of mechanisms that should be preserved or enhanced to have a stable and efficacious democratic system.

It is necessary to articulate a conception of democracy that is opposed to the dominant pluralist conception, which is based mainly on the equilibrium between opposing interests and the avoidance of monopolization of authority by any of their holders. I defend a version of democracy based on participation, deliberation, and consensus. Agreements reached after broad deliberation, in which all of those affected participate, approximate the moral correctness of decisions more closely and reliably than any other procedure of collective decisionmaking. □

DEFINING THE MORAL VALUE OF DEMOCRACY

To avoid the fallacies of undue abstraction and partial valuation, we must define what justifies undertaking the dangerous process of constitutional reform. For securing the moral value of democracy, the primary requirement is preservation of the rule of law. Latin American democracies in general, and Argentina in particular, are now subject to a rather different threat from that which loomed over them in the past. People traditionally feared a military coup that would interrupt the normal working of democratic institutions. This threat seems to have vanished in most of the region, but it may have been replaced by a more insidious one: the incremental "depletion from the inside" of democratic institutions arising from the undermining of the separation of powers. Restrictions on the independence of the judiciary, for example, leave institutions without the capacity to respond to widely perceived injustices and inequities (such as massive corruption). Marginalizing large sectors of society from the democratic process—whether because of increasing inequalities that make their participation less effective, their own apathy and skepticism in the face of previous evils, or manipulation of public opinion through control of the media—erodes the mechanisms of representation and control.

This process creates in many Latin American countries what Guillermo O'Donnell has called "delegative democracy."[1] These countries may have stable and perhaps efficient political systems in terms of the outcomes some expect from them, but they are extremely deficient in regard to their moral democratic value.

The rule of law means there is a system of legal standards that are stable, general, nonretroactive, and public and that are applicable and administered impartially to all sectors of the population without discrimination. This requires an independent judiciary—that is, a judicial power whose decisions are not influenced by the desire to favor one political, economic, or social group over others.

A direct relationship may exist between the concern for preserving the rule of law and the concentration of economic and social power in society. Consider the Hobbesian theorem that under certain conditions self-preservation leads social actors to agree to the constitution of a leviathan to guarantee mutual agreements of nonaggression. Concern for the rule of law thus increases when powerful economic groups (mainly because of their size) can no longer meet secretly to negotiate among themselves and with those holding political power. Given that the recent process of privatization in Argentina has produced a remarkable oligopolization of the economy, a derivation of that theorem would be that in Argentina it is no longer in the interest of powerful social and economic agents to maintain the rule of law through the creation of a state whose rules are not determined by any one agent or by any coalition of agents.[2]

This is particularly alarming when we take into account the inroads that were made in the independence of the judiciary and other bodies of control during the administration of Carlos Menem. These maneuvers included, among others, the packing of the Supreme Court, the dismissal of members of the Court of Accounts (which was later replaced by a new organ controlling government accounts and staffed by political appointees), the dismissal of the head of the agency that controls irregularities in public administration, the subordination of federal prosecutors to the Ministry of Justice, and the appointment of hosts of new judges—all with close ties to the government.

We can also conjecture that one way to promote a deconcentration of social and economic power is by reinforcing the rule of law. There is little doubt that such a deconcentration is required by the moral conception of democracy described earlier. When social and economic power becomes concentrated, participation in the political process becomes less and less equal and hence less and less democratic. A critically necessary constitutional reform in Argentina is, therefore, the strengthening of the rule of law by securing the independence of the judiciary and other institutions that can check the influence of unequal social and economic power. The first step would entail the specification of the maximum number of justices on the Supreme Court, which would prevent packing the court.

But something more adventurous could be attempted. For instance, the new Bolivian constitution (if it wins final approval) will require a two-thirds majority in both houses of Congress for approval of appointments to the highest courts and other controlling bodies. Such a reform in the

Argentine constitution might secure the independence of courts and agencies from the control of any one party. A more far-reaching reform would be the creation of a special Constitutional Court with the right of both concrete and abstract judicial review and with the power to make its decisions binding on the lower courts.

Another possibility would be the creation of a Council of Judicial Power in the European style, formed mainly by judges and representatives of the legal profession, with the power to nominate justices in the court system. Further beneficial reforms would be the separation of the office of federal prosecutors from the executive branch so as to make it completely independent, the formation of a congressional agency for overseeing the financial dealings of the government, and the establishment of an ombudsman. □

ARGENTINE HYPERPRESIDENTIALISM

These reforms, although indispensable, would not completely eliminate the tendency of those with political power to undermine the rule of law and dominate the judiciary. That tendency arises from a deeper feature of the Argentine political system: its hyperpresidentialism. Hyperpresidentialism, the concentration of economic and social power, and the deterioration of the rule of law mutually reinforce each other. Neutralizing hyperpresidentialism would be a way of strengthening the rule of law and decentralizing power—all of which would, in turn, enhance the moral quality of the democratic system.

The roots of hyperpresidentialism, both de jure and de facto, lie in the 1853 Argentine constitution, which sought the creation of a strong presidency. The intellectual author of that document, Juan Bautista Alberdi, argued explicitly for a departure from the model of the U.S. constitution. In response to the history of Argentine civil strife, he favored following the 1813 Chilean constitution, which provided for a sort of elected king—an office that was democratic in its origin but absolutist in its exercise.

Argentine presidents differ from their U.S. counterparts in that they do not need to seek legislative confirmation when appointing members of their cabinet or other executive offices. The Argentine constitution also gives the executive very broad regulatory powers by means of decree, and it allows the president to declare a "state of siege"—a suspension of habeas corpus and other guarantees in case of external war or internal strife. Not only can the president independently enact the state of siege during the long periods of congressional recess, but he or she is also the only person who can freely exercise that power by arresting people or moving them from one point in the country to another. The Argentine president's term of office also used to be longer than that of the U.S. president (six years and four years, respectively), although his or her reelection was prohibited. [The 1994 constitutional reform changed these rules to a four-year term and eligibility for one additional term; see Postscript.]

Even more important than the explicit provisions in favor of hyper-presidentialism are those resulting from the constitutional power of the federal government to intervene in provincial governments—even to the point of dismissing their elected officials and appointed authorities. Despite the dominant opinion of scholars that this constitutional article refers to a power of Congress, presidents—with the consent of some courts—have interpreted the provision as applying to the executive branch.

The power of veto over congressional bills has also been interpreted by presidents as including subsections of a bill that is otherwise enacted. The hyperpresident thus has power to reformulate the very structure of congressional legislation. This was declared unconstitutional by the Supreme Court in *Colella*, but that decision was widely ignored, since findings of Argentine courts are binding only for the case being considered.[3]

The Supreme Court has restricted the right of Congress to delegate its powers to the executive.[4] This is, nevertheless, a common practice of the legislative branch. Another important source of presidential powers comes through agencies like the Central Bank, which—despite their creation by Congress—operate under exclusive presidential control. It has been said, for example, that the Central Bank is more powerful than Congress.

The most important inroad hyperpresidents have made into legislative powers (with the consent of the courts) is their capacity to enact decrees in cases of "necessity and urgency."[5] This capacity, which is endorsed by some constitutional lawyers on the basis of the example of parliamentary executives, is a source of enormous power: Menem, for instance, has enacted at least twice as many decrees of necessity and urgency as all of the former civilian presidents combined. These decrees have ranged from important issues, like freezing bank deposits, to banal ones, like regulating traffic in Buenos Aires.

A final example of the de facto assumption of powers by hyperpresidents is the capacity to grant pardons. This power has been acquired by presidents despite the fact that the Argentine constitution seems even more explicit than that of the United States in restricting pardons to people who have been convicted—a form of pardon that is much less intrusive on the workings of the judiciary.

Part of the dynamism behind the formation of hyperpresidentialism in Argentina is the backlash against practices developed during military regimes. During these periods, the only institution in operation that is mandated by the constitution is the presidency, which thus absorbs not only legislative powers but also the power to remove and to appoint members of the judiciary and the governors of the provinces. Upon the reestablishment of democracy, the most blatant unconstitutional powers are removed from the executive branch, but others that do not so clearly contradict the text of the constitution remain in force.

The powers of the president are also reinforced by a dynamic inherent in the democratic process. Tradition and the proportional electoral system in the lower house make political parties highly disciplined entities. Incumbent presidents and presidents-to-be are usually the leaders of their parties. Even when parties have adopted internally democratic and open decisionmaking rules, their leaders have continued to possess enormous leverage in deciding, among other things, candidacies for elective positions. This means members of Congress who belong to the president's party are extremely sensitive to his or her wishes with regard to the extent of their respective powers.

Something similar happens with judges. During military rule, when life tenure is not respected, most judges develop "conditioned reflexes" for maintaining a low profile. This inclination sometimes carries over into democratic regimes when those judges remain in office. Even when judicial tenure is respected, the president dominates the Senate, which must confirm appointees. He or she thus holds the key for promotion, as well as the possibility of securing appointments for political friends. Therefore, it is not surprising that in Argentina judges are extremely reluctant to challenge the powers of the presidency. □

DYSFUNCTIONALITIES OF PRESIDENTIALISM

Many political scientists have noted the serious dysfunctionalities displayed by presidential systems.[6] Statistical evidence reveals their weaker stability compared with parliamentary and mixed systems. These dysfunctionalities are especially dangerous when presidentialism in Latin American countries is combined with features of European parliamentary political systems, such as proportional representation and disciplined political parties. The dysfunctionalities may also be exacerbated when the presidential systems are hyperpresidential in character.

These dysfunctionalities are often ignored because scholars and lay people accept yet another fallacy, "decisionism," which consists of thinking that the important thing in the design of institutions is to allow them to make decisions. But many weak democratic bodies are perfectly able to make decisions; in fact, the weaker they are, the more decisions they tend to make (as could be witnessed during the last months before President Raúl Alfonsín resigned). What should be taken into account is not only the formal power of a democratic agency to make decisions but also the effectiveness of those decisions, which depends on whether the decisions in question receive consensual support.

Argentina's hyperpresidentialism produces formally strong presidents who, more often than not, are actually very weak as a result of the lack of consensual support. Isabel Perón, the weakest Argentine president of the twentieth century, was formally so strong she could enact a "decree of urgency and necessity" to order the military to "annihilate subversion." This was the case because the main weakness of presidentialism, especially hyperpresidentialism, is its inability to mobilize consensus. Let us consider several factors.

Presidentialism allows the formation of governments that lack strong popular support. This occurs mainly when the electoral system gives the victory to the candidate with the largest number of votes, which may be far less than a majority. A notorious example is that of Chile's President Salvador Allende, who in 1970 attempted to achieve far-reaching structural transformations with less than 37 percent of the popular vote. The election of President Arturo Illia of Argentina in 1963 is also an example: The blank ballot in favor of the proscribed Peronist Party outnumbered Illia's support. Runoff elections are another mechanism that creates an artificial majority, which can vanish the moment the president confronts his or her first controversial measures. The case of President Fernando Collor de Mello in Brazil provides an apt example.

Second, the rigidity of the presidential term of office exacerbates the problem of the lack of consensus: When presidents lose their popularity, there is no way to form a new government in response to the emerging political consensus. (Some Latin American presidents have had to continue governing while enjoying less than 5 percent support in public opinion surveys.) Impeachment is not a desirable mechanism for resolving the discrepancy between government and public opinion. This procedure requires an accusation of crime or malpractice and an extraordinary majority in Congress, which is extremely difficult to obtain in a hyperpresidential system. The impeachment of Collor de Mello in Brazil in 1992 is an exception that can be explained in part by the weakness of that country's political parties. Resignation is also unsuitable, since, as was demonstrated by Alfonsín, stepping down is seen as an act of betrayal of the popular mandate.

Third, the dynamics of confrontation between parties (provoked by the zero-sum game of presidentialism) lead to serious problems between the president and Congress.[7] Regardless of whether opposition parties dominate (as was the case with the Senate during Alfonsín's administration) or the president's party has a majority in the legislature (as happened with Menem), the quality of consensus is impaired. In the first case, two discordant expressions of political will exist unreconciled; in the second case, docile submission prevails instead of a constructive dialogue.

Fourth, hyperpresidentialism operates against the formation of coalitions. Since power is concentrated in the executive (and ministries have only minor political importance), there is a strong incentive to savagely oppose the president to increase the opposition's likelihood of winning the next election. Under these circumstances, there is little reason or room to use resources to create a coalition, and so another opportunity for building political consensus is lost. As Arend Lijphart has pointed out, such a consensus is required in divided societies that face serious crises.[8]

Finally, the extreme personalization of power in hyperpresidentialist systems is not conducive to the formation of political consensus. Although wide and enthusiastic support may be achieved by a charismatic president, this popularity is not necessarily converted into support for his or her governmental programs. Conversely, support for a president's program, however valuable, may be jeopardized by purely personal problems, such as corruption scandals and physical or mental illnesses.

Presidentialism and especially hyperpresidentialism produce an executive branch that has enormous formal powers but that frequently lacks the consensus required to implement policy. This means immensely strong hyperpresidents—in the formal sense—are often remarkably weak in their capacity to have their policies carried out successfully. The weakness of hyperpresidents does not, however, imply strength in other democratic bodies. The case of Argentina shows that formal omnipotence in the executive branch is achieved at the expense of other democratic bodies, which are often seen as irrelevant. A formally strong, but in fact weak, hyperpresidentialism means a weak democracy *tout court*.

This leads back to my conjecture about the interrelatedness of hyperpresidentialism on the one hand and the strength of the rule of law and the concentration of economic power on the other. Hyperpresidentialism is both a cause and an effect of the weakness of the rule of law. The hyperpresident acquires excessive powers because of the submission of courts and legislatures to the presidency; these bodies, in turn, are further weakened as the president increasingly invokes those powers, using them at least partially to undermine the authority of the other two branches. The link between the rule of law and the concentration of economic power exists because hyperpresidentialism is conducive to the concentration of such power, and concentrated economic power frequently does not require the rule of law to sustain itself.

Because hyperpresidentialism is a poor system for counteracting the concentration of social and economic power, it also tends to undermine the moral quality of the democratic process itself. The reverse is true as well: Powerful social and economic actors prefer to deal with a sole agent that does not operate through public deliberation. The incentive for influential groups is to weaken the presidency to strengthen their own position. □

TARGETING HYPERPRESIDENTIALISM

Reform of the Argentine constitution must focus on changing the structure of the country's hyperpresidentialist system. A constitutional reform that accepts a prefabricated "package" of political institutions or that is designed to achieve secondary values, such as efficiency or stability, however, will not enhance the moral quality of the evolving democratic process.

Among the problematic packages is pure parliamentarism. Its defect is not so much its alleged tendency toward unstable cabinets, as illustrated by the Third and Fourth French Republics and by Italy. Cabinet instability is not necessarily synonymous with regime instability, and it may also be alleviated by continuity in public administration and by devices like the constructive vote of no confidence found in the German constitution. Instead, I believe pure parliamentarism, if applied to Argentina, would have two different serious shortcomings. First, because prime ministers are elected (or informally selected) by legislatures instead of being popularly elected, parliamentarism weakens the connection between the people's votes and the formation of governments. This situation would certainly be viewed by the general public as a major reversal for representative, participatory democracy—which, in turn would affect the legitimacy of the government and its ability to marshal popular support.

The second shortcoming of pure parliamentarism is that it may lead to a situation in which the two largest Argentine parties, the Radicals and the Peronists, have nearly equal support and a small party holds the balance of power between them. The excessive leverage of minor but pivotal parties negatively affects the quality of the democratic process, as has been the case in Israel.

Mixed systems—such as those that exist in France, Portugal, Finland, and Iceland—may combine the advantages of both presidentialism and parliamentarism: the direct election of the chief executive, as in presidential systems, and the flexibility of parliamentarism. However, as Juan Linz has suggested, a mixed system may also combine their shortcomings: the rigidity of presidentialism and the indirect selection of the prime minister.[9]

To sort out this problem, one must unseal the package to observe the inner workings of mixed systems. These systems are defined by three features, two derived from parliamentarism and one from presidentialism. First is the separation of the office of the head of government from the office of the head of state. The second feature is the intervention of Parliament in the formation of government. The third—presidentialist—feature is the intervention of the electorate in government formation.

The first feature is particularly important, since tensions between the two offices can be resolved more easily when they are not concentrated in one individual. The head of state acts as a moderator who is not immersed in day-to-day politics and who represents the unity of the nation and the continuity of the democratic institutions. The head of government is responsible for carrying out specific policies, debating with the opposition, and competing with the opposition for the favor of the electorate. The Argentine people resent it when the president, whom they expect to fulfill the first role, is seen as performing the second—even though it is plainly necessary for him or her to do so.

The second feature gives the mixed system its flexibility. The need for confidence (or lack of censure) for continuity of the government serves as an escape valve in crisis situations, prevents deadlocks between Parliament and the executive, and allows for the formation of coalitions when they are needed.

The third feature is very important for overcoming the main shortcomings of parliamentarism. It avoids the indirect expression of the popular will by giving the electorate direct influence on the formation of government and by breaking the ties between evenly matched major parties so smaller ones do not gain disproportionate leverage.

The big problem, however, is how the second and third features should be combined. In existing mixed systems, the head of state (that is, the president of the nation) is popularly elected, and he or she has the power to appoint a prime minister who is also subject to the confidence of Parliament. Here some dilemmas emerge. An elected president is supposed to have important powers such as in France the responsibility for foreign relations and defense. This creates a delicate equilibrium between the president and the prime minister, since the different areas of government are closely interrelated.

Another possibility is found in the Portuguese mixed system, which concentrates all of the powers of normal government in the prime minister and his or her cabinet. This system was also proposed in the Second Report of the Council for the Consolidation of Democracy in Argentina.[10] The idea was that this system would have a dual dynamic. When the president had majority support in Congress, he or she would dominate the government, based on the power to appoint or dismiss the prime minister without fear of opposition by Congress. But when the president lost his or her majority in Congress, the mixed system would transform itself into a parliamentary one, since the president would have no other option but to nominate a prime minister supported by the opposition.

In a country like Argentina, however, it is doubtful that in a crisis situation a popularly elected president, without formal powers of government, would refrain from invoking his or her political legitimacy to interfere with the action of government. In countries with presidential traditions, strong pressures would exist to endow an elected president with more powers than those constitutionally prescribed. Thus, an inherent tension is present between the officeholder who has the greatest democratic political legitimacy and the officeholder who has the formal powers of government.

But now that we have unsealed the package of the mixed system, we can look into its constituent elements more closely and suggest combinations that might avoid these risks. For instance, the Center of Institutional Studies in Buenos Aires has proposed a kind of mixed system that to date has not been instituted anywhere, although it is similar to proposals made in the Netherlands, Italy, and Brazil—and most important—is similar to the Israeli law that will go into effect in the next election, scheduled for 1996. The crux of the proposal is that it is not the head of state but the head of government who should be popularly elected. This structure would unify the powers of government and political legitimacy in one office of the head of government. It would avoid the indirectness of the parliamentary system but would maintain the advantage of separating the two offices of head of state and head of government.

Above all, this system would preserve the main advantage of parliamentary systems, since the candidates who seek to lead the government must gain the confidence of Parliament if no candidate has won more than 40 percent of the popular votes (if more than 40 percent has been achieved, he or she would automatically accede to the office). Moreover, Parliament could censure the head of government by a three-fifths majority.

It can be argued that a serious shortcoming of this kind of system is that a popularly elected official is subject to dismissal by another branch. This objection is solved by the proposal—and in the new Israeli law, the rule—that in the case of censure new elections will be held for both the head of government and the legislature. Likewise, if the head of government decides to dissolve Parliament, the same two new elections must be held. Thus, an irreconcilable conflict between the two bodies that enjoy popular legitimacy is solved by the voters who are the source of that legitimacy.

Because of the importance of symbolism, the proposal of the Center of Institutional Studies calls the elected head of government not just a "prime minister" but the "President of Government," whereas the head of state is simply called the "Head of State." The popular acceptance of the new system may be helped by the fact that the people will continue to vote for a president (the President of Government) and that the changes will gradually be better understood. At first, some confusion will exist about the exact role of the Head of State (who will be designated by an extraordinary majority of Parliament and who should not belong to any political party). The new Head of State will have to make an effort to gain the respect of the people and will need to prove that having only ceremonial functions does not make the position irrelevant. Regarding the other important change—the possibility of censure—people will begin to understand it when it is applied. But since censure occurs only in truly critical situations, given the required three-fifths majority, it will be welcomed as a way of solving an obvious deadlock.

Both this diagnosis and the proposed remedy require further discussion. In this debate, it is of crucial importance that proponents and opponents avoid the serious fallacies discussed earlier, which stand in the way of rational institutional experimentation. □

EDITORS' POSTSCRIPT

Tragically, Carlos Nino died suddenly in 1993. The amendments to the Argentine constitution adopted in August 1994 were a far cry from the drastic reform he advocated, but they introduced a few elements—which he favored—aimed at tempering the excessive powers of hyperpresidents. The presidential term of office was reduced from six to four years, although presidents can now be reelected once. The president continues to be both head of state and head of government, but a new executive office resembling a prime ministership was created: that of the chief of the cabinet, who is "responsible for the general administration of the country." The president appoints the chief of the cabinet without congressional approval, but the chief of the cabinet can be removed by a congressional vote of censure (requiring absolute majorities of the members of both houses). He or she must send monthly reports to Congress and can be summoned by Congress to report on specific matters.

Moreover, the president's ability to legislate by decree has been limited. "Decrees of necessity and urgency" must be submitted to Congress within ten days of their issuance. A new Council of the Magistry—made up of political appointees, representatives of the judiciary, representatives of the bar, and academics—will be responsible for proposing judicial appointments and for the operation of the courts. Finally, the new constitution also provides for overseeing the independent ombudsman ("Defender of the People") Nino advocated. □

NOTES

1. Guillermo O'Donnell, "Delegative Democracy," *Journal of Democracy* 5, no. 1 (January 1994): 55–69.

2. A small number of economic groups now controls, among many other things, the large providers of public services.

3. *Ciriaco Colella C./S.A. Fevre y Basset v. otro*, Vol. 268 Fallos, pp. 352–364 (August 9, 1967).

4. *Delfino y Cía*, vol. 148 Fallos, pp. 430–438 (June 20, 1927).

5. *Rafael A. Peralta Rodriguez C./ Nación Argentina*, Tomo 314, Vol. 1 Fallos, pp. 704–709 (July 23, 1990).

6. See Juan J. Linz and Arturo Valenzuela, eds., *The Failure of Presidential Democracy* (Baltimore: Johns Hopkins University Press, 1994).

7. Juan J. Linz, "Presidential or Parliamentary Democracy: Does It Make a Difference?" in ibid., pp. 3–87.

8. Arend Lijphart, *Democracy in Plural Societies: A Comparative Exploration* (New Haven: Yale University Press, 1977), esp. p. 224.

9. Linz, "Presidential or Parliamentary Democracy."

10. Consejo para la Consolidación de la Democracia, *Reforma constitucional. Segundo dictamen del Consejo para la Consolidación de la Democracia* (Buenos Aires: EUDEBA, 1987).

PART THREE

The Design of Market Economies

CHAPTER TEN

■

Privatization in Central Europe: Can It Be Designed?

Éva Voszka

Privatization of state-owned enterprises is a fundamental task for all governments that aspire to transform a centrally planned economy into a market economy. Central European countries share an understanding that privatization is more than simply the transfer of individual firms from state hands to other proprietors: It is the precondition and the main instrument for rebuilding the entire economic system. The task is not only to fit state-owned enterprises into a functioning market but also to convert the ownership structure of a nation as a whole.

A basic dilemma for these governments is whether it is possible to build a mechanism for a decentralized market by applying a comprehensive, homogeneous privatization strategy, carried out by centralized governmental institutions. In other words, can governments design privatization?

In this chapter I examine the Hungarian experience in comparison with the experiences of Czechoslovakia and Poland.[1] I argue that all three governments have attempted to design ownership change. They have succeeded to differing degrees—not only in terms of privatized assets or enterprises but also in regard to the impact of programs, guidelines, and centralized decisionmaking on the transformation of the proprietary structure. The success of "design" can be measured by evaluating the stability of, versus shifts in, governmental privatization policies and by assessing the relationship between the programs as they are announced and their implementation.

At the beginning of the privatization process in the late 1980s and early 1990s, formerly socialist countries applied different approaches to conversion. At the outset, experts suggested typologies based either on published strategies and an analysis of the implementation of the initial programs or on such factors as key actors, resources necessary to acquire property rights, and method of asset valuation.[2] I suggest here a typology of the possibilities for designing privatization that takes into account the dynamics of the process since 1990.

Factors that play a significant role in the creation of the privatization framework include the social and political preconditions of the collapse of the old regime, the way in which new structures emerged, and the division of power following free general elections.[3] I concentrate on the "fine structure" of inherited economic preconditions, the differences in prior economic reforms, and, consequently, differences in specific characteristics of the planned economy as a starting point for transformation.[4]

Although it is widely believed that pre–1989 economic reforms created favorable preconditions for rebuilding the economic system, this assumption may be only partially true. The increase in enterprise autonomy and the subsequent weakened dependence on state and party decisions, the spread of small private entrepreneurships, deregulation of price and wage systems, and so forth, facilitated the shift to a market economy. At the same time, this transition has greatly complicated prospects for planning and control. I argue that the greater the erosion of the traditional planned economy preceding the political transformation, the more difficult it will be for the government to effectively design the procedures for privatization.[5]

To be sure, weakness of design does not necessarily mean privatization is slower or less efficient. Positive value is not attached to the concept of design. Nor does the hypothesis indicate that a recent experience with economic reforms is the only factor influencing the process. It is just one of numerous elements but one that integrates important preconditions. □

MACROECONOMIC CONDITIONS: PRIVATIZATION STRATEGIES

The transformation of Hungary, Poland, and Czechoslovakia has occurred in an environment of deep economic crisis. As Tables 10.1, 10.2, and 10.3 indicate, production has decreased every year since 1990. Inflation has been in the two- and sometimes three-digit range, and unemployment has grown from a negligible level to between 5 and 13 percent. The state budget deficit has increased in Hungary and Poland, whereas the external financial equilibrium (despite a high starting rate of indebtedness) proved to be manageable—although each country used different methods to cope with it. A comparison indicates the relatively better position of Czechoslovakia than the other two countries along nearly every dimension, including unemployment levels and budget deficits. Nevertheless, all three countries

TABLE 10.1 Macroeconomic Conditions in Hungary (1990–1992)

	1990	1991	1992
Gross domestic product (GDP) (previous year = 100 percent)	− 3.6	− 11.0	− 5.0
Inflation (percent)	29.0	35.0	23.0
Unemployment (percent)	1.7	8.5	11.4
Budget deficit in percentage of GDP)	− 0.3	− 5.0	− 7.4
Balance of payments (in percentage of GDP)	1.3	1.1	1.0

Sources: Adapted from Central Statistical Office; Ministry of Finance; Arnold Ludányi, *Magyaroszág és a kelet-európai átalakulás 1992-ben* (Hungary and the Transformation in Eastern Europe) (Budapest: Pénzügykutató Rt [Financial Research, Ltd.], 1993).

TABLE 10.2 Macroeconomic Conditions in Poland, 1990–1992

	1990	1991	1992
Gross domestic product (GDP) (previous year = 100 percent)	− 11.6	− 9.0	− 2.0
Inflation (percent)	550.0	70.0	40.0
Unemployment (percent)	6.3	11.8	13.6
Budget deficit (in percentage of GDP)	− 1.0	− 4.0	− 8.0
Balance of payments (in percentage of GDP)	0.9	− 2.0	− 0.6

Sources: Adapted from W. Grzegorz Kolodko, *Stabilisation, recession et croissance dans les economies post-socialistes*, Economic Prospective Internationale 1992–1993 (Vienna: Wiener Institute for Wirtschaftsvergleichung, 1992); Arnold Ludányi, *Magyaroszág és a kelet-európai átalakulás 1992-ben* (Hungary and the Transformation in Eastern Europe) (Budapest: Pénzügykutató Rt [Financial Research, Ltd.], 1993).

face shrinking markets, low profitability, instability and unpredictability in the business environment, and scarcity of internal and external financial resources. These factors—some of them caused or at least brought to light by stabilization efforts—obviously have an unfavorable influence on converting the ownership structure.

TABLE 10.3 Macroeconomic Conditions in Czechoslovakia, 1990–1992

	1990	1991	1992
Gross domestic product (GDP) (previous year = 100 percent)	− 4.0	− 15.9	− 7.0
Inflation (percent)	7.0	58.0	11.0
Unemployment (percent)	1.0	6.6	5.2
Budget deficit/surplus (in percentage of GDP)	− 0.3	2.2	0.01
Balance of payments (in percentage of GDP)	2 0.3	2.1	2.2

.Adapted from W. Grzegorz Kolodko, *Stabilisation, recession et croissance dans les economies post-socialistes*, Economic Prospective Internationale 1992–1993 (Vienna: Wiener Institute for Wirtschaftsvergleichung, 1992); Arnold Ludányi, *Magyaroszág és a kelet-európai átalakulás 1992-ben* (Hungary and the Transformation in Eastern Europe) (Budapest: Pénzügykutató Rt [Financial Research, Ltd.], 1993).

The conditions for privatization are challenging not only because of the economic depression and the complexity of the task, which requires systemic change, but also because of the scope of the task. Planned economies are traditionally characterized by the overwhelming role of state ownership. Some differences are found among the three countries analyzed here. According to official estimates, the contribution of the private sector to gross domestic product (GDP) at the time of political transformation was 4 percent in Czechoslovakia, 13 percent in Hungary, and 29 percent in Poland.[6] These figures are the result of dissimilarities in the nature of the planned economies (for example, agriculture has never been nationalized in Poland) and of the variation in reforms within the framework of those economies. The reform process in Czechoslovakia had been blocked by the intervention of the Soviet Army in 1968. In the other two countries earlier decades were characterized by economic reform disrupted by internal struggles and reversals. A primary component of change was a tolerance for increasing the role of the private sector. In Hungary, since the beginning of the 1980s, legislation even encouraged private-sector activity.

Another component of reform was located within the state sector itself and involved the relationship between the government apparatus and firm management. Although mandatory planning survived in Czechoslovakia, it was loosened significantly in Poland and was abolished altogether in Hungary.[7] The goal of these changes was to increase enterprise autonomy.[8] Decentralization of the decision-making system meant, among other things, strengthened bargaining positions for large enterprises in their negotiations with government ministries for financial resources and preferences. The informal influence of these enterprises was accompanied by formal decentralization, which meant firms were assigned more and more ownership rights formerly held by the government.[9] The final step was the introduction of self-governing bodies: workers' councils in Poland and the so-called enterprise councils in Hungary.[10] Enterprise councils, consisting of both employee and management representatives (but dominated by the latter group), had statutory authority to determine business strategy and organizational structure, to appoint the firm's chief executive, to make decisions on mergers and splits, and to form joint ventures and companies involving state property.

Thus, Hungary and Poland were pioneers in eroding the traditional planned economy, although in somewhat different ways. The breakup of the hierarchy in Poland led to a strong working class and trade unions, whereas in Hungary an oligarchical interdependence existed between central political institutions and enterprise management.[11] In any case, given that for decades central planning has coexisted with market features in these two countries, the classical model for a planned economy had in essence already collapsed. The political transformation during the early 1990s has not essentially changed this situation.

This is also reflected in the privatization process. Czech researchers worked out a nine-point list of "specific circumstances" that influenced the shape of the privatization process.[12] Two of these points concern the new political situation, but the rest—including the size of the private sector, certain alliances in the economy, the strength of different interest groups, institutional and cultural background, the financial situation of state enterprises, and public budgets (measured in particular by levels of external disequilibrium)—can be regarded as the consequences, or the extension, of previous economic reforms.

The general features of a planned economy—such as the dominance of state ownership, tight formal or informal central control over enterprises (and their highly concentrated, monopolistic structure), loose connections to Western markets, and the entire syndrome of soft budget constraint—however, resulted in some similar developments.[13] Because of the challenge presented by the unprecedented task of privatizing an entire economy, and because many economists remained or became influential advisers and even politicians, the newly elected governments devised comprehensive privatization strategies.[14] Legal frameworks and new institutions for converting the ownership structure emerged in the three countries in early 1990. Although the objective of designing privatization was widespread, the content and the processes themselves—which were already underway before the political transformation—differed in Hungary, Poland, and Czechoslovakia. □

THE MODEL OF RECIPROCITY:
SPONTANEOUS PRIVATIZATION

Three forms of spontaneous privatization began in Hungary in 1988 under the socialist regime. The first version involved the transformation of large factories into groups of individual companies. Driven by shrinking markets coupled with the evaporation of budgetary subsidies, which led to serious liquidity problems, several dozen large Hungarian enterprises created companies from their factories. The majority owner of the shares was the former central administrative unit of the enterprise. Although this new organization was called a "holding center," its legal form remained that of a state-owned enterprise. In other words, majority shares were owned by a "holding" created from the former enterprise center, which preserved the form of a state-owned entity. Minority shares, on the other hand, were acquired mainly by state-owned banks through debt-equity swaps and by customers and suppliers, most of which were also state enterprises.

A second version of spontaneous privatization saw Hungarian firms entering into joint ventures with foreign investors, which enabled enterprises to contribute only a small part of their assets toward the formation of each new company.[15] The third version, in Hungary often called "hidden privatization," meant assets (or at least income) were transferred from state enterprises to small new companies that were founded by managers or strong internal groups with in the same firms.[16] In contrast to the first version, the second and third ones resulted in privatization in the strict sense of the word.

The key actors in spontaneous privatization were the managers of state-owned enterprises. The state itself played a relatively passive role. The formal precondition for the managers' decisionmaking power was created by an earlier decentralization of ownership rights, which had aimed at maintaining the viability of the firms and preserving managerial positions. In the basic transformation model, top management had to negotiate only with the directors of factories over the details of creating the new companies out of existing factories and the allocation of assets and liabilities. Costs or prices were not considered because of the marginal role of external investors. This approach resulted, however, in organizational decentralization, as well as internal financial pressure to seek external capital. To avoid bankruptcy, the holding companies were often forced to find new owners and additional funding, usually by selling the majority shares of one or several companies. In this phase, as well as under the joint-venture model, sale prices were not a crucial factor for managers.

Thus, symmetrical groups in horizontal relations bargained over privatization. Without involving government organizations, managers of enterprises and occasionally foreign investors made decisions about the commercialization of state enterprises and the sale of state assets. Bargaining often involved clearly defined exchanges of favors, such as top management awarding managerial positions to factory directors in exchange for their support of commercialization. According to the categories proposed by Károly Polányi, spontaneous privatization can be described as a process dominated by reciprocity.[17]

Unlike Hungary, no systematic information about spontaneous privatization is available in Czechoslovakia. Some features of hidden privatization—pumping profits from state enterprises into private companies owned by the management or taking over assets through rental (leasing) contracts—were soon abolished by law. Spontaneous processes seem to be less widespread because of the more centralized system that existed prior to political transformation—which led to management's weaker position, both formally and informally.

Not surprisingly, however, features similar to the Hungarian developments also occurred in Poland. Nevertheless, criticism of spontaneous processes started earlier and was stronger than was the case in Hungary, with its detractors describing it as "nomenclatura" privatization.[18] Polish civil society, through organizations such as the workers' councils and the Solidarity trade union, became the primary force opposing the old regime. They viewed spontaneous privatization as a "theft of collective wealth," which should have become the property of the workers in the firm. Because preconditions in Hungary were different, the transformation of state enterprises into a group of companies could be regarded as an unbroken continuation of reforms that were strengthening enterprise autonomy and managerial positions without inducing real privatization.

Nevertheless, the Hungarian government criticized spontaneous privatization. Blame was placed first on the nonmarket nature of transformations. Specific complaints included the avoidance of publicity and competition, "selling out," and preservation of power. The criticisms can be better explained, however, by the limits of centralized control over privatization rather than by its nonmarket characteristics. Centralization of privatization-related decisionmaking power was one of the first actions of the new government following the free parliamentary elections. The creation of a central organization for privatization is a common feature of all three countries: Poland's Ministry of Ownership Change (MOC), Czechoslovakia's Ministry of National

Property Administration and Privatization, and Hungary's State Property
Agency (SPA). ☐

THE FIRST ATTEMPT AT A MARKET MODEL:
CENTRALIZED PRIVATIZATION

The foundation of ministries or agencies for privatization meant the centralization of decisions concerning ownership change. In all three countries the new organizations took over rights from branch ministries. In
addition to centralization within the government, this step meant the centralization of decisions from enterprises to state administration in
Hungary and Poland, where management-initiated spontaneous privatization had occurred before. In Poland, however, workers' councils
reserved the right of veto in any ownership change, which proved to be
effective in practice. The possibility of Hungarian enterprise councils ini-
tiating transformation or privatization did not vanish. Nevertheless,
above a low-value limit, since 1990 all deals involving state assets have
been controlled by the State Property Agency.

In its role as seller, the SPA—the key actor in the phase of centralized
privatization between summer 1990 and fall 1991—tried to pursue market criteria. Sales were based on competitive procedures (auctions or ten-
ders). The main objective was to increase the revenues of the state and to
modernize the economy through a "big jump," which was expected to
result in a simultaneous change in the structure of ownership, production, and market. The "active" programs initiated centrally (the first and
second privatization programs, small privatization, and the building
industry and wine programs) were aimed at the sale of majority shares.
The general intention was to sell the enterprises without splitting up or
restructuring; consequently, most of the potential buyers were international investors.[19] Price was considered the most important criterion in
negotiations.

The active programs moved very slowly. For example, of the
twenty enterprises targeted in the first privatization program, only
four were sold by the end of 1992. Others, at best, were transformed
into companies without involving private capital. The second privatization program has never truly gotten underway, although small privatization is an exception in this respect as well. The sale of the more than
three hundred enterprises involved was completed by 1993 (although
the sale often occurred by selling leasing rights rather than assets or
shares).

The degree of centralization of decisionmaking was limited, too.
Because it was unable to control all deals, the SPA approved—without
requiring many revisions—most proposals concerning small assets,
which constituted the majority of its cases.

Hungary was not unique in these developments. After setting up ministries of ownership change, both Czechoslovakia and Poland also applied models of centralized privatization. Privatization involving smaller units—retail trade and restaurants—was started at an early stage everywhere and has been progressing with fair success (Table 10.4). Apart from this, however, Poland and Czechoslovakia did not launch comprehensive active programs but tried to sell firms one by one. Privatization through liquidation became a special type of conversion in Poland. Initiated by enterprises or branch ministries, liquidation had to be negotiated with and approved by the MOC. The majority of liquidations resulted in employee buyouts.[20]

In Poland, with the exception of liquidation, privatization by sale has been less extensive than in Hungary—in part because of resistance to foreign investors.[21] Other explanations include the existence of Poland's designed mass privatization program and Czechoslovakia's voucher privatization. Hungary, nevertheless, turned to a more decentralized model. □

THE SECOND ATTEMPT AT A MARKET MODEL: DECENTRALIZED PRIVATIZATION IN HUNGARY

A decentralized privatization model was introduced in Hungary in fall 1991. The poor results of centralized models and the rivalry between different government institutions—especially involving the Ministry of Finance, which accused the SPA of inefficiency and power-mongering—drove this change.

The new model was not used in isolation but was applied simultaneously with other, existing techniques. The so-called self-privatization program initially involved smaller enterprises, but it was extended to larger ones in the second round, which was launched in spring 1992. Self-privatization means most of the seller's rights were assigned to consulting firms selected and deemed to be reliable by the SPA. These firms became key actors in the process, and the goal was to achieve the quickest possible sale for the highest possible price.[22] Thus, as had been the case with centralized sell-offs, acquiring revenue was the main goal of self-privatization. In the transformation phase, however, consultants received assignments from the firms in question; therefore, they had to consider the requirements set by management. Because of this and the relatively small size of the enterprises involved, in most cases sales occurred without splitting up or restructuring the entities involved.

Although there was some international participation, most buyers were Hungarians—including those involved in the many employee buyouts. In the latter cases, shares were divided among a large number of small investors. Nevertheless, the controlling interest was usually concentrated in a few hands, so in one sense these cases can be classified as

TABLE 10.4 Privatization in Hungary, Poland, and Czechoslovakia c. 1992

	Hungary[a]	Poland[b]	Czechoslovakia[c]
Restitution and compensation claims			
Total claims filed	1,500,000.00	> 100,000.00	50,000.00
Total claims settled	400,000.00		10,000.00
Small privatization			
Number designed	10,000.00	no data	43,013.00
Number privatized	7,637.00		31,021.00
Large privatization			
Number of enterprises transformed into companies[d]	602.00	2,100.00[e]	1,492.00[f]
Assets involved (billion Hungarian forints [HUF], Czechoslovakian korunas [kcs])	1,364.00		238.00[f]
Companies founded with part of enterprise assets	670.00		
Assets involved (billion HUF)	81.40		
Number of firms privatized[g]	130.00	385.00	120.00[f]
Assets involved (billion HUF, kcs)	142.90		133.30[f]

[a]By the end of 1992.
[b]By mid-1992.
[c]By the end of 1991.
[d]Under supervision of the State Property Agency and the Ministry of Ownership Change.
[e]Some preparation.
[f]Voucher privatization, first and second round.
[g]Under supervision of the State Property Agency and the Ministry of Ownership Change. Incomplete data (privatization means a transfer to private owners of more than 50 percent of the shares).

Sources: Adapted from Péter Mihályi, Progress in Privatization, 1990–1992 (Geneva: United Nations Economic Commission for Europe, 1993); Arnold Ludányi, Privatizáció Lengyelországban (Privatization in Poland) (Budapest: Financial Research, Ltd., 1993); Michael Mejstrik and James Burger, Vouchers, Buyouts, Auctions: The Battle for Privatization in Czechoslovakia (Prague: Centre for Economic Research and Graduate Education, Charles University, 1993).

"management buyouts."[23] The participation of domestic investors in privatization received growing financial support. A preferential credit program called the "existence loan" was introduced in early 1992, and its terms have been improved repeatedly. State-run loan-guarantee institutions were established in early 1993.

Both centralized and decentralized privatization can be regarded as market methods since they are characterized by competitive sales in which price plays an important role in negotiations. Although in both cases sale is based on competitive bidding by means of auction, selection of bids is determined not only by price but also by criteria that are introduced incrementally, including the commitment of additional investments or promises of employee retention. Often, these prerequisites are not advertised before tendering shares. The SPA is obliged to enter into a contract with the bidder who makes the best bid. The agency is free, however, to evaluate bids for potential trade-offs in regard to these sometimes conflicting criteria.

The market characteristics of self-privatization have been limited by the growing financial and administrative dependence of consulting firms on the SPA. Consultants have increasingly had to carefully consider the explicit and the inferred wishes of the SPA, which controlled the awarding of contracts.[24] The second important nonmarket feature was the introduction, in the second round of the program, of a sales price minimum equivalent to at least 80 percent of the calculated value of the assets. Since only the SPA could issue the special permit required to sell enterprises below the 80 percent limit, the agency had the power to either block privatization or offer the company a chance for survival and give the consultants their fees. These decisions obviously belong to the category of administrative redistribution of incomes and positions. □

MODELS OF REDISTRIBUTION

At the beginning of the 1990s, many Western experts regarded Hungary as a country in which privatization strategies were dominated by external sales and truly market-conforming methods, but redistribution also appeared—not only mixed with mainly market techniques but also as a separate model.[25] The first steps in this direction were enacted in 1990–1991 and involved allocating assets free of charge—in part to institutions (such as churches, local governments, and social security funds) and in part to persons once deprived of their property.[26] The preconditions for the extension of redistribution were established by privatization laws passed in summer 1992, which dictated that goods must be collected and the rights of disposition centralized prior to any kind of distribution.

One of the most important new features of the so-called privatization laws was the creation of Hungary's State Holding Company (SHC), whose purpose was to manage state-owned firms that were not marked for full or partial privatization in the short run. One-hundred and sixty-three organizations with about 1,500 billion forints (HUF) in assets were assigned to the SHC.[27] By means of compulsory corporatization, all other state-owned firms were placed under the SPA's direct control. This second important feature of the new laws meant the termination of enterprise councils and the reclaiming of a legal proprietary position by government institutions. If corporatization is not accompanied by immediate privatization, the majority shareholder of the firms is the SPA.[28] Thus, following the decentralization of decisionmaking, centralization of all ownership rights was completed by the end of 1993.

This kind of renationalization meant the rate and method of privatization were entirely at the discretion of the SPA (or the SHC). The objectives of privatization changed accordingly. The establishment of the SHC emphasized asset management and the restructuring of state-owned firms. Thus, a considerable part of the economy came to be controlled by a bureaucratic organization that was able to influence indirectly the distribution of income throughout the economy by setting the prices and allocating supply orders. Additionally, this enabled an allocation of profits and assets among the different companies of the SHC, which also gave the holding the ability to redistribute property.

A new privatization strategy was adopted by the Hungarian government at the end of 1992, aimed at creating a strong, proprietary middle class. In addition to preferential loans and privatization leasing, the new instruments—designed to increase demand for state assets—included free credit vouchers distributed without any personal investment or collateral. Although the program only began in spring 1994 with a moderate package of 5 to 10 billion HUF, it greatly resembled the mass privatization proposals in Poland and Czechoslovakia.

Similar redistribution features had occurred earlier in Poland and Czechoslovakia. Restitution and compensation were also present, although in somewhat different forms.[29] Another general feature was the attempt by the state to reclaim an ownership role. As in Hungary, the basic method was corporatization of state enterprises. In Czechoslovakia the centralization of ownership rights, like that of decisions on privatization, meant changes occurred mainly at the government level. The proprietary role of branch ministries was taken over by the Funds of National Property, one fund for each republic and one for the federation. The funds act as shareholders, like their Hungarian counterparts, until the privatization of a firm is completed.[30]

In the Polish case, in contrast to Czechoslovakia but similar to Hungary, corporatization meant renationalization and the elimination of workers' councils. The MOC became the new shareholder. Not surprisingly, enterprises and workers' councils strongly resisted the plan. Since these groups reserved the right of veto (unlike the case in Hungary), compulsory corporatization has not been enacted, so the process in Poland is moving slowly.[31]

This is true not only for the transformation of state enterprises into companies but for the entire privatization process. Because of political compromises, the Polish privatization law—which passed as early as 1990—listed all possible methods of sale and final ownership structures but failed to set clear priorities.[32] The Polish government, however, worked out a comprehensive mass privatization program intended to privatize, at least partially, several hundred large commercialized enterprises through free distribution of vouchers among citizens. Although more than 180 firms were selected for the first wave of mass privatization prior to mid-1992, the program was rejected by Parliament in early 1993.[33] The obvious reasons were the political weakness of the government and the strength of the proponents of internal employee buyouts, which was rooted in the aspirations of the Solidarity Union and workers' councils. Yet according to the draft bill, the owners had to be outsiders, namely, closed-end investment funds. Vouchers could have been used for purchasing the shares of these intermediaries, but they could not be used to buy the shares of the firms directly.

The Czechoslovakian voucher program was more successful in terms of enacting mass privatization. According to the original method of computerized public offering, individuals bid with voucher points for shares of 1,492 firms with a total book value of 568 billion crowns.[34] The voucher points are not transferable, and bids must to be repeated until a satisfactory level of supply-demand equilibrium is achieved. Bidding thus solved the crucial problem of asset valuation and complemented redistribution with market-type mechanisms. Citizens were supposed to acquire directly the shares of the firms involved in the program. Because of the low level of interest at the outset, the government encouraged the establishment of investment funds. More than four hundred intermediaries were founded, most of the largest ones by state-owned banks. Intermediaries control two-thirds of all investment points, and the top ten control 40 percent of the points.[35]

The progress in mass privatization in Czechoslovakia is partially the result of the strength of the government and the weak opposition from firms. At the early stage of privatization policy formulation, open debates occurred between "gradualists" and "radicals." The latter group has controlled policy issues since 1990 and has pushed for voucher privatization with the goal of rapid transformation. At the outset, management resisted change, mainly by refusing to deliver information to the state administration. Such attempts soon became illegal and were eliminated in practice.[36]

Management resistance was further weakened by inherited economic mechanisms. Because of the lack of substantial reforms, the autonomy of firms and of the private sector in general has been relatively weak in Czechoslovakia. Thus, strong opposition to the government proposal has not arisen.[37] In addition, voucher privatization has promised an ownership position (although not a very stable one) to wide segments of the population.

Nevertheless, we must not forget that contrary to the main goal of voucher privatization—speeding up the transformation—in reality the process is moving slowly. By 1992 only the first wave had been launched, changing the ownership structure of just over one hundred firms (Table 10.4).[38] No evidence is yet available on the performance of these new companies. Moreover, in Czechoslovakia voucher privatization is only one part of a larger privatization process.[39] After the establishment of the two independent states, both new governments seemed to revise privatization policies by turning to standard methods of ownership change.[40] □

SIMILARITIES AND DIFFERENCES

At the beginning of the 1990s, several experts classified the Czechoslovakian, Hungarian, and Polish privatizations in terms of preferences concerning targeted actors, resources required, or valuation of assets. As developments have unfolded, however, experts are finding more similarities than had been anticipated, and initial strategies on which the typologies were based have proved to be fairly unstable.

Similarities include the *institutional system*. In all three countries, central governmental organizations were set up to handle privatization and manage state assets. Centralization of decisionmaking was followed by the attempt to recentralize all ownership rights. The intention of the state to reclaim its proprietary position has also been a general characteristic. Renationalization has appeared in the form of corporatization, eliminating the formal influence of branch ministries and bodies charged with enterprise self-governance. The institutional system reflects the desire of all of the governments to design the privatization process and to reestablish the traditional bureaucratic practices and decisionmaking mechanisms in the new organizations.

Other models exist in all three countries, such as restitution or compensation for certain groups of individuals and the free assignment of state assets to institutional owners (such as local governments, social security funds, and churches). Small privatization of the retail trade and certain service sectors was started early and progressed relatively quickly everywhere. These similarities indicate that the methods for privatization in all three countries are *mixed;* there is no homogeneous procedure for changing ownership structure.

The dynamic aspect of this statement is less valid for Czechoslovkia, however, where the voucher program—although not an exclusive technique—was the primary and most stable model for privatization of large firms. Government design was the most successful here, at least during the implementation stage (the results remain to be seen). I have argued that this is at least partially the result of the lack of earlier reforms. In contrast, in Hungary and Poland—the two reform-socialist countries—politically influential groups were more divided, and they urged the use of different priorities in changing the ownership structure.

From the beginning, Poland designed privatization as a mixed process that opened the way for a variety of techniques and potential proprietary groups. Government attempts to recentralize decisions and reclaim ownership rights have faced the strongest opposition in that country. Workers' organizations and enterprise managers preserved formal rights of agreement and informal influence on commercialization and privatization; consequently, the MOC had limited powers. Poland also never established a central institution for state-asset management. Whereas the opposition slowed down transformation, government priorities shifted from preferring internal (employee) ownership (enacted in the privatization law of 1990) to direct sale and, later, to redistributive institutional privatization through a voucher program. These programmatic shifts nevertheless failed to have a significant impact on actual processes.

Hungary seems to fall between the two extremes regarding the implementation of designed privatization and the stability of the processes. The Hungarian government was more successful in recentralization and renationalization than its Polish counterpart, at least from the formal-legal point of view. The true controlling power of the State Property Agency in privatization deals, however, has remained rather limited, and its role as asset manager for temporary state-owned firms seems to be even weaker. Lacking at the outset a comprehensive law on privatization, the government pledged itself to sales on a competitive basis. Yet parallel to centralization of all proprietary rights, even Hungary turned in the direction of (semi-) free distribution methods. The mixed and unstable framework for privatization, unlike the Polish case, did not paralyze the transformation but made it more flexible. The social structure and "business" culture in Hungary are traditionally bargain oriented. The actors in the privatization process have the social experience to expect that laws can be evaded and rules negotiated. This situation did not change after the political transformation. All players can try to enforce their interests with a good chance of success, whatever the official rules of the game. In contrast, Poland has a tradition of open and sharp social confrontations, which has hindered it from following the Hungarian path of hidden compromises and negotiations and which has thus stalled the Polish transformation in several respects. □

NOTES

1. Czechoslovakia and Poland were chosen as comparisons because of their relatively advanced stage of privatization. Because of reunification, the former East Germany has very specific preconditions, whereas in most post-Yugoslavian states transformation processes were blocked by the civil war. Other countries are characterized more by privatization *plans* than by actual changes.

2. Branko Milanovic, *Privatization in Post-Communist Societies* (Washington, D.C.: World Bank, 1990); David Stark, "Path Dependence and Privatization Strategies in East Central Europe," *East European Politics and Societies* 6, no. 1 (1992): 17–54.

3. Ellen Comisso, "Property Rights, Liberalism, and the Transition from Actually Existing Socialism," *East European Politics and Societies* 5, no. 1 (Winter 1991): 162–188; László Bruszt and David Stark, "Remaking the Political Field in Hungary: From the Politics of Confrontation to the Politics of Competition," *Journal of International Affairs* 45, no. 1 (1991): 17–54.

4. The approach reviewed here is close to the term *path dependency* used in Stark, "Path Dependence and Privatization Strategies in East Central Europe."

5. István Csillag, "A reprivatizáció" (The Reprivatization) in *Tulajdonreform* (Ownership Reform) (Budapest: Pénzügykutató Rt., 1988) pp. 129-134; György Matolcsy, ed., *Lábadozásunk évei* (Years of Recovery) (Budapest: Privatizációs Kutatóintézet, 1991).

6. *Progress in Privatization, 1990–1992* (New York: United Nations Economic Survey of Europe, 1993), pp. 191-216.

7. Formal and informal autonomy of firm management increased only after the 1989 Czechoslovakian revolution, leading to the dismantling of the central planning agency and the weakening of branch ministries. See Michael Mejstrik and James Burger, *Vouchers, Buyouts, Auctions: The Battle for Privatization in Czecho-Slovakia* (Prague: Centre for Economic Research and Graduate Education, Charles University, 1993).

8. The term *enterprise* is used for the traditional socialist organizational form of firms, whereas *company* refers to the new form, owned either by the state or by private investors.

9. This is discussed in detail in Erzsébet Szalai, *Gazdasági mechanizmus, reformtörekvések és nagyvállalati érdekek* (Economic Mechanisms, Reforms, and Interests of Large Enterprises) (Budapest: Közgazdasági és Jogi, 1989).

10. The anatomy of these organizational changes is summarized in Tamás Sárközy, *Egy gazdasági szervezeti reform sodrában* (In the Stream of an Economic Organizational Reform) (Budapest: Magvetô, 1986).

11. Bruszt and Stark, "Remaking the Political Field in Hungary"; András Nagy, *Åtmenet? Honnan—hová?* (Transition? From Where, and Where To?), Institute of Economic Sciences (Budapest: Közgazdaságtudománi Intézet, 1993).

12. Ales Capek and Alena Buchtikova, *Privatization in the Czech Republic: Privatization Strategies and Priorities* (Budapest: International Workshop on Privatization in Eastern Europe, 1993): 1687–1737.

13. János Kornai, *The Economics of Shortage* (Amsterdam: North Holland, 1980); János Kornai, "The Hungarian Reform Process: Visions, Hopes and Reality," *Journal of Economic Literature* 24, no. 4 (1986): 1687-1737.

14. These strategies were influenced by the recommendations of the International Monetary Fund and the World Bank.

15. It follows from the nature of spontaneous privatization that exact data for its scope are unavailable. The Privatization Research Institute estimates the number of firms involved to be approximately 250 with assets of 130 billion HUF. See György Matolcsy, ed. *Lábadozásunk évei* (Years of Recovery), Research Institute of Privatization (Budapest: Privatizációs Kutatóintézet, 1991), p. 226. For a summary review of the process, see, for example, Mária Móra, *Az állami vállalatok (ál)privatizációja* (Pseudo-Privatization of State Enterprises), Research Institute of Economy (Budapest: Gazdaságkutató Intézet, 1990); István János Tóth, "A spontán privatizáció mint kormányzati politika" (Spontaneous Privatization as Government Policy), *Külgazdaság* 9 (1991), pp. 67-78; and Éva Voszka, *Két ur szolgája: az önprivatizáció* (Servant of Two Masters: Self-Privatization) (Budapest: Pénzügykutató Rt, 1993).

16. The scope of "informal" or "hidden" privatization is sometimes estimated to be as large as that of official privatization. The methods that do not transgress the legal framework include inter alia transfer pricing in favor of small private companies, thus depleting state assets. These small companies from the management or internal enterprise groups can also lease firm assets at favorable conditions or simply extract useful experience and business contacts—that is, the market—from their former employers.

17. Károly Polányi, *Az archaikus társadalom és a gazdasági szemlélet* (The Archaic Society and Economic Philosophy) (Budapest: Gondolat, 1976).

18. John Earle, Roman Frydman, and Andrzej Rapaczynski, *The Privatization Process in Central Europe* (Prague: Central European University Press, 1993); Arnold Ludányi, *Magyaroszág és a kelet-európai átalakulás 1992-ben* (Hungary and the Transformation in Eastern Europe) (Budapest: Pénzügykutató Rt, 1993).

19. Small privatization was an exception in several respects. Firms operating mainly in retail trade were separated, with shops being sold one by one and international buyers formally disqualified.

20. Privatization through liquidation is also possible in Hungary. In that country, however, it cannot be regarded as centralized, because the SPA has no decisionmaking rights in such cases. A liquidation process that may result in privatization is managed by specialized private or state-owned consulting firms. See Ludányi, *Magyaroszág és a kelet-európai átalakulás 1992-ben*.

21. According to the 1990 law on privatization, only 10 percent of the firm's shares can be sold to foreigners without special government permission.

22. Consultants are chosen from a list provided by the SPA, and the costs of commercialization are paid by the firm. Any payment by the SPA to the consultants, however, is conditional on the full or partial privatization of the firms. Fees include a rate adjusted to sales price plus a bonus for early completion.

23. For an overview of self-privatization, see Éva Voszka, "Spontaneous Privatization: Preconditions and Real Issues," in John Earl, Roman Frydman, and Andrzej Rapaczynski, eds., *Privatization in the Transition to a Market Economy* (New York: St. Martin's Press, 1993). Similar results with respect to employee buyouts have been estimated by Dorottya Boda, *Vezetôi és dolgozói tulajdon* (Management and Employee Ownership) (Budapest: Munkaügyi Kutatóintézet, 1992).

24. The SPA organized monthly meetings to provide instructions for experts.

25. Mihályi, *Progress in Privatization, 1990–1992*; see also Milanovic, *Privatization in Post-Communist Societies*.

26. Compensation involved nearly one million people and about 80 billion HUF. By the end of 1992, state-owned shares were bought for about one billion HUF worth of compensation notes issued by the beneficiaries or secondary buyers of the notes. Social Security will receive state assets in the amount of 300 billion HUF; however, the transfer has not yet started. No reliable data exist on growing ownership by churches and local governments.

27. Another sixty-two firms that remained in long-term state ownership were left under the control of ministries, mainly those of agriculture and transport.

28. In 1992, the SPA made 40 percent more decisions covering twice as many assets than it had made the previous year. More than half of these decisions resulted in corporatization and represented a share of nearly 97 percent of the assets concerned. The average percentage of shares held by the SPA is as high as 75 percent.

29. For more details, see Mihályi, *Progress in Privatization, 1990–1992*, and John Earle, *Voucher Privatization in Eastern Europe* (Prague: Central European University, 1992).

30. For more details, see Earle, *Voucher Privatization in Eastern Europe*.

31. Ludányi, *Magyaroszág és a kelet-európai átalakulás 1992-ben*.

32. Barbara Blaszczyk and Marek Dabrowski, *The Privatization Process in Poland* (Budapest: International Workshop on Privatization in Eastern Europe, 1993).

33. As a compromise among different political forces, the proposal was passed by the Polish Parliament in mid–1993. Earle, *Voucher Privatization in Eastern Europe*.

34. Ibid.

35. Mejstrik and Burger, *Vouchers, Buyouts, Auctions*.

36. Ibid.

37. This situation does not mean, however, that firm management has no influence on the process. Managers can exercise a certain degree of control by elaborating privatization proposals. If their plans are chosen by the ministries over the competing proposals, the process may result in management buyouts or buy-ins. Ibid.; Brigita Schmöglerová, *Privatization in Transition: Some Lessons from the Slovak Republic* (Budapest: International Workshop on Privatization in Eastern Europe, 1993).

38. During the first wave, 1,492 firms were involved, representing assets of 586.6 billion korunas. Most of the investment went through the newly established investment funds, set up mainly by commercial banks.

39. Experts emphasize that this fact is "little understood in the West" (Earle, *Voucher Privatization in Eastern Europe*). The share of vouchers in approved privatization projects is only 38 percent for business units and 49 percent for assets (Mejstrik and Burger, *Vouchers, Buyouts, Auctions*). Moreover, the division of the country into two republics, and the progress in voucher privatization, may lead to some changes in privatization policies. The Czech Ministry of Privatization, for instance, intends to place more emphasis on "standard privatization methods—that is, selling.

40. Mejstrik and Burger, *Vouchers, Buyouts, Auctions*; Schmöglerová, *Privatization in Transition*.

CHAPTER ELEVEN

———————— ■ ————————

Obstacles to Economic Reform in Brazil

Juarez Brandão Lopes

Processes of economic liberalization are shaped not only by the actions of elites and other groups interested in restructuring the economy but also by the incentives and constraints those groups face. Central to an understanding of economic reform is the study of the obstacles that can block or distort liberalization, determine the paths it follows, or affect its timing. These obstacles may arise from agency (the mobilization of groups negatively affected by liberalization), institutions (which may produce structures that inhibit reform or make it extremely difficult), or culture (the influence of values and beliefs opposed to, or otherwise inconsistent with, liberalization).

The case of Brazil is especially important to the analysis of these issues. Brazil's experience with statized and highly protected industrialization was more successful than Argentina's or Chile's, and this situation generated—over the decades in which the model was implemented—a web of powerful interests, institutions, and beliefs that inhibited conversion. This is the reason large-scale economic liberalization began later in Brazil than in Argentina or Chile. In this chapter I discuss many of these obstacles and the ways in which they affected economic policy during the past three decades. □

BRAZIL'S SEMIDEVELOPMENTAL STATE

Brazil has had great difficulty achieving economic reform and stabilization even with fifty years of successful industrialization under state guidance. Between 1929 and 1987, the annual average compound growth rate

195

was 5.4 percent; between 1950 and 1980 alone, the average rate reached 6.8 percent.[1] By the late 1970s, Brazil was one of the success stories of import-substitution industrialization, achieved under the supervision of what could perhaps be called a semidevelopmental state.[2] To this record, however, one must add Brazil's dismal social performance: one of the worst income and regional inequalities in the world and an enormous number of people living in poverty. This social situation actually worsened in the 1960s, and in spite of high growth in the 1970s, it did not improve. By 1980 the per capita income of Brazil's richest state was about 8.6 times that of the poorest.[3] The historical record shows a continuous deterioration of income distribution during the high-growth period, ameliorated only somewhat in the second half of the 1970s when the Gini Index declined from 0.589 (in 1976) to 0.562 (in 1981).[4]

What political and institutional characteristics of the Brazilian situation can help us understand the recent failures? I treat this question by examining the roots of the current situation as they developed during the military regime when it undertook to legitimize itself through a new round of investments (the Second Development Plan [II PND]). At the same time, the regime went on with its ambiguous "political opening" and in this context made the first failed attempt to introduce the needed economic reforms. I continue with an analysis of the political and institutional obstacles to the stabilization and reform efforts of the second half of the 1980s and the early 1990s (with special attention to the Cruzado Plan and the Collor Plans), treating in turn the fragmented party system, the relations between the presidency and Congress, the relationship between federalism and the fragility of coalitions, the relations between the executive and the bureaucracy and state enterprises (all penetrated by heterogeneous private interests), and the long-term uncertainty up to the present regarding the basic institutional rules. A comparison is made with Argentina, the other important case of economic reform occurring simultaneously with democratization. I focus on the Argentine plans under Alfonsín and Menem to further clarify the analysis of the Brazilian case. In the end, I comment briefly on the ongoing efforts at stabilization and reform being undertaken in Brazil with the Real Plan.

The military regime in Brazil (1964–1985) preserved Congress, the parties, and elections (maintained, during the harshest years in the early 1970s, as an almost completely empty facade). The relatively free 1974 senatorial elections resulted in a serious defeat for the military government and showed that the previous "economic miracle" had not legitimized the regime. President Ernesto Geisel, however, was committed to gradual and guided "liberalization." During his administration (1974–1979), the II PND implemented an impressive wave of import substitution in intermediate and capital goods. That ambitious program resulted in an enormous expansion of the foreign debt and growth of inflation. Once the state's capacity to finance the plan from its savings was exhausted, external borrowing and the so-called inflation tax became the only possible sources for investment. The II PND was formulated, financed, and implemented within the state—with foreign monies—using state and mixed enterprises. This was a reiteration of the traditional methods of the semidevelopmental state. Political analysts feel Geisel's decision to embark on an ambitious new phase of industrialization—to "complete" the industrialization of the country—was closely linked to his strategy of political liberalization, with both tactics aimed at the legitimation of the regime.[5]

The implementation of the II PND had dire economic consequences and was not without political costs. Arriving at the same time as the second oil shock and the explosion of international interest rates, the plan resulted in the enduring fiscal crisis of the state. Initially, it disguised the crisis and thus postponed the implementation of the steps required for adjustment. Geisel's strategy of guided political liberalization relied on continuous manipulation of the party and the electoral system. The 1977 political package was aimed at avoiding a repetition of the 1974 defeat, but it also meant that the government shifted alliances. Power moved from the highly industrialized southeast section of Brazil to new, regionally dispersed industrial centers that were located in the center-north and the northeast, where the II PND located the bulk of its investments. As I will show, these economic and political changes were at the root of some of the political and institutional obstacles to economic reform during the 1980s (which have continued into the 1990s). This "flight forward from the [world] crisis," as the decision to implement the II PND has been called, meant the postponement of adjustment and put Brazil among those cases in which adjustment takes place not before but simultaneously with democratization—a situation that has significant effects for adjustment.[6]

Throughout the 1980s, Brazil stagnated and had enormously high inflation rates, averaging 199 percent per year during the period from 1980 to 1988.[7] By the end of the 1980s, Brazil was nearly bankrupt, with virtually no capacity for investment and with huge foreign and internal debts. To service its debt and finance its expenditures, the state was obliged to pay extremely high rates of interest. At the root of this situation was Brazil's failure to reform its economy. ☐

STABILIZATION AND REFORM PROGRAMS

The stabilization programs during the final period of the military regime (1979–1983) could not prevent the growth of inflation and, combined with the debt crisis in 1982, helped to throw the country into one of the worst recessions in its history. Although the failure of stabilization attempts during the military regime is not my main focus, it is important to recall the social and political conditions that led to the return of civilian rule, as this is undoubtedly significant for the modality of economic adjustment that is my concern: the situation that exists when adjustment and democratization take place simultaneously.

The return to civilian rule was preceded by the revocation of Institutional Act 5 (1978), on which the most dictatorial features of the regime were based, and by the passage of the Act of Amnesty (1979), which led to the return of most of Brazil's exiled politicians. When strong popular demand for direct elections failed to make Congress reform the Brazilian constitution, the opposition accepted the entire legal and institutional framework of the military regime, including indirect elections. The 1984 election was won by the opposition when a sizable segment of the political forces supporting the regime defected to join the opposition.

Brazil was only beginning to come out of its deep recession.[8] João Figueiredo, the last general of the military regime and the first president to face the economic crisis, also confronted a strong union movement that had surfaced in 1979 and that was able to defy the existing labor legislation and mount strikes, which spread outward from the industrial core of the country.[9] Thus, the democratization process began not only with the military having achieved no significant economic adjustment but also with high levels of inflation and social discontent.

Following the return of civilian rule in 1985, Brazil implemented several stabilization and reform plans, ranging in diversity from the heterodox 1986 Cruzado Plan (which was inspired, as was the Austral Plan in Argentina, by theories of inertial inflation) to the strictly orthodox monetarist 1988 Summer Plan.[10] A new constitution was passed on October 5, 1988, and Fernando Collor de Mello was elected in the 1989 direct presidential elections. The day after his inauguration in March 1990, he decreed a new economic package—the Collor Plan I. This plan was followed by three others during his administration; in all, there have been nine stabilization plans since the 1985 redemocratization.[11]

The plans were inspired by different philosophies and proposed methods to integrate the Brazilian economy into the international economy. All were predominantly stabilization plans, although they sometimes included features with other objectives. All of the plans failed. In each case, after a period of low inflation (the duration of which shrank in every new round), inflation would rapidly peak again until Brazil reached quasi-hyperinflationary levels (see Figure 11.1).[12]

The stabilization plans were often accompanied by reforms, such as fiscal adjustment, liberalization, and privatization; only in the case of the two Collor plans in 1990 did these reforms achieve any significant results or continuity.[13] To analyze political and institutional impediments to economic reform, I focus mainly on the 1986 Cruzado Plan and the Collor

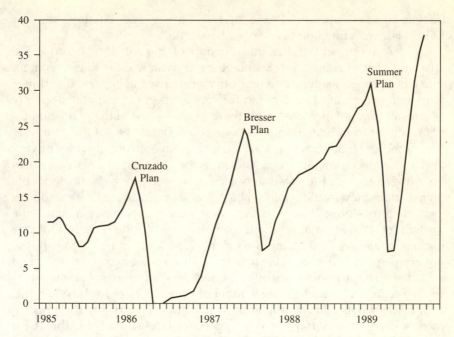

FIGURE 11.1 Brazil: Inflation Rates, 1985–1989[a] (percentage per month with a three-month moving average)

[a]As calculated by the general price index of the Brazilian research institute Fundação Getúlio Vargas.

Source: *Coyuntura Economica,* various issues.

plans of 1990. These plans demonstrate the effects of different institutional contexts before and after the 1988 constitution, and political analyses of them reveal the major obstacles to reform. □

The Cruzado Plan

This plan actually consisted of several versions, all of which were ill conceived, ineffective, and inappropriate to the problems at hand; additionally, serious institutional obstacles blocked their implementation. Of the economic reform packages created during the 1980s, however, the Cruzado Plan was the most ambitious and lasted the longest. The initial version—launched in February 1986—changed the monetary unit, dismantled the elaborate indexation system, froze prices, and raised the minimum wage by 15 percent. After mandating an 8 percent across-the-board increase, it left salaries and wages to be settled through union-management negotiation.[14] Its popularity was instantaneous, enormous, and highly visible. Inflation dropped to zero, business picked up, and President José Sarney and Finance Minister Dilson Funaro gained immense popular support.

A few months after the introduction of the initial version of the Cruzado Plan in February 1986, however, it became clear to government officials, business leaders, and economic and financial experts that things were not going well. The demand for consumer goods expanded greatly as a result of wage increases (both those given as part of the plan and others resulting from bargaining). Growing uncertainty about the continuation of the Cruzado Plan in mid-1986 resulted in both anticipatory buying and the expectation of salary increases by employers. With business booming, there was little resistance from that sector, since businesspeople were certain they would soon be able to raise prices as well. Goods disappeared from stores; hidden overpricing was prevalent; and, later, the growth of the internal market, combined with the stability of the exchange rate, resulted in rapid erosion of the trade balance. In July, the government introduced measures to reduce demand (the so-called *cruzadinho*), but they were insufficient and delayed more substantive corrective action until after the November elections (Cruzado II). When this action was finally taken, following a landslide victory for the government's party, it was too late.[15] The plan collapsed, and the threat for hyperinflation returned. The rapidly diminishing external reserves, reaching U.S.$3.9 billion in February 1987, led to the declaration of a unilateral moratorium on the payment of interest on the foreign debt.

The failure of the Cruzado Plan, following the euphoria it had raised, combined with the widespread blame placed on President Sarney and the politicians of the government's Brazilian Democratic Movement Party (PMDB), had vast repercussions. Ultimately, the failure disallowed the possible success of any new plan. The viability of subsequent plans was threatened by (1) a popular discrediting of economic packages in general, particularly price freezes unilaterally decreed by the government without the participation of civil society; and, consequently, (2) the 1988 constitution's substitution of "provisional measures" (for executive decrees), which significantly restricted the discretion of the executive to implement economic plans without prior approval by Congress.[16] □

The Collor Plans

The adoption of reform plans arising from events during the period between the 1989 presidential elections and the inauguration in 1990 faced serious sociopolitical obstacles. The Sarney government, and politicians in general, were held in very low esteem on the eve of the elections, and the economic situation had worsened considerably. This helps to explain why the two candidates in the second round of the presidential election, which occurred in November 1989, were the leftist candidate of the Workers' Party (PT)—Luis Ignacio (Lula) da Silva, a former metallurgical worker—and a political outsider—Fernando Collor de Mello, a virtual unknown at the time of his nomination. The latter campaigned against professional politicians and bureaucratic privilege and was elected not only because of his campaign but also because of widespread fear of the Left. One should note that a minority government was inevitable: Given the two contending electoral coalitions whichever side won would hold only 5 to 8 percent of the congressional seats.[17]

From election day until Collor took office in March 1990, the economic situation continued to deteriorate. A hyperinflationary spell began in February. There was widespread fear that Collor would institute austerity measures immediately upon taking office, which could include confiscation of financial assets. A frenzied change of position regarding financial assets followed among investors and savers, with a run first on the dollar and gold and then on savings accounts, in the belief that these would not be touched because of their broad use by the poorer segments of the population.

On the day he took office, Collor initiated Collor Plan I, which through a series of provisional measures, combined heterodox and orthodox features—that is, a drastic blockage of financial assets (70 percent of the total, including savings and current accounts), a rapid freeze of wages and prices, and firm fiscal adjustment.[18] In light of the severity of the measures, opposition to and criticism of the plan were at first rather mild and were restricted to deputies on the Left (the PT and the Democratic Labor Party). Inflation fell rapidly to almost zero.

In addition to the plan, decisions were also taken to liberalize trade, deregulate the economy, and speed up the privatization process. During the Collor administration, trade liberalization progressed gradually but deeply. It differentially affected consumer goods, where protection was dismantled more rapidly and widely than in the case of capital and intermediate goods. Industrial deregulation and policies to increase competition were more limited in scope. Antimonopolistic measures, which often took the form of price control mechanisms, were also a part of stabilization efforts. Privatization started in a limited way, with twenty-two enterprises slated for transformation in 1992.[19]

Interests affected by the privatization program expressed their opposition more openly than had been the case with trade liberalization. Opposition manifested itself in Congress and in the regions where enterprises likely to be privatized were located, and it involved battles in the judiciary as well. The participation of state-enterprise employee pension funds and domestic private firms in the privatization auctions softened opposition attitudes, including those of nationalist segments of the military. Two points should be emphasized: First, groups—rooted in civil society—that actively proposed liberalization and privatization failed to appear during that period; second, elites may have accepted the programs more readily because they were designed and implemented by the same technocratic bodies that had led the planning of previous developmental industrialization projects.

It is surprising that the drastic Collor Plan could be implemented at all and that it met with wide acceptance if not outright approval. Although some of the provisional measures had difficulties passing, the major ones were approved by Congress within the required thirty days. After the short episode of hyperinflation in February 1990, the boldness of the measures taken by the government was probably related to the widespread belief that the economic situation was extremely serious and to the legitimacy conferred upon Collor because of his success in the two rounds of the presidential election. It may also have been related to Collor's fame as a political maverick who was free from connections to the major political parties.

Similar factors also explain the undoing of the plan. As inflation began to rise again and the president's popularity dropped, increasing conflicts appeared between the president and Congress. Executive actions also experienced setbacks as the result of decisions by the judiciary. Still, almost up to the final months of 1990, local business and international confidence remained high.

By December 1990, inflation was back to 20 percent per month, and in January 1991—again with no political negotiation—a new freeze was adopted. It also failed. In May, Finance Minister Zélia Cardoso de Mello resigned under considerable internal and external pressure. In mid–1991, President Collor began political negotiations, and by 1992 he had reorganized his cabinet along more politically acceptable lines. However, in mid–1992 grave accusations of widespread corruption were leveled of at high levels of the government, including the presidency. Collor was suspended from office in September and impeached in December. Surprisingly, although inflation rose even more, the government did not lose control of the economic situation, and social and political chaos was avoided during the unprecedented process of impeachment. Vice President Itamar Franco took office December 29, 1992.

The Collor years left a mixed inheritance. Brazil suffered a major recession in 1990, during which GNP dropped almost 7 percent, and two years of stagnation followed. The initiation of trade liberalization and privatization programs occurred alongside a disastrous administrative reform. The public internal debt was reduced by about 30 percent, but high levels of monthly inflation returned, which the widely respected Finance Minister Marcilio Marques Moreira managed to control.

Economists, politicians, and elites in general experienced some important shifts in attitude toward the end of the Collor administration. Additionally, more concrete changes took place in the organization of private enterprises. In both dimensions, Collor government initiatives appear to have acted as an important catalyst. A consensus began to form around attitudes considerably different from those prevailing during the populist and developmental phases of Brazilian industrialization. The Brazilian state began to be regarded as having grown too much and as having been too interventionist, and industry came to be seen as inefficient and overprotected from foreign competition. An agreement gradually coalesced that recognized the need to reform the state, partially privatize state enterprises, liberalize trade, and deregulate.[20]

Moreover, the Collor administration's initiation of programs of trade liberalization and privatization, combined with the opportunity presented by the long recession, stimulated private enterprise—especially the multinationals—to prepare to face fiercer competition at home from imports and to venture abroad to compete in external markets that were opening up. By the mid–1990s, the restructuring of private firms was proceeding apace. Efforts at greater competitiveness are occurring through productive reorganization toward models of "lean" production (with much subcontracting and use of franchising) rather than through great technological investments (although this is also taking place). Also significant are the frequent declarations by industrialists, managers, and business associations indicating that, in their specific case, economic recovery will not necessarily mean that rehiring will occur.[21] □

POLITICAL AND INSTITUTIONAL FACTORS INFLUENCING ECONOMIC REFORM

The Cruzado and Collor stabilization plans were fairly different in conception, and they occurred at different political conjunctures. The euphoria of the Cruzado Plan was never repeated, and frustration in the interim with three other failed plans influenced Collor's plan and its implementation. Importantly, the plans are separated by the 1988 constitution. In spite of these differences, some political and institutional factors have remained the same during this period and help to explain the difficulties encountered with Brazil's stabilization efforts.

The Presidency, Congress, and the Party System

Brazil is noted for its strong presidency, which during democratization has been coupled with weak presidents. Before redemocratization, Figueiredo was weakened by a strong popular movement for direct elections; this may help to explain the insufficiencies of the Delfim Neto stabilization plans in 1979, 1981, and 1983. Sarney was an incumbent vice president who lacked the legitimacy of the popular vote and who joined the democratic coalition at the eleventh hour, splitting from the party of the military regime. He achieved the presidency because the elected president died prior to inauguration. During the first two years of Sarney's administration—including the year of the Cruzado Plan—he governed with a cabinet chosen by the deceased president and with the PMDB, which had opposed the military regime and to which he belonged only formally.

Collor's electoral coalition won a very small percentage of the vote, and during his first months in office Collor relied entirely on an ephemeral legitimacy derived from the significant majority he had received during the two rounds of the presidential election. As is often the case with charismatic leaders, when Collor's plans began to fail his popularity waned and his vulnerability surfaced.[22]

Collor was an antiparty politician who was elected as a result of specificities of the Brazilian political system—that is, the amorphous nature of its parties and the fragmentation of its party system.[23] Amorphous parties have deep roots in the country's political history, and during democratization their shapelessness has been exacerbated. But Collor's election was also the result of the enormous and rather unpredictable influence a candidate's carefully built media image can have on elections in a majority system, irrespective of parties. Collor won the first round of the election on the basis of his television campaigning against professional politicians and the privileged bureaucratic elite, who were becoming increasingly demoralized.[24] The electoral law distributes free television and radio time to the candidates according to the number of seats the parties supporting them hold in Congress. Even with much less time than the major parties, Collor won the first round of the election on the basis of the antipolitician image he built through the media.

Let us return to the issue of the strength of the Brazilian presidency as an institution. In 1990, being antiparty was problematic for Collor because the 1988 constitution had established a much stronger Congress, which shifted the traditional equilibrium with the still strong presidency. The presidency's formal prerogatives are ampler than those of the U.S. presidency, especially because of the existence of the partial veto and the executive's ability to initiate legislation.[25] Scott Mainwaring has argued that because of the amorphous nature of parties and the fragmentation of the party system, Brazilian presidents have difficulties in getting Congress to support their political agenda. They generally depend on fluid and weak coalitions that cross party lines, or they attempt to bypass Congress through appeals to popular support.[26]

At the root of the fragility of government coalitions is the fragmentation of the party system. Although the multiplicity of Brazilian parties is mostly the result now, as before the military regime, of traits of the electoral system and the heterogeneity of the socioeconomic structure, the manipulation of the electoral and party systems by the authoritarian regime in an attempt to continue gradual and controlled political liberal-ization had a long-term impact.[27] Party identities inherited from the democratic period (1946–1964) were destroyed, and politicians accepted an electoral law with very low entrance requirements for the formation of parties. Consequently, almost a dozen parties were formed, although almost none have distinguished themselves programmatically. They are also undisciplined: Secession by individuals or groups of state represen-tatives motivated by personal interests or regional issues is common and tolerated. Similarly, deputies and senators often change parties or remain in Congress with no party affiliation, which illustrates that individual, electoral interests are often placed before party affiliation. The resulting lack of cohesion is amply demonstrated by congressional votes on crucial issues.[28] Blocs—which cut across parties on the basis of religion, environ-mental issues, and so forth—are common, and these interests have prece-dence over party interests.

Brazil has almost always had minority presidents. Electoral coalitions are ad hoc arrangements that have little to do with the coalitions that sup-port the government. The latter are fragile and impermanent and are glued together by the president's patronage and clientelism. Frequent reforms of the cabinet, distribution of ministerial positions and of high-level offices, and the opportunistic creation of new ministries enable a president to solidify coalitions—often uselessly, in light of the frequency with which local and state politics overwhelm party cohesion.[29] Of course, the durability of the coalition depends on the popularity of the president. Sarney's popularity during the Cruzado Plan, derived as it was from the price freeze, was not a useful instrument since it could not gar-ner him support for the corrective and unpopular actions that were required to make the plan successful. In other words, from the point of view of stabilization, Sarney had support for doing the wrong thing—persisting with the price freeze with no correction.

Federalism, Regional Inequality, and Fragile Coalitions

One aspect of the fragility of coalitions is especially noteworthy: the importance within Congress of state-level politics. In Brazil, governors "coordinate" their states' representatives. *Bancadas estaduais*—groups in Congress that are organized by state without regard for party affiliation or participation in federal-level government coalitions—are often crucial in deciding congressional votes. The several *bancadas* hold a de facto veto power over proposed legislation that affects states' interests. It is easy to imagine the decisive importance of this situation for stabilization plans.

The dynamics of state-level politics is demonstrated in a variety of ways. For example, interests of different states can coincide, and their joint resistance may prove overpowering. The issue of the transfer of federal fiscal resources to states and municipalities, as required by the 1988 constitution, without a new apportioning of the functions and responsibilities among the three levels of government is a case in point. Some change in the present situation is under consideration by the finance ministry and is thought by many economists to be crucial to helping solve the fiscal crisis. Both the federal government and state-level governments—especially the richer ones—have considerable powers of patronage, which will influence the outcome.

States at different levels of development also represent different interests. The more developed states have a relatively lower level of representation in Congress.[30] Public support for economic reform is greater in the richer states, and pressures for reform of the system of representation—a highly conflictive issue—are increasing.

These characteristics of the political system were exacerbated by the democratization process. Especially since implementation of the 1988 constitution, which resulted in a much stronger Congress without the institutional means to guarantee congressional responsibility, the political cost of building the needed coalitions has increased.

The Executive and the Bureaucracy

The system of fragile party coalitions often results in deep fractures within the executive branch. Political interests based on individual and narrowly electoral considerations, coupled with the penetration of private interests in the upper levels of the bureaucracy, divide in half-hidden ways ministry from ministry, a ministry from its subordinated agencies, and "the palace" (the president and his or her close entourage in the executive mansion) from one or another ministry. A well-documented situation involved the divergences between core teams of the planning and the finance ministries during the design and implementation of the Cruzado Plan, which, of course, had prejudicial consequences for the success of the plan.[31]

When industrialization was a top political priority, parties and coalitions were permeated by a relatively consistent developmental ideology and could be counted on to carry out projects in spite of splintering and conflicts. Today a greater diversity of political interests exists, reflecting a much greater heterogeneity of the socioeconomic structure of the country.[32] Instead of a growth situation in which everyone gains even when inequality increases, the situation today is one of dividing losses arising from stabilization and adjustment. In the developmental period, efficiency was needed only in specific areas of the state bureaucracy to accomplish the development of Brazil's industrial capacity. Currently, the adjustment program demands much more consistent effort in all parts of the state apparatus, making it increasingly clear that the reform must encompass the entire state.[33] Little room remains for inefficiency and backwardness.

Since the 1930s, attempts at administrative reform of the bureaucratic apparatus of the Brazilian state have failed. Developmental programs were carried forward by the creation of new agencies, "pockets of efficiency," that were insulated from the common administrative body where patronage was unchecked. These, using the terminology of Peter Evans, could be called cases of localized "embedded autonomy" of given agencies of the state, with a given set of social bonds within the appropriate sections of the economy and society that create institutionalized channels for the continual negotiation of goals and policies.[34] With the demise of the developmental model and its ideology, ties between government agencies and private organizations have degenerated, assuming the simpler character of the penetration of private interests in the apparatus of the state and unrelated to general goals and policies. This process of "privatization" of the state is made easier by the amorphousness of the party system and the impermanent coalitions that are temporarily achieved through patronage and clientelism.[35]

State Enterprises and Privatization

The case of state enterprises illustrates the relationship between government agencies and private organizations and the process of privatization. Their autonomy of operation and ties to certain sectors of the economy functioned effectively during developmental industrialization; now— when the objectives are stabilization, privatization, deregulation, and trade liberalization—state enterprises have become barriers. With the onset of the fiscal crisis and the lack of investment funds, the efficiency and success of the past, along with privileges for their functionaries (vis-à-vis employees in the bureaucracy), gave way to vested interests and a narrower, corporative esprit de corps. In several respects, state enterprises turned into formidable hurdles for stabilization and privatization programs.

The autonomy of state enterprises permits them, and ties to governors or elected representatives empower them, to resist and frustrate the federal government's efforts to cut expenses. Ties to suppliers, importers, exporters, and all kinds of special interests make them unwilling collaborators with plans for privatization or with deregulation efforts that may hurt privileged and protected interests.

Uncertainty of Institutional Rules

Uncertainty about institutional norms has been and continues to be a powerful obstacle to economic reform. Planners have experienced continuing postponement of a solidification of the country's institutional context, and uncertainty still prevails about the ultimate shape of the institutions that will govern Brazilian social and economic life. Thus, institutional uncertainty has been an intrinsic ingredient of the drawn-out democratization process. It reflects the contradictions of the democratic transition under the aegis of the heterogeneous Democratic Alliance, which united the old opposition to the military regime with the politicians who had split from the party that supported the regime. Sarney's government inherited many of the institutions and the legislation of authoritarianism. The constituent Assembly prolonged the uncertainty, even with respect to the form of government—whether monarchy or republic, presidentialism or parliamentarism. The 1988 constitution specified a plebiscite in 1993 to decide the form of government; the result was a republic and presidentialism. The new constitution also specified a constitutional revision, beginning in October 1993, aimed at a broad reform of the fiscal and social security systems, along with other steps deemed necessary for economic adjustment.

The Constituent Assembly's design of the 1988 constitution reflected Brazil's fragmented party and political systems. The constitution is a long, detailed, and sometimes inconsistent document. Many of its provisions require the enactment of more specific legislation.[36] After several years, few of these laws have been approved by Congress. The constitutionality of laws and executive decrees based on articles of the constitution is continually challenged by the judiciary. Judicial decisions have frequently invalidated legislation deemed essential for economic plans, making more problematic the resolution of the state's fiscal crisis.

Social Consequences

Industrialization initially took place in an atmosphere of significant inequality in Brazil's distribution of income. By the end of the 1970s, this situation was slightly reversed. Then, in the 1980s economic stagnation, low growth, and the successive failures of stabilization plans reasserted the historical tendency toward income inequality, with the Gini Index reaching 0.635 in 1989. The social gains of the high economic growth in the 1970s, which led to a decrease of absolute poverty, were wiped out in the 1980s. By 1988, Brazil had returned to the 1970 level of poverty—almost 40 percent of its households were poor.[37]

Paradoxically, in the 1980s some progress occurred in social conditions that reflect state action, including sanitation, education, nutrition, and health conditions. Political liberalization and democratization had an effect, and popular demands for better conditions were met at least in part.[38] □

COMPARISON WITH ARGENTINA

Brazil and Argentina are two cases of reform efforts that occurred simultaneous with, rather than before, democratization. In Argentina, crucial policies and events occurred during the Radical Party government of Raúl Alfonsín (1983–1989)—the first president following redemocratization—and the Peronist Party government of Carlos Menem (1989 to the present).[39] In June 1985, Alfonsín launched the Austral Plan, which was the first attempt to combine heterodox policies (monetary reform and a price freeze) with heavily orthodox fiscal and monetarist policies. Government economists had come to believe that the economic crisis had originated in the foreign debt and in the state's fiscal crisis. The Argentine government made an enormous effort to reduce the budget deficit, and it reached agreements with the International Monetary Fund and the World Bank about the needed structural reforms.

Even though it took the first steps toward liberalization and privatization, the reform government was unable to control inertial inflation and "chronic dollarization." Most important, it was unable to convince Argentina's dominant classes about the explosiveness of the state's fiscal situation.[40] Thus, it was unable to tax the proprietary classes (its fiscal proposals were diluted by Congress in 1987) and could not avoid huge capital flight. By mid–1989 the government was drowning in hyperinflation, and—in the midst of the worst economic and social disaster Argentina had ever known—the country awaited the transfer of office to President-elect Carlos Menem (in June 1989).[41]

This exceptional social and political context worked to Menem's advantage. With "the persuasive force of an economy adrift, social chaos, and institutions at risk," his political choices widened enormously.[42] In a complete turnabout that went against all of the traditions of Peronism, Menem proposed radical policies of neoliberal structural reform. To convince economic actors of the authenticity of his conversion, he appointed a neoliberal minister of the economy who was identified with the internationalized bourgeoisie. He gave first priority to trade liberalization and privatization, thus aligning with the world of big business. With a clear majority of Peronists in both houses and the Radicals providing at least a quorum, Congress passed laws that amounted to a delegation of legislative functions to the executive—enabling the executive to determine which enterprises would be privatized, what limits would exist to the liberalization of trade, and how control of antidumping would be implemented. Nevertheless, because the country had not tackled the problems of fiscal crisis, inertial inflation, and chronic dollarization, two new episodes of hyperinflation struck—in December 1989 and again in early 1990.

In early 1991, reduction and consolidation of the internal debt permitted the adoption of the Cavallo Plan.[43] The government guaranteed a fixed exchange rate for australes to dollars and promised absolute fiscal discipline. Annual inflation began to drop, and in 1991 it reached only 84 percent; the interest rate fell to 3 percent per month—which had previously been the daily rate! Between 1985 and 1991, the social costs of the series of plans were extremely high; nevertheless, as William C. Smith noted, "no Argentine government, military or civilian, has been able to make such all-encompassing changes."[44]

Democratization has taken place in both countries in the midst of economic crises, which the former military regimes did nothing or very little to mitigate. The problems encountered by the first democratic governments in the two countries were dramatically different and were much more serious in Argentina. Prior to the debt and fiscal crises of the 1980s, Argentina had undergone a long economic decline, a military defeat, and a revolutionary threat; moreover, it had experienced a short period of unsuccessful neoliberal policies in the late 1970s during the ministry of Martínez de Hoz. Since that time, de-industrialization and capital flight had been prominent features of the Argentine economy.

Brazil was in a much more favorable situation. The country had experienced considerable growth since the 1930s. External adjustment had been accomplished in the early 1980s before democratization, and soon reserves of hard currency began accumulating. Both Brazil and Argentina, however, faced severe foreign debt and state fiscal crises.

One can speculate that Brazil's successful development made it possible for the country's political and economic elites to ignore the need for thorough structural reforms, so ingrained were the patterns of behavior and attitudes appropriate to the developmentalist state (in spite of the incompleteness of its project). It makes sense to speculate that Brazil's successful development made it possible for the country's political and economic elites to ignore the need for thorough structural reforms. Moreover, the patterns of behavior and attitudes appropriate to the developmentalist state were deeply ingrained in these groups. On the other hand, Argentina's much more serious economic situation forced that country's elites to recognize at an earlier stage the need to confront the state's fiscal crisis. As the rate of capital flight shows, the commitment of these elites with Argentina's fate are not very strong. In fact, the Austral Plan and its successors failed, and they ended in disaster: hyperinflation. However, Alfonsín's plans, from the Austral Plan on, had greater consistancy than those adopted by Brazil, and they were less permeated by electoral concerns than was the case in that ountry. Compared to Brazil, Argentine parties were not amorphous and the party system was not fragmented; thus, policies could be followed more consistently for longer periods.[45] They nevertheless failed.[46]

When, however, hyperinflation was added to the economic crisis in mid 1989, social and political chaos resulted. In the words of Luiz Carlos Bresser Pereira, society became more willing to accept "higher transition costs." More appropriately, Vicente Palermo and Juan Carlos Torre observed that in a hyperinflationary context—in which the motivation is "to flee from an unbearable present or from the fear of returning to a past whose extreme hardness was experienced. . . material costs get smaller instead of greater as economic stabilization becomes effective."[47] One should add that matters were only facilitated at this juncture by the fact that stabilization and reform were undertaken by a president from the Peronist Party, who by tradition should have strongly opposed neoliberal policies.

Brazil faced problems of a magnitude similar to those of Argentina. During the 1980s Brazil's economy continued to grow.[48] Only at the beginning of 1990 did the country witness a short spell of hyperinflation, followed by three years of recession and stagnation. Because Brazil grew intermittently during the crisis, the elite failed to recognize the gravity of the state's fiscal situation and took longer than did the elite in Argentina to acknowledge that the crisis required a complete overhaul of the state itself. □

CONCLUSION

Given the country's political institutions, is the Brazilian economic situation without a remedy? Is Brazil condemned to an endless alternation between stabilization plans and controlled megainflation? Is the cure to be found only after two or three more bouts of hyperinflation? What are the prospects for Fernando Henrique Cardoso's Real Plan?

After the impeachment of Collor, Vice President Itamar Franco took office, with general promises of support from the parties instrumental to the impeachment. As the 1994 presidential campaign began, the situation appeared to be "politics as usual." The government coalition was as fragile and ambiguous as ever, and controlled inflation was at a level as high as ever. Government economic measures continued to be challenged successfully in the judiciary. Splits in the center parties occurred every day. The date appointed for the constitutional revision, as stipulated in the 1988 constitution, was a matter of dispute in Congress,[49] and the revision took place before all of the candidates for the presidency had been chosen by the parties. Only one important amendment was approved, which created a temporary "social emergency fund" deemed essential for sheer governability to the end of 1995. This almost complete inactivity revealed the unwillingness of all political sides in Congress to put workable reforms of the constitution into the hands of an unknown winner. There was a visceral ambiguity on the part of politicians of all persuasions, with half wanting efficacious economic policies and half fearing those policies might succeed. It was felt that the political faction that solved the economic enigma was sure to be the winner in the elections. The major problem was how to constitute a majority out of factions with such a great diversity of interests.

Not everything, however, was opposed to the reform. Public opinion and general attitudes, as already noted, had changed in its favor.

In the first half of 1994, a new reform package, the Real Plan, was begun under then–Finance Minister Fernando Henrique Cardoso. All of its measures had been adequately discussed before its implementation, and rather than including a freeze of wages and prices, it consisted mainly of a skillfully introduced monetary reform. The first stage contained a complete indexation to the real value unit, an index tied to the dollar. In July 1994, the government introduced this unit, which involved a physical change of all money in circulation.

Before this date, Cardoso had resigned from the finance ministry to run for president, with the support of an ample spectrum of parties ranging from the Center-Right to the Center-Left. In June, polls showed the candidate of the Workers' Party, Lula, was still far in front of Cardoso. Less than a month after the introduction of the new money, inflation had dropped drastically, the real was worth much more than the dollar, and the political situation had changed dramatically. In October, in the first round of the election, Cardoso was elected by a substantial majority.

During 1995, however, the old obstacles of the institutional framework began to reappear. The electoral coalition did not translate into a clear majority, which was needed to approve the constitutional amendments for the economic reform. Demonstrations against specific reforms (mainly against that of the social security system) made their first appearance.

The economic and political situation, however, appears to be much improved over that prevailing during former plans. First, because the stabilization program seems firm, inflation is under control.[50] Foreign reserves remain high in spite of the world financial crisis provoked by the Mexican devaluation. Second, because the stabilization and reform programs began *before* the election, the president was elected on a clear plank of "defense of the real" to continue the needed reforms, as were all of the governors, deputies, and senators of the coalition. As was said earlier, a workable temporary fiscal adjustment was approved as part of the constitutional revision, and it is likely to be extended by Congress for two or three years, even if the constitutional amendments that should constitute the main body of the economic reform take longer to pass.

Success in approving the more permanent reforms may be a matter of political ability and muddling through. Not all the clouds have disappeared from Brazil's horizon, but it has been a long time since it has been as clear as it is today. □

NOTES

1. Angus Maddison and Associates, *The Political Economy of Poverty, Equity, and Growth: Brazil and Mexico* (New York: Oxford University Press, 1992), table 1–2, p. 6.

2. In the mid–1930s, import-substitution industrialization gained popularity. See Celso Furtado, *A formação econômica do Brasil* (Rio de Janeiro: Editora Fundo de Cultura, 1959). Peter Evans, discussing the efficacy of the state in implementing industrial transformation, distinguishes among three types: developmental states, such as Japan, Taiwan and Korea, predatory states, such as Zaire, and "intermediary" cases, such as Brazil and India. The latter are defined as states that failed to be consistently developmental. See Evans, "The State as Problem and Solution: Predation, Embedded Autonomy and Structural Change," in Stephan Haggard and Robert Kaufman, eds., *The Politics of Economic Adjustment: International Constraints, Distributive Conflicts and the State* (Princeton: Princeton University Press, 1992) pp. 132-181.

3. See Madison and Associates, *The Political Economy of Poverty, Equity, and Growth*, Table 4–2, p. 81.

4. For a recent thorough discussion of income inequality in Brazil, see Regis Bonelli and Guilherme Luiz Sedlacek, "A Evoluçao da distribuiçao de renda entre 1983 e 1988," in José Márcio Camargo and Fábio Giambiagi, eds., *Distribuição de renda no Brasil* (São Paulo: Editora Paz e Terra, 1991), pp. 47–67. The Gini Index measures the degree of inequality within a population. It ranges from a value of 0 (zero), representing perfect equality, to a value of 1, representing the maximum possible level of inequality (i.e., the wealthiest person would receive all the income in a given society).

5. See Guilherme Leite da Silva Dias and Basilia Maria Baptista Aguirre, "Crise político-econômica: As raízes do impasse," and Brasílio Sallum Jr. and Eduardo Kugelmas, "O leviatã acorrentado: A crise brasileira dos anos 80," both in Lourdes Sola, ed., *Estado, mercado e democracia: Politica e economia comparadas* (São Paulo: Editora Paz e Terra, 1993), pp. 280–299 and 300–318, respectively. See also Lourdes Sola, "The State, Structural Reform and Democratization in Brazil," in William C. Smith, Carlos H. Acuña, and Eduardo A. Gamarra, eds., *Democracy, Markets and Structural Reform in Latin America* (New Brunswick: Transaction Press, 1994) pp. 151-181.

6. On the "flight forward from the crisis," see Sola, "The State, Structural Reform and Democratization in Brazil." There were three unsuccessful stabilization programs in the final years of the military regime, in 1979, 1981, and 1983. All three programs ignored the inertial nature of inflation and were marked by populist overtones. Inflation went from 50 percent per year in 1979 to 200 percent per year in 1983. See Luiz Carlos Bresser Pereira, "The Failure to Stabilize," keynote speech to the conference Brazil: Economic, Political, and Social Reform, Institute of Latin American Studies, University of London, February 18–19, 1993. See also Haggard and Kaufman, eds., *The Politics of Economic Adjustment*.

7. Maddison and Associates, *The Political Economy of Poverty, Equity, and Growth*, table 1–3, p. 8.

8. The economy recovered significantly in the second half of 1985. But there was still fear that the Cruzado Plan might cause a recession, as had happened in

Argentina following the implementation of the Austral Plan. See interview with André Lara Resende, in Alex Solnik, *Os pais do cruzado contam por que não deu certo (Depoimentos a Alex Solnik)* (Porto Alegre: L & PM Editores, 1987), pp. 157–160.

9. For the social and political contexts of the economic crisis, see Thomas Skidmore, *The Politics of Military Rule in Brazil, 1964–1985* (New York: Oxford University Press, 1988).

10. Roberto Frenkel, one of the fathers of the Austral Plan, was a visiting professor at the Catholic University in Rio de Janeiro in the early 1980s when the inertial theory of inflation was being developed. Interview with Persio Arida, in Solnik, *Os pais do cruzado contam por que não deu certo*, p. 78.

11. See the brief characterization of each of the plans (1979–1992) in Bresser Pereira, "The Failure to Stabilize," pp. 4–5.

12. During the last fortnight before the inauguration of Collor in March, 1990, prices began to climb exponentially. Because of the elaborate indexation system, inflation never amounted to a true monetary debacle, however.

13. Bresser distinguishes two plans during the first nine months of the Collor presidency: Collor Plan I, March to April 1990, and what he calls the Eris Plan (named for the then-president of the Central Bank), May to December 1990. Bresser Pereira, "The Failure to Stabilize," p. 5.

14. Some of the original formulators of the inertial theory of inflation participated in the preparation of the plan along with other economists. In their writings they defended the concept that strategies to combat inertial inflation should have no distributive effect. The fact that salary increases were even included points to the fact that the political role of some of the economists—as participants in the opposition party during the military regime—overshadowed their technical role. For a thorough political analysis of the Cruzado Plan, see Lourdes Sola, "Choque heterodoxo y transición política sin ruptura," *Desarrollo Económico* 28, no. 112 (January-March 1989): 483–524.

15. The party won more than three-fourths of the senatorial seats and 54 percent of the seats in the Chamber of Deputies. See Scott Mainwaring, "Democracia presidencialista multipartidária: O Caso do Brasil," *Lua Nova* 28/29 (1993): 24–26.

16. A provisional measure, decreed by the executive, goes out of effect if it is not approved by Congress within thirty days. Under the old constitution, executive decrees remained in force permanently if they were not voted down by Congress within thirty days following their promulgation. Actions resulting from provisional measures can now also be invalidated if a measure is voted down by Congress, a rule that was not in force for executive decrees.

17. See Mainwaring, "Democracia presidencialista multipartidária."

18. See Luiz Carlos Bresser Pereira, "Economic Reforms and Economic Growth: Efficiency and Politics in Latin America," in L. C. Bresser Pereira, J. M. Maravall, and A. Przeworski, eds., *Economic Reforms in New Democracies* (Cambridge: Cambridge University Press, 1993), pp. 49–50.

19. See the excellent summary of these programs in Sola, "The State, Structural Reform and Democratization in Brazil," pp. 250–254. See also Gustavo Franco and Winston Fritsch, "Los avances de la reforma de la política comercial y industrial en Brasil," J. Vial, ed., *Adonde vá América Latina? Balance de las reformas económicas*

(Santiago: CIEPLAN, 1992) pp. 135-157. Reduction of tariffs was planned to go in steps, dropping from around 40 percent to an average of 20 percent by 1994. By and large, the goals have been fulfilled. The free trade treaty among the four countries of the southern cone—MERCOSUR—is an important part of the country's liberalization objectives. During the period 1990–1992, trade among these countries increased 75 percent, from $3.6 to $6.3 billion. Argentina is already Brazil's second-largest trade partner (after the United States). The goal was to achieve a free trade area by the end of 1994, that would eliminate differences among the countries in their fiscal, exchange, and monetary policies. Things proceeded almost on schedule. Obstacles to the fulfillment of the objectives did appear—of which Brazil's failure to stabilize its economy was an important factor. See "Integração ainda encontra barreiras," Edição Especial, *O Estado de São Paulo* (March 26, 1993).

20. Note the observations on changes in the "cognitive map" of elites, whose expectations had been formed in the context of the state-led economy. See Sola, "The State, Structural Reform and Democratization in Brazil."

21. Among other discussions of productive restructuring, see Leda Gitahy, *Estudo da competividade da indústria brasileira: Relações de trabalho, política de recursos humanos e competividade: Reestruturação produtiva e a empresa* (Campinas: University of Campinas, 1993); and reports on organizational changes in enterprises in newspapers such as *O Estado de São Paulo, A Folha de São Paulo,* and *A Gazeta Mercantil* (São Paulo), several dates in 1991 and 1992. An important piece of evidence is the fact that although economic recovery has occurred since the end of 1992, unemployment remains high (5.6 percent from October of 1992 to July of 1993). See "PIB cresceu 5,49 por cento no primeiro semestre," *O Estado de São Paulo* (September 23, 1993), p. B–6.

22. See Max Weber, "Foundations and Instability of Charismatic Authority," in H. H. Gerth and C. Wright Mills, *From Max Weber: Essays in Sociology* (London: Kegan Paul, Trench, Trubner and Co., 1947), pp. 248–250.

23. The most famous antiparty politicians were Getúlio Vargas (1951) and Jânio Quadros (1961), whose lives ended in tragedy. Vargas committed suicide in 1954, and Quadros resigned in 1961 after only seven months in office. For an analysis of presidents against parties and their relationship with Congress, see Mainwaring, "Democracia presidencialista multipartidária," pp. 42–49.

24. This was in part the result of the failure of the Cruzado Plan and of the flagrantly clientelistic character of Sarney's final years, particularly apparent in his attempt to extend his mandate by means of manipulation of Congress through a supra-party bloc.

25. For more information on the "provisional measures," see note 16.

26. See Mainwaring, "Democracia presidencialista multipartidária."

27. The heterogeneity of the socioeconomic structure is also related to the inarticulateness of the social actors. No leader or leaders from business associations or unions have stepped forth to represent either the industrialists or the workers. There was frequent talk about "social pacts" as components of stabilization plans (the Pact of Moncloya in Spain was readily taken as a example). The impossibility of the task, given the Brazilian situation, soon became abundantly clear.

28. Constituent Assembly voting on controversial issues is revealing. Of the six major parties, only two leftist parties—the PT and the Democratic Labor Party—showed any consistency. See Mainwaring, "Democracia presidencialista multipartidária," table 10, 38.

29. Mainwaring's article contains numerous examples of these characteristics of coalitions, taken both from the 1946–1964 period and after democratization began in 1985. See ibid.

30. This is an inheritance from the military regime (see the episode discussed earlier of the "shift in alliances" that occurred in 1977 during the Geisel government). For the Chamber of Deputies, the 1988 constitution kept the same minimum and maximum numbers of seats (eight and seventy, respectively) by state.

31. See the candid testimonies of the creators and implementers of the plan made several months after its failure, in Solnik, *Os pais do cruzado contam por que não deu certo*, pp. 34, 36, 40, 54.

32. On this point see José Luis Fiori, *Ajuste, transición y governabilidad: El enigma brasilero* (Washington, D.C.: Inter-American Development Bank, 1993). Fiori argues convincingly that many of the obstacles that impede stabilization programs are structures inherited from the developmentalist period.

33. Fiori affirms, "As in the 1930s, there will be no progress without a profound institutional reorganization of the state (of which the redemocratization process is a central part), a reorganization of the productive structure, a redefinition of the relations of the state with markets and civil society, and a clear demarcation of new rules of participation. . . a profound transformation that goes much further than what economic policies alone can accomplish" [my translation]. See ibid., p. 16.

34. On the failure during the 1950s to introduce a meritocratic system, insulated from clientelistic pressures, see Mainwaring, "Democracia presidencialista multipartidária," pp. 30–31. On "embedded autonomy," see Evans, "The State as Problem and Solution." Evans quotes data from Barbara Geddes that compare the accomplishment of the goals of President Kubitschek's development plan by the special organs created by him (102 percent of efficiency) with the accomplishment of those goals by the traditional bureaucracy (32 percent).

35. The accusations that became part of the impeachment process were suggestive of the ties established among private interests, parts of the bureaucracy, and certain members of Congress and Congress's connection with patronage politics. It is important to note that these relationships function as obstacles to reform and also to indicate their connection with the nature of the political system.

36. Certain norms—approved by the Constituent Assembly when it thought the government would be parliamentary—are inadequate for present system with its presidentialist organization.

37. On income distribution, see Bonelli and Sedlacek, "A evolução de distribuição de renda entre 1983 e 1988" on the Gini Index, see Camargo and Giambiagi, eds., *Distribuição de renda no Brasil*, p. 115. On absolute poverty, see Mauricio Costa Romão, "Distribuição de renda, pobreza e desigualdades regionais no Brasil," in ibid. The complete series is 1960, 41.4 percent; 1970, 39.3 percent; 1980, 24.4 percent; and 1988, 39.3 percent.

38. After examining data showing improvement in social indicators, Vilmar Faria wrotes, "I am convinced . . . that the strong political mobilization that characterized the decade, associated with the progress in popular organization and with the reiteration of free and democratic elections, explains, in diverse ways, a great portion of this advancement" [my translation]. Faria, "A conjuntura social brasileira: Dilemas e perspectivas," *Novos Estudos Cebrap* 33 (July 1992): 111.

39. For interpretations of economic reform in Argentina, see Vicente Palermo and Juan Carlos Torre, "A La Sombra de la Hiperinflación: La Política de Reformas Estructurales en Argentina," paper presented at the Seminario Regional sobre Reformas de Política Pública, Santiago, Chile, August 3–5, 1992; and Bresser Pereira, "Economic Reforms and Economic Growth." See also William C. Smith, "Conflicto distributivo y política macroeconómica en Argentina," *Revista Mexicana de Sociologia* 1 (1991): 71–105, and William C. Smith, "Estado, mercado e neoliberalismo na Argentina pós-transição: A experiência Menem," in Sola, ed., *Estado, mercado e democracia*, pp. 194–231.

40. Bresser Pereira noted that "in Argentina there was true or effective dollarization of the economy for several years before, during, and after hyperinflation," which posed additional difficulties for its stabilization. See Bresser Pereira, "Economic Reforms and Economic Growth," p. 47.

41. On May 14, Carlos Menem received 52 percent of the vote versus 39 percent for Angeloz, the Radical candidate. Given the business cycle, these results show the cohesion of the parties.

42. See Palermo and Torre, "A la sombra de la hiperinflación," p. 7.

43. Measures taken by Néstor Rapanelli and especially by Antonio Erman González during the 1990 included rescheduling of short-run private assets in the banks (January), a strong fiscal shock (March), tax collection reforms (July), acceleration of privatization or liquidation of state enterprises (August), and amnesty for repatriation of dollars (December). Note that the intensity and magnitude of the privatization program, in addition to playing a significant political role, has also played an economic role in both financing the public sector and backing the external sector of the economy, accounting significantly for the increased capital inflows. See Chapter 13.

44. See Smith, "Estado, mercado e neoliberalismo na Argentina póstransição," pp. 212–221, for appraisals of the Cavallo Plan and of the social costs of all of the plans since 1985.

45. With the failures and his consequent loss of popularity, Alfonsín had increasing difficulty dealing with both his party and Congress. Argentine employers' and workers' organizations are also better articulated within civil society than is the case in Brazil. Party identity had been weak during Brazil's democratic period (1946–1964), and the identities formed during those years were destroyed by the military regime.

46. Bresser Pereira was puzzled by this failure, since it "was not caused either by incompetence or populism." He added that years of economic deterioration had "weakened the [elite's] sense of and concern for the national interest in Argentina" The huge capital flight was a particular indication of this. See Bresser Pereira, "Economic Reforms and Economic Growth," p. 46.

47. See Palermo and Torre, *A la sombra de la hiperinflación*, pp. 16–17.

48. Between 1980–1987, the annual average growth rate for Argentina was negative, −0.6 percent, whereas for Brazil it was 2.4 percent. See Maddison and

Associates, *The Political Economy of Poverty, Equity, and Growth*, table 1–2, p. 6. During the early 1990s, after the Collor Plan, the record was even more dismal: Following a decline in GDP of more than 6 percent in 1990, two years of almost no growth occurred (1.3 percent and 0.7 percent, respectively). Economic recuperation began only toward the end of 1992. During the first half of 1993, GDP registered a growth rate of approximately 5.5 percent. See "PIB cresceu 5,49 por cento no primeiro semestre," p. B–6.

49. It was argued that the result of the plebiscite maintaining the form of government (republic and presidentialist) annulled the constitutional stipulation to hold a constitutional revision. Amendments to the constitution were much easier to pass during the revision, since they needed to by approved by only a simple majority of the vote.

50. Inflation in February 1995 was about 1.5 percent.

CHAPTER TWELVE

———————— ■ ————————

The Multiple Roles
of Privatization in Argentina

Roberto Frenkel and Guillermo Rozenwurcel

ECONOMIC RESTRUCTURING, LIKE other instances of large-scale social change, is a process of collective action in which actors' rationality should be empirically ascertained. This means their motives for acting in specific ways should not be simply taken for granted (for instance, by assuming that policy choices are dictated by the intrinsic superiority of these policies on the basis of such criteria as efficiency or equity) and that the relationship between action and consequences should be considered problematical (i.e., the extent to which the objective consequences of action are those intended by the actors is empirically variable). Policy choices are the result of knowledge and interests, but often the interests of policymakers or of the groups they represent have overriding importance as determinants. These interests may be individual or private rather than collective or public, and they frequently focus on areas of social life that are different from those to which the policy is oriented (e.g., economic policy may reflect the political rather than the economic interests of policymakers and other groups). Also, policy outcomes are the result of many factors other than policymakers' intentions: other groups' agency, institutional mechanisms, cultural processes, and so forth.

In this chapter we focus on privatization—the central dimension of economic liberalization—and on the case of Argentina, one of the most radical instances of privatization in Latin America. Our purpose is to ascertain the motives that guided the Menem administration when it embarked on the privatization drive. We also look into some of the objective consequences of large-scale privatization in Argentina.

Hyperinflationary episodes in 1989 and 1990 left the Argentine economy in a critical situation. In addition to huge fiscal imbalances, massive capital flight, and swift demonetization, prices rose almost 5,000 percent in 1989 and more than 1,300 percent in 1990; meanwhile, real investment collapsed, and output dropped 6.2 percent in 1989.[1] At the end of March 1991, the Argentine government announced a new stabilization policy based on the full convertibility of the domestic currency at a fixed exchange rate established by law, and a 100 percent backing of the money base with foreign reserves. The government also instituted sharp fiscal adjustment aimed primarily at increasing tax revenues.

At the same time, the government hastened its market-oriented program of structural reforms. Privatization of public firms was one of the key elements of that program: Its scope was large, its implementation was quick, and its impact was significant in a variety of ways. From a short-term perspective, privatization revenues were crucial as a means to temporarily finance the fiscal deficit, as well as to reduce the public debt and close the external gap generated by the stabilization plan. Privatizations also enhanced the government's credibility and dramatically changed the country's economic environment.

The new plan effectively stabilized the economy. The fiscal balance improved remarkably, and optimistic expectations and a favorable international context triggered an impressive inflow of private capital and a rapid process of remonetization. As a result, inflation dropped dramatically, and economic activity rapidly recovered.

By the end of 1993, however, Argentine domestic inflation had not yet fully reached international levels. This fact, coupled with a fixed nominal exchange rate, provoked the real appreciation of the domestic currency. Meanwhile, despite its significant revival, aggregate investment was still fairly low, and prevailing incentives directed growth toward the nontradables sector.

Against the backdrop of a falling real exchange rate, trade liberalization caused an abrupt increase in imports. As exports remained stagnant, the trade balance sharply deteriorated, and the current account—which had run a surplus in 1990—turned into a growing deficit.

Furthermore, the fragility still displayed by the public sector had dimmed the prospects for stabilization. Regardless of the importance of the achievements in tax revenues, nonfinancial current expenditures grew significantly because of the still unresolved crisis in the social security system and the lack of fiscal adjustment in the provinces. In such a context, privatization revenues, investment cuts, and the decline in international interest rates have played a key role in keeping the public-sector borrowing requirements under control. Nevertheless, this is clearly not a permanent solution.

To tentatively assess the progress of fiscal reform in Argentina, we discuss the multiple roles played by privatization within the context of that country's Convertibility Program and of the recent performance of the Argentine economy and its fiscal accounts. □

RECENT MACROECONOMIC AND FISCAL PERFORMANCE

The Convertibility Program announced in March 1991 achieved considerable success in overcoming hyperinflation and stabilizing the Argentine economy.[2] Annual inflation dropped to 17.5 percent in 1992 and to only 7.4 percent in 1993, a remarkably low rate when compared with historical levels (see Table 12.1). A fixed exchange rate, swift trade liberalization, and a sharp fiscal adjustment were the key factors that explained this outcome, but legal deindexation of nominal contracts, price agreements in some strategic industries, and other incomes-policy measures were also important at the initial stages of stabilization.

Regarding the fiscal situation, the improvement has also been significant—even allowing the government to produce a surplus in the overall fiscal balance during recent years: 0.7 percent of gross domestic product (GDP) in 1992 and 1.8 percent of GDP in 1993 (Table 12.1). Several factors contributed to the favorable evolution of the fiscal accounts.

First, beginning in the early 1990s tax receipts increased dramatically. The impressive improvement in tax performance was mainly the result of economic recovery, a much lower inflation rate, better collection and control procedures, and an increasing public willingness to pay existing taxes. As a result, fiscal pressure at the federal level reached an unprecedented 16.6 percent of GDP in 1992, whereas current income (which also includes nontax revenues) amounted to 17.5 percent of GDP the same year. These values remained roughly constant in 1993 (see Table 12.2).

Nonfinancial current expenditures also displayed a growth trend over the same period, however, climbing to about 15 percent of GDP in 1991, 1992, and 1993, mainly as a consequence of an adverse evolution of transfers to both the social security system and the provinces. The appreciation of the Argentine currency also contributed to this trend. The resulting primary savings were 2.5 percent of GDP in 1992 and 2.6 percent in 1993. This level, although much higher than the one attained in 1991, was roughly similar to that of 1989 and was even lower than that of 1990 (Table 12.2).

The evolution of current savings, in contrast, proved to be much more favorable, reverting from a negative 2.7 percent of GDP in 1989 to a positive 1.4 percent in 1993. An unexpectedly swift decrease in foreign debt interest payments, which declined from 4.4 percent of GDP in 1989 to 1.0 percent in 1993, helped explain that outcome (Table 12.2). Indeed, the lower interest payments were the consequence not only of a reduction in

TABLE 12.1 Key Economic Indicators, 1988–1993

	1988	1989	1990	1991	1992	1993[a]
Percentage change in						
Real GDP	−1.90	−6.2	0.1	8.9	8.7	6.5
Industrial production	−4.9	−7.1	2.0	11.9	7.3	4.5
Consumer price index						
(CPI) (end-period)	387.7	4,923.3	1,343.9	84.0	17.5	7.4
Real Exchange Rate						
CPI U.S./Argentina	103.1	127.3	82.6	56.2	49.6	47.9
(1983=100)						
Individual real wages	101.4	82.0	85.8	87.0	88.1	86.7
(1983=100)						
Public-sector borrowing						
requirement (PSBR)[b]	3.3	4.8	1.8	0.8	−0.7	−1.8
Total money resources[c]	17.8	11.5	5.0	7.5	11.4	18.2
Investment rate[d]	18.6	15.5	14.0	14.6	16.7	17.9
National savings rate[d]	19.5	17.8	17.7	14.9	13.9	15.8
Export coefficient	9.5	13.1	10.4	7.7	6.6	6.3
Import coefficient[d]	6.2	6.6	4.6	6.1	8.1	7.9
External accounts						
(U.S.$ billion)						
Trade balance	3.81	5.37	8.28	3.70	−2.64	−3.70
Real services	−0.26	−0.26	−0.32	−0.93	−1.05	−1.22
Financial services	−5.13	−6.42	−6.12	−5.63	−4.59	−3.97
Current account	−1.57	−1.29	1.90	−2.83	−8.55	−8.97
External debt	58.50	63.30	61.00	63.70	65.00	68.00

[a] Estimated.

[b] Shown in percentage of change from year to year.

[c] Including dollar deposits in the financial systems, shown in percentage of change from year to year.

[d] Current prices, shown in percentage of change from year to year. Sources: United Nations Economic Commission for Latin America and the Caribbean, *Indicadores macroeconómicos de la Argentina,* (Santiago: United Nations, 1992, 1993, and 1994); Argentine Ministerio de Economía, Dirección Nacional de Investigaciones y Análisis Fiscal, *Evolución de la Recaudación Tributaria* (Buenos Aires: Ministerio de Economía, 1992, 1993, and 1994); and authors own estimates.

the country's foreign indebtedness, brought about by privatizations and debt-equity swaps, but also resulted from a simultaneous and sharp decline in international interest rates. The cash revenues arising from privatizations, extremely low levels of public investment, and an almost balanced consolidated budget of public firms also contributed to the overall fiscal surpluses generated by the national government in 1992 and 1993.

In particular, the privatization process, which had begun in 1990, evolved at an extremely fast pace. The calls for bids attracted offers from a large number of local and international companies. By the end of 1992, most public utilities and oil fields had already been privatized. In 1993, moreover, the government undertook the privatization of the Yacimientos Petrolíferos Fiscales (YPF), the state-owned oil company and Argentina's largest concern. As a first step in that process, 40 percent of the company's shares were sold to domestic and international investors in June 1993. No major steps were undertaken in 1994, but the government announced its intention to complete the process in 1995 by privatizing the few companies still in public hands and selling its remaining shares of the already privatized firms.

The immediate beneficiary of this process has been the Argentine government. Including the sale of YPF shares, it has collected around U.S.$17.3 billion since the beginning of the effort at privatization: U.S.$9.5 billion in cash, the remainder taken at the market value of all other payments involved (see Table 12.3). So far, these funds have been an important factor in explaining the government's rough compliance with International Monetary Fund fiscal targets, as well as its ability to service the public debt without resorting to inflationary financing of public expenditures.

The implementation of the Convertibility Program has also brought about a large increase in all monetary aggregates. The abrupt drop in inflation and the economic recovery resulting from stabilization caused the demand for money to rise steadily. Privatization and the expanding money needs of the public were the two major domestic determinants underlying the strong capital inflow that has taken place since the beginning of the program. As a result, private capital inflows amounted to nearly U.S.$26 billion in 1991–1993, whereas total monetary resources (in pesos and dollars) rose from 5 percent of GDP in 1990 to 18.2 percent three years later (see Table 12.1).

Economic activity also underwent an outstanding expansionary phase. Indeed, the GDP growth rate stood at 8.9 percent in 1991, 8.7 percent in 1992, and 6.5 percent in 1993 (Table 12.1). The performance of industrial output was also impressive: Its growth rate was 11.9 percent for 1991, 7.3 percent for 1992, and 4.5 percent for 1993 (Table 12.1). The huge capital inflow induced by both domestic stabilization and a positive external environment was the key factor in this trend.

TABLE 12.2 National Public-Sector Accounts, 1988–1993 (% of GDP)

	1988	1989	1990	1991	1992	1993
Current income	13.8	14.7	14.0	15.5	17.5	17.3
Tax revenue	11.9	12.9	12.5	14.2	16.6	16.1
Nontax revenue[a]	1.9	1.8	1.5	1.3	0.9	1.2
Nonfinancial current expenditures	12.4	12.6	11.1	14.4	15.0	14.7
Personnel	2.9	2.6	2.2	2.9	2.4	2.5
Transfers to social security system	3.7	3.3	4.0	5.0	5.3	5.7
Transfers to provinces	4.2	5.0	3.7	5.0	5.6	5.2
Other expenditures	1.6	1.7	1.2	1.5	1.7	1.3
Primary savings	1.4	2.1	2.9	1.1	2.5	2.6
Interest payments	2.6	4.8	3.2	1.6	1.7	1.2
Foreign debt	2.4	4.4	2.9	1.3	1.4	1.0
Domestic debt	0.2	0.4	0.3	0.3	0.3	0.2
Current savings	−1.2	−2.7	−0.3	−0.5	0.8	1.4
Capital income	0.3	0.5	0.4	1.2	1.4	1.0
Privatizations (cash)	0.0	0.0	0.3	1.2	1.3	0.9
Others	0.3	0.5	0.1	0.0	0.1	0.1
Capital expenditures	2.5	2.0	1.3	1.2	1.5	0.6
Public-sector borrowing requirements	3.4	4.2	1.2	0.5	−0.7	−1.8

[a]Nontax revenue includes the public firm surplus.

Sources: Economic Commission on Latin America, "Indicadores macroeconómicos de la Argentina," 1992, 1993, and 1994; Dirección Nacional de Investigaciones y Análisis Fiscal, "Evolución de la Recaudación Tributaria," 1992, 1993, and 1994; and authors' own estimate.

TABLE 12.3 Financial Results of the Privatization Process, 1990–1993
(in U.S.$ million)

Sector/ Form of	Cash Transference	Amorti- zation	Transferred Foreign Debt	Total Liabilities	Amorti- zation of Foreign Debt
Telecom/Sale of stock	2,279.0	1,264.3	—	3,543.3	5,029.0
Airlines/ Direct sale	190.1	394.1	—	584.2	1,313.8
Railways/ Concession	—	—	—	—	—
Electricity/ Direct sale	1,283.1	1,258.5	1,003.0	3,544.6	2,516.9
Harbors/ Concession or direct sale	12.3	—	—	12.3	—
Roads/Concession	—	—	—	—	—
TV and radio/ Concession	—	—	—	—	—
Petroleum/ Sale of stocks	1,806.8	—	—	1,806.8	—
YPF/Concession	3,040.0	953.3	—	3,993.3	1,271.1
Gas/Direct sale	658.0	1,498.9	1,110.1	3,267.0	2,997.9
Water and sewage/ Concession	—	—	—	—	—
Petrochemical/ Sale of stocks	53.5	26.8	—	80.3	132.0
Ships/Direct sale	59.8	—	—	59.8	—
Steel/Direct sale	143.3	15.9	250.0	409.2	30.0
Public real estate/ Direct sale	3.2	5.8	—	9.0	13.0
Others/Direct sale or concession	4.5	0.7	—	5.2	3.3
Total	9,533.6	5,418.3	2,363.1	17,315.0	13,307.0

Source: Authors' own calculations based on Ministry of Economy, Informe Económico—
Año 1993 2, no. 8 (Buenos Aires, 1994).

Economic recovery was led by consumption, which experienced a boom as a consequence of the repatriation of capital from abroad and because of the increased availability of private-sector credit. The boom was so strong that, somewhat paradoxically, it strengthened the decline in the national savings rate produced by the debt crisis and the hyperinflationary episodes that followed. As a result, national savings was only 13.9 percent of GDP in 1992 and 15.8 percent of GDP in 1993 when it had been 19.5 percent of GDP in 1988 (Table 12.1).

Aggregate investment also showed a significant improvement. According to official data, in effect, gross fixed capital formation grew from 14 percent of GDP in 1990 to 17.9 percent of GDP in 1993 (Table 12.1). To date, this improvement has enabled the economy to recover the investment rates that prevailed in the mid–1980s before the hyperinflationary outburst but after the debt crisis. Nevertheless, these rates are substantially lower than the ones observed in the 1970s.

Meanwhile, the substantial growth in private-sector money demand had allowed the Central Bank to accumulate a considerable sum of foreign currency since 1992. As a result, the stock of international reserves (excluding gold) added over U.S.$15 billion by the end of 1993. This amount is equivalent to almost one year of imports.

Other foreign-sector indicators also evolved in a favorable way. After complex negotiations, a final agreement with the creditor banks was signed in December 1992 under the auspices of the Brady Plan, thereby normalizing Argentina's relations with the international financial community. As already mentioned, privatizations and debt-equity swaps contributed to cutting down the stock of foreign debt by more than 8 percent between 1989 and 1992. Moreover, as a proportion of GDP, foreign debt fell from 38 percent in 1989 to 26 percent in 1992, even though the appreciation of the domestic currency was partly responsible for this result. Interest-due payments, in nominal terms and also as a percentage of both total exports and GDP, diminished as well because of both the reduction in foreign debt and the fall in international interest rates.

The Convertibility Program, despite all its achievements, did not perform as well regarding relative prices. In fact, the rapid growth of aggregate demand, and the persistence of implicit defensive pricing rules inherited from the high-inflation period—especially in the sectors providing services—made convergence of domestic inflation toward international rates a slow process. Under the convertibility scheme, this caused a sizable appreciation of the domestic currency, thus impairing the competitiveness of the tradables sector. Indeed, the real exchange rate, which at the beginning of the program was almost 34 percent above its average level in the second quarter of 1990 (generally accepted, even in the government's view, as a reasonable reference for this variable), fell another 15 percent from April 1991 to the end of 1992.

Real appreciation, coupled with trade liberalization and a booming domestic demand, induced a sudden worsening of the trade balance. Total imports grew rapidly in both volume and value, from an extreme low of U.S.$4.1 billion in 1990 to U.S.$16.8 billion in 1993. Total exports, in turn, remained stagnant (around the ceiling attained in 1990 in the aftermath of hyperinflation when they reached U.S.$12.4 billion). As a result, the huge U.S.$8 billion trade surplus achieved in 1990 was cut by more than half in 1990, and it has turned into a growing deficit since 1992: U.S.$2.6 billion that year and U.S.$3.7 billion in 1993. Meanwhile, the deficit in real services declined sharply as well, with tourism expenditures abroad largely accounting for this outcome. In spite of a sizable reduction in financial services—from U.S.$6.1 billion in 1990 to U.S.$3.9 billion in 1993—the deterioration in foreign trade and real services caused the current account balance to revert from a U.S.$1.9 billion surplus in 1990 to a U.S.$2.8 billion deficit in 1991, which soared to a U.S.$8.9 billion deficit in 1993 (Table 12.1).

The rapidly growing deficit in Argentina's current account during 1991 and 1992 was totally financed through the capital account. In fact, the impressive amount of capital inflows even made possible a sizable increase in foreign reserves, which grew from U.S.$2.3 billion in 1991 to almost U.S.$4 billion in 1993. Private-sector capital movements were mainly responsible for this outcome, accounting for a U.S.$2.5 billion inflow in 1991 and an outstanding U.S.$11.5 billion inflow in each of the following two years. Privatizations were one of the key factors underlying this process. The repatriation of flight capital and the reopening of international credit markets to domestic firms were equally important.

From this analysis, it appears that Argentina's economic prospects are influenced simultaneously by conflicting factors. On the positive side, the rate of inflation continues to decline, foreign reserves appear strong enough to sustain the credibility of Argentina's economic policy, and the agreement reached with foreign creditors under the Brady initiative has eased Argentina's access to voluntary lending in the international financial markets.

Nevertheless, many difficulties still lie ahead. From a long-term perspective, the rate of investment is still low, and its current growth is geared primarily toward production for the domestic markets and the nontradables sector, with the recently privatized public utilities leading the process. Moreover, almost all of the expansion in aggregate investment has been financed by foreign savings. National savings, on the other hand, have not yet reacted to ongoing structural reforms and continue to show a striking decline.

Additionally, the rigidity imposed on the exchange rate policy by the Convertibility Program will make it difficult to reverse the real appreciation of the domestic currency and will probably aggravate the problems of the tradables sector, as well as the current account deficit. As a result, the external balance will remain highly dependent on the continuity of substantial capital inflows, making the overall economic environment too fragile to absorb potentially destabilizing external shocks.

The other source of potential trouble for the prospect of Argentina's economic stabilization is the fragility the public sector still displays. Although the achievements in tax revenues have been impressive so far, nonfinancial current expenditures have recently shown a dangerous increase. Thus, the exogenous reduction in foreign interest payments, privatization revenues, and investment cuts all were critical in keeping fiscal accounts under control. Nevertheless, this is clearly not a permanent solution. □

THE ROLE PLAYED BY PRIVATIZATIONS

The privatization of public firms was one of the major goals of President Menem's administration. In the market-friendly literature and in the current rhetoric employed by many developing country governments, privatizations—along with deregulation—are viewed as tools for enhancing both the productivity of existing resources and the efficiency of investment decisions. Indeed, they are expected to produce such effects through their incentives for private initiative and creativity and are thus supposed to work mainly through microeconomic channels.[3]

Nevertheless, Argentine privatization seems to have served other purposes as well. With outstanding performances in both the relative magnitude of the privatized assets and the speed exhibited in completing the process, Argentina's privatization program has played a crucial role that was very different from that advocated by the World Bank-inspired market-friendly approach to structural reforms.

As was the case with the tax policy, two different stages of privatization can be identified. The first occurred during 1990 and the first quarter of 1991, whereas the second is associated with the Convertibility Program launched in April 1991. During the first stage, the economic situation was very bad. Even though the government had managed to curb the second hyperinflationary outburst in March 1990, inflation remained very high (fluctuating around a 10 percent monthly rate), and a recessionary trend persisted throughout the rest of the year.

In this context, a primary function of the privatization program was to respond to political economic considerations. When the persistence of the economic crisis damaged the credibility of the administration, officials—hoping to regain the support of the business community—pointed to the continuity of the privatization effort as proof that the government was sticking to its original commitments. At the same time, the public was asked to accept privatization as the only possible way out of the economic crisis.

Given the political constraints, the administration submitted the first major privatizations to tight deadlines. To not delay the process, officials dismissed or postponed a thorough consideration of truly important economic issues, such as the pricing policy of the privatized firms or the establishment of regulatory frameworks in response to the new reality.

The second function of privatization was related to macroeconomic stabilization. In fact, the narrowness of the domestic financial markets—aggravated by two hyperinflationary episodes and the compulsory rescheduling of short-term bank deposits and public bonds in January 1990—made it compelling to find a temporary way to finance the remaining fiscal gap so the intended adjustment could have sufficient time to produce its full effects. Privatization revenues now served that purpose, as had been the case earlier with the bridge loans provided by multilateral institutions.

The government's political and financial constraints in 1990 led to the selection of those public firms that were most attractive to the private sector: ENTel (the public telephone company) and Aerolineas Argentinas (the state-owned airline). The new owners of both firms were granted extremely high real tariffs, as well as the preservation of quasi-monopolistic conditions in their respective markets. The government also initiated the privatization of oil fields.

The Convertibility Program launched the second stage in the privatization process. Economic stability helped the government recover credibility and made political considerations less prominent in orienting that process. However, given the clear aversion still evidenced by domestic financial markets in meeting government requirements and despite a significant improvement in tax performance, privatization cash receipts—coupled with the sharp decline in foreign debt interest payments—proved vital in closing the fiscal gap in 1991 and 1992.

In fact, in 1991 privatization cash receipts were slightly higher than primary savings and covered almost all foreign interest payments. Primary savings more than doubled the following year, but privatization cash revenues still represented over 50 percent of those savings and equaled almost 100 percent of foreign interest payments in 1992 (see Table 12.2).

Privatizations were also critically important in reducing of the outstanding public debt. From the beginning of the program until the end of 1993, the government had already rescued the equivalent of about U.S.$13.3 billion (face value) in titles of both domestic and foreign public debt. In particular, the exchange of public foreign debt titles for equity constituted the bulk of the first two major privatizations (ENTel and Aerolineas). These operations alone enabled the government to rescue U.S.$6.5 billion in foreign debt bonds (about 20 percent of the debt with commercial banks at that time), therefore making it possible for Argentina to join the Brady Plan.

The revenues from the privatization of the YPF, which initially included the sale of 40 percent of the company's shares, amounted to slightly less than U.S.$2.5 billion. Nearly half of that sum was destined to pay federal debts to the provinces; the rest was used to diminish the government's long-standing debt with pensioners.

In addition to contributing to strengthening the fiscal situation, privatizations also played a key role in the evolution of Argentina's external accounts. Capital inflows had been crucial in closing a current account's growing imbalance since the beginning of the Convertibility Program, and privatization cash revenues were an important component of these inflows: More than one-third of the private capital account surplus in the period 1991–1993 can be attributed directly or indirectly to privatizations.

In regard to their long-term impact on efficiency and growth, it is widely acknowledged that the sustainability of the current stabilization process and the prospects of growth resumption in the Argentine economy are very much contingent on two factors: (1) an increase in both the national savings rate and the investment rate and (2) an improvement in the competitiveness of the tradables sector.

Let us consider first the different ways in which the domestic private sector can finance the purchase of public firms. At the macroeconomic level, there are four options (plus possible combinations): (1) an increase in private savings, (2) a drop in private investment, (3) an increase in private-sector demand for credit, or (4) a decline in private-sector demand for financial assets. The first two options imply that the private-sector financial surplus (deficit) is growing (diminishing). The third and fourth options imply that given the private sector financial balance, the composition of that balance is changing.[4]

From this point of view, privatizations could have a positive effect on growth provided they cause an increase in private savings while keeping public savings constant, thereby enabling an increase in aggregate investment. Given that the additional private savings will be transferred to the public sector, this means the government must not use privatization earnings to meet current expenses or debt payments.

In the Argentine case, however, privatizations were financed not by private savings but by a combination of greater private foreign indebtedness (option 3) and the repatriation of flight capital (option 4). Moreover, prevailing incentives since the beginning of the Convertibility Program have been such that the massive capital inflows helped finance not only privatizations but also a boom in private consumption, thereby inducing a sort of crowding-out effect on private savings.

Considering the evolution of the fiscal accounts (see Table 12.2), it is also evident that privatization earnings did not fund higher levels of public investment but, rather, replaced other financing sources that were unavailable to the government during the recent period. In that sense, one could argue that the use of privatization revenues to meet current expenses and debt payments had a crowding-out effect on aggregate investment.

Privatizations could have a positive effect on growth in a different way. Most privatization contracts impose investment commitments on the new owners of the formerly public firms, which are expected to have a favorable effect on the productivity of those firms. But to improve over-all competitiveness, those productivity gains must spill over to the rest of the economy. To make privatizations more attractive, however, the government authorized significant increases in the prices charged by the formerly public firms, which are now at a historical peak in real terms. This situation, coupled with the real appreciation of the domestic currency, is impairing the competitiveness of the economy.

A timing problem is also connected with the sustainability of stabilization because privatized firms are located mainly in the nontradables sector. Even if a proper regulatory framework could ensure that productivity gains would be passed on to the rest of the economy, the positive effects of an investment spurt in the nontradables sector on the economy's international competitiveness would be far from immediate. In the meantime, the government may have to face the familiar trade-off between a growing external imbalance and recession, thereby jeopardizing the prospects of the stabilization effort. □

CONCLUSION

The current performance of the Argentine economy provides new evidence for the ongoing debate about the proper sequencing between stabilization and fiscal reform. If anything, the Menem administration's initial failure to stabilize the economy, as well as its subsequent success under the Convertibility Program, confirmed that when inflation surpasses a certain threshold, stabilization cannot wait until the structural reforms reshape the public sector according to market-oriented principles. Some kind of shock therapy is needed first to bring inflation down to less disruptive levels (under 20 percent). The Convertibility Program accomplished this by successfully establishing the exchange rate as the nominal anchor of the economy.

Of course, this does not mean fiscal reform is irrelevant; rather, such reform concerns not the implementation of stabilization but its sustainability. The Convertibility Program imposed severe constraints on the government's ability to finance fiscal imbalances. Two different stages can be distinguished according to the way in which these constraints were met. During the first stage, the priority was to increase fiscal revenues by any means. During the second stage, which is still in progress, more attention has been paid to allocative and distributive considerations.

The outstanding recovery of tax revenues is probably one of the most significant economic changes that has taken place since 1990. Stabilization, coupled with a dramatic expansion of output, no doubt played a major role in this recovery.

It would be a mistake, however, to credit that improvement exclusively to macroeconomic factors. In fact, immediately after Menem's inauguration, political conditions created by hyperinflation enabled the government to force Congress to pass an entirely new legal framework. This had been unthinkable in the past, and it laid the foundation for the forthcoming structural reforms. Against that background, the government launched a vast privatization program and a comprehensive tax reform process, which were largely the cause of the powerful response of fiscal revenues during the Convertibility Program. Regardless of its long-run effects, the sharp fiscal adjustment brought about by this rapid increase in fiscal receipts has been decisive for the credibility and sustainability of the stabilization program.

Despite all of the positive changes achieved by the fiscal reform during this short period, several questions remain. First, once privatization revenues have been exhausted, the tax system must be able to ensure on a permanent basis a level of revenues consistent with public expenditures. On the one hand, tax performance during 1993 seems to suggest that federal tax collection is approaching a ceiling that will not be easy to exceed. On the other hand, political pressure, conflicting demands for better social services, and the appreciation of the domestic currency have kept public expenditures on a growth path.

Additionally, many of the structural reforms already in place will also require significant public funds to finance imbalances that will inevitably arise during the transition. The social security reform is probably the best example. In a long-term perspective, to keep the fiscal deficit under control, the government must pace public-sector reforms with the evolution of the revenue generating capacity of the tax system.

Finally, a few remarks should be made about the various roles played by the privatization program. In fact, despite the standard justification based on long-term efficiency, privatizations to date have basically served short-term, macroeconomic purposes. In 1990, when the economy was still in a deep crisis, privatizations helped the government regain credibility. Privatization revenues have also been very important as a means to temporarily finance the remaining fiscal imbalances, as well as to reduce the outstanding public debt. Ultimately, privatization has been critical in closing the external gap generated by the stabilization plan.

It is still too early to appraise the long-run impact of privatizations on the Argentine economy. Little improvement has occurred in aggregate savings and investment. Because of the lack of an appropriate regulatory framework, productivity gains in privatized firms have not spilled over to the rest of the economy. This, in turn, has prevented an advance in overall competitiveness. At least one aspect of the process, however, seems irreversible: the dramatic change in Argentina's political economy. New private monopolies enjoy substantial economic power. At the same time, the public sector, which is supposed to control these powerful groups, has been left extremely weak as a result of the crisis of the 1980s. It is very difficult to foresee the outcome of this new environment. □

NOTES

1. Output remained constant in 1990.

2. For a more detailed discussion of the fiscal reform, particularly regarding the tax system, see Guillermo Rozenwurcel, "Fiscal Reform and Macroeconomic Stabilization in Argentina," paper presented at the seminar Tax Reform and Macroeconomic Policy in Developing Countries, sponsored by the Indian Statistical Institute and the International Development Research Center, New Delhi, August 25–28, 1993.

3. For a detailed description of the privatization process, see Myrna Alexander and Carlos Corti, "Argentina's Privatization Program," *CFS Discussion Paper Series*, no. 103 (Washington, D.C.: World Bank, 1993). An assessment of its impact on the external sector can be found in José M. Fanelli and José L. Machinea, "Capital Movements in Argentina," *Serie Economía*, no. 99 (Buenos Aires: CEDES, 1994); and Daniel Chudnovsky, Andrés López, and Fernando Porta, "La Nueva Inversión Extranjera Directa en la Argentina. Privatizaciones, Mercado Interno e Integración Regional," mimeo (Buenos Aires: CENIT, 1994). For an analysis of the micro- and macroeconomic consequences of privatization, see Pablo Gerchunoff and Guillermo Cánovas, "Las privatizaciones en la Argentina: impactos micro y macroeconómicos," mimeo (Buenos Aires: Instituto Torcuato Di Tella, 1993).

4. This point is also discussed in José M. Fanelli, Roberto Frenkel, and Lance Taylor, "The World Development Report 1991: A Critical Assessment," in *International Monetary and Financial Issues for the 1990s: Research Papers for the Group of Twenty-Four*, Vol. I (New York: United Nations, 1992).

CHAPTER THIRTEEN

■

The Design of
Markets and Democracies:
Generalizing Across Regions

Arend Lijphart and Carlos H. Waisman

In this concluding chapter, we discuss the role of institutional design in the processes of political and economic transformation underway in Eastern Europe and in the most industrialized countries of Latin America. In particular, we examine how the two processes interact and how this interaction affects the possible outcomes of the overall transition to capitalism and democracy. Next, we turn to the different strategies pursued by economic and political reformers and the expected and actual consequences of their policies; we also speculate about the long-term outcomes of the overall transformation. We then reach several conclusions about the explanations proposed by our authors. Finally, we revisit the issue of similarities and differences between regions, with an emphasis on the latter. □

THE LOGICS OF ECONOMIC AND POLITICAL
TRANSFORMATION

There are three possible sequences between economic and political liberalization. To give them Latin American labels, they would be the Chilean pattern, in which privatization, de-regulation, and the opening up of the economy precede democratization; the Venezuelan one, in which the liberalization of the economy takes place within the context of democratic institutions that have been in place for several decades; and finally the Argentine sequence, in which economic liberalization and the consolidation of democracy take place more or less simultaneously. East European countries and most industrialized countries in Latin America, including

Argentina but also Brazil, fit this last pattern. The three sequences are fraught with dangers, but the third is the least favorable because economic liberalization and the consolidation of democracy are governed by opposing social logics.

Privatization, deregulation, and the opening up of the economy are impelled by the logic of differentiation. Their first impact is to increase social differentiation in both the vertical and the horizontal senses: Polarization between rich and poor as a whole intensifies, and so does polarization between "winners" and "losers" within each social class and also between sectors of the economy and regions of the country. If and when the open market economy is successfully constituted, these discontinuities diminish because of two factors: the operation of market mechanisms themselves and the redistributive policies carried out by the states of prosperous societies. The transition, however, could be long, and its success is not at all certain.

The consolidation of democracy, on the other hand, is governed by the logic of mobilization. The political context of a new democracy renders the mobilization of those affected by economic liberalization more likely because of the lowering of the costs of political action in relation to what was the case in the predemocratic period. Moreover, new democracies create incentives for political entrepreneurship, for in the new political conditions labor and political activists must secure and organize social and political bases. Economic liberalization presents them with an inventory of grievances that easily translates into a political agenda.

These two logics have the potential for inhibiting each other and, consequently, for blocking or derailing economic liberalization, the consolidation of democracy, or both. This is why the third and, unfortunately, the most common pattern listed earlier is less favorable than either of the other two: In the Chilean sequence, the political consequences of the social dislocation produced by economic liberalization are contained by an authoritarian regime; in the Venezuelan pattern, the social order facing dislocation can draw from the capital of legitimacy accumulated by democratic institutions over several decades.

And yet, economic liberalization and the consolidation of democracy are occurring simultaneously in several Latin American countries and in most of Eastern Europe, and to date no blockage or derailing has taken place as a consequence of the interaction between these processes. The breakup of Yugoslavia and the consequent civil war among several of its constituent republics were caused by underlying ethnic cleavages, and they have little to do with political mobilization caused by economic liberalization. In many countries, an impressive consensus exists among state and economic elites and even labor and some of the parties of the Left and the Center that had supported state socialism or economic nationalism in the past.

The reason for the fact that the two opposing logics discussed earlier have not yet clashed lies in the operation of three "cushions," or moderating factors, that inhibit political mobilization. These can be classified into structural, cognitive-ideological, and institutional factors. The first and the second are already operating, in a spontaneous manner. The third is the factor whose materialization involves deliberate social action.

The structural cushion simply consists of the fact that economic liberalization weakens and even destroys the power bases of the coalitions supporting the institutions of the ancien régime (managers and workers in the command economy, rent-seeking entrepreneurs, and unions in autarkic industrial economies) and, in general, of those hurt by trade liberalization, privatization, and deregulation. Entrepreneurial elites, both public and private, face the choice between recycling themselves into competitive capitalists or being driven out of business. The mobilization of labor—which has been weakened by deindustrialization, increased unemployment, and the growth of poverty—is inhibited by the labor reserve generated by these very processes. In many Latin American countries (but not in all), such a labor reserve was a structural trait of the ancien régime, and, in most nations of the two regions, its growth was a manifestation of the crisis of that regime. The existence of this labor reserve, the most effective deterrent of workers' political action, explains the weakness of labor resistance to economic liberalization.

Cognitive-ideological factors have both external and internal sources. From abroad, centrist economic nationalists as well as leftists have been affected by both the collapse of communism and the apparent success of the Thatcher-Reagan economic policies. Internally, a process of political learning has occurred, produced by the protracted stagnation and illegitimacy of the ancien régime. The cumulative effect of these cognitive processes has been the acceptance by economic and political elites of two interrelated propositions: First, state socialism and autarkic capitalism are not viable in the long run; second, only an open capitalist economy and a liberal state can sustain over time both economic growth and political legitimacy.

The third factor is the design or redesign of the basic economic and political institutions in these societies. The main purpose of this book has been to deal with this process, its causes, and its consequences. □

DESIGNING DEMOCRATIC INSTITUTIONS: CHOICES AND CONSEQUENCES

With regard to the design of democratic institutions, the basic assumption underlying this volume has been that two kinds of institutions are of the greatest importance: electoral systems and executive-legislative relations. This assumption is clearly borne out by the chapters in Parts One and

Two: Democratizing politicians in both Eastern Europe and Latin America have been particularly concerned with, and have spent a great deal of their time and energy on, calculating the advantages and disadvantages of the different options and negotiating systems that are as close as possible to their most preferred designs.

At the same time, our experts on the political systems of the two regions add a number of important nuances and qualifications. One is that these basic choices are not dichotomous. In practice, the choice of electoral systems is usually not between pure proportional representation (PR) and undiluted majoritarianism but among a range of options that include combinations of majoritarian and proportional elements and PR systems with different degrees of proportionality. Similarly, the choice in systems of executive-legislative relations is often not the dichotomous one between pure presidentialism and pure parliamentarism but includes intermediate systems, as well as possibilities within each of the two basic types. The second qualification is that the influence of different electoral and executive-legislative designs may be very strong, but their impact is not fully determinate and predictable. In fact, constitutional designers often attribute too much significance to the choices to be made. Finally, other aspects of democratic design should not be overlooked.

The two main categories of electoral systems that election theorists use are plurality and other majoritarian systems (like the majority runoff) on the one hand and PR on the other. But in practice, these categories have not been the alternatives for electoral designers. Instead, in both regions, as the chapters by Barbara Geddes and Dieter Nohlen make particularly clear, election laws have most frequently steered a middle course: They have mixed elements of both majoritarian and proportional rules, and they have tended to use moderate—or impure—forms of PR. PR systems can vary a great deal with regard to their degree of proportionality between votes cast and seats won and in their friendliness toward small parties depending mainly on the district magnitude (the number of representatives elected per district) and the electoral threshold (often a fixed minimum percentage of the total vote required for a party to win any seats). For instance, a hypothetical party, with 5 percent of the vote nationwide and an even distribution of its vote, is not likely to do well in ten-member districts but will fare rather well in twenty-member districts; this same party will also do well with a 2 percent threshold but will not do well if the threshold is raised to 6 percent. Typically, the new PR rules in both regions have used relatively low magnitudes and relatively high thresholds.

There are very few examples of pure majoritarianism. Even the systems with a clearly majoritarian intent, the Chilean and recent Mexican systems, do not have a completely majoritarian form. In Mexico, as Juan Molinar Horcasitas shows, the mixed system, coupled with the "governability clause," has assured a legislative majority to the largest party even if that party falls short of a majority of the votes—similar to the usual pattern in pure plurality countries like the United Kingdom and Canada. The Chilean electoral law is technically a PR system but one with the lowest possible district magnitude a PR system can have—namely, two representatives per district. As Peter Siavelis and Arturo Valenzuela demonstrate, however, this system operates very much like a majoritarian one.

Similarly, the presidential-parliamentary dichotomy has not dominated the constitutional debates in the two regions. Instead, the intermediate form of a semipresidential government—with both a popularly elected president and a prime minister who is subject to the confidence of the legislature—has been fairly popular. Poland provides an excellent example. With much less success, reform-minded Latin Americans have tried to move away from pure presidentialism, but their goal, too, has tended to be to adopt semipresidential rather than parliamentary institutions. An important example is the proposal, mentioned by Carlos Nino, of Argentina's Council for the Consolidation of Democracy, which Nino headed. And in his chapter, Nino recommends yet another, highly creative variant: a kind of semiparliamentary regime with a directly elected prime minister and a mainly ceremonial president elected by the legislature. More important, the political debate has focused on the question of the formal powers to be given to the president and, in Eastern Europe, on the issue of whether presidents should be directly elected. Furthermore, powerful chief executives can be and have been created regardless of whether they are called "presidents"—for instance, as Jerzy Wiatr points out, President Lech Walesa in the immediate aftermath of his popular election—or "prime ministers"—for instance, the Hungarian prime minister who, according to György Szoboszlai, has been made into a much-too-dominant leader.

Whereas electoral and presidential-parliamentary systems have important consequences, and democratic reformers in both regions have been strongly aware of these consequences, it is also true that the formal electoral laws and the rules governing executive-legislative relations are not exclusive determinants. One of the best-known propositions in political science concerns the link between electoral systems and party systems: The more proportional the electoral system, the more fragmented the party system is likely to be. Two of our chapters, however, focus on the at least equally forceful impact of a country's underlying social and ideological divisions.

The 1991 election in Poland yielded an extremely fragmented party system in both houses of Parliament. Many foreign observers immediately concluded that extreme PR was responsible for this result. In fact, however, the Polish electoral law for the Sejm (lower house) was not really hyperproportional. The average district magnitude was only slightly more than ten representatives, and 15 percent of the seats were set aside as bonuses for the larger parties (those receiving more than 5 percent of the total vote). By comparative standards, this is moderate rather than extreme PR. As Stanislaw Gebethner convincingly argues, moderate PR resulted in extreme multipartism as a reflection of the fragmentation of Polish society. Even stronger evidence is the fact that the Senate election also produced a highly fragmented party system, even though the electoral system was pure plurality.

As Siavelis and Valenzuela show, the two-member-district election arrangement in Chile provides a very strong impetus for a two-party system. The great advantages this system gives to the two largest parties and the disadvantages for smaller parties are roughly on a par with those of plurality systems. Nevertheless, the new electoral rules have been unable to change the threefold division into right, center, and left that has been strongly embedded in Chilean society for decades.

Similarly, a president's power clearly depends on more than his or her formal constitutional prerogatives and the prestige conferred by direct election. An additional and particularly critical factor, as both Geddes and Nohlen, as well as Juarez Brandão Lopes, emphasize, is the party system. Presidential power is enhanced under two fairly different conditions: a strong pro-presidential party in the legislature or a large number of weak and ineffective parliamentary parties. Since the party system is influenced in part by the electoral system, this means that system has an indirect impact on executive-legislative relations as well.

Finally, two of our chapters make the important point that the electoral system and executive-legislative relations have played too prominent a role in the minds of, and negotiations among, constitutional engineers. Both Szoboszlai and Nino argue that various other critical elements have been neglected in the new democratic designs and that these should be given much greater attention. And they both emphasize the need for institutional devices to limit executive power whether in a parliamentary system, as in Hungary, or a presidential system, as in Argentina. They agree on the need for strengthening the role of the judiciary, and Szoboszlai further recommends other measures to spread power, such as decentralization and referenda. □

DESIGNING A MARKET ECONOMY: CHOICES AND CONSEQUENCES

The transformation of a state socialist or an autarkic and statized capitalist economy into an open market economy presupposes three processes: privatization of public firms, deregulation, and the opening up to world markets. Privatization is the key aspect of this transformation, for it leads to the drastic reduction of the scope and power of the state, the creation (in state socialist societies) or strengthening (in highly protected and statized capitalist societies) of the private bourgeoisie, and the constitution or revitalization of the network of private associations that make up the core of civil society.

The chapters in Part Three show important commonalities between privatization processes in Eastern Europe and those in Latin America. First, the transitions in the two regions took place as a consequence of a profound economic and political crisis of the ancien régimes. Éva Voszka depicts the critical economic situation in the former Czechoslovakia, Hungary, and Poland at the beginning of the transition: These economies were experiencing a combination of recession, high inflation, and high unemployment. In the case of Argentina, Roberto Frenkel and Guillermo Rozenwurcel describe the conditions in which privatization began in that country: huge fiscal imbalances, massive capital flight, hyperinflation, and the collapse of real investment. Lopes makes the highly plausible claim that the late inception of economic liberalization in Brazil was a result of the fact that Brazil avoided the economic (and political) convulsions that afflicted Argentina in the 1970s and 1980s.

Second, in both regions the dismantling of the ancien régime was carried out by the state elite (or a segment thereof). In the former Communist states, this is true not only in the sense that the regimes imploded, and—in cases such as Poland, Hungary, and Czechoslovakia— this implosion took the form of a "revolution from above." In addition, in these societies a segment of the old state and economic elite became a main beneficiary of the privatization process—that is, it "recycled" itself into a part of the new bourgeoisie. Voszka refers to the phenomenon of "nomenclatura capitalism" in Poland and describes "spontaneous privatization" in Hungary. And in Latin America, both the process of massive privatization in Argentina, described by Frenkel and Rozenwurcel, and the belated and more limited one Lopes documents for Brazil are the result of actions taken by the state elite and supported by central segments of the bourgeoisie. They can also be described as revolutions from above.[1]

Third, privatization is a contested process that triggers resistance within the society, especially from important segments of the elites and of the state itself. Voszka shows that in the case of Poland, privatization was slowed by opposition from managers and workers' councils. And Lopes argues that in Brazil, powerful government firms, in alliance with the governments and congressional deputies from states negatively affected by economic liberalization, have been a formidable hurdle for stabilization and privatization programs.

It follows from the chapters in this section that the understanding of the process of the construction of open market economies would be enhanced by further analysis of three important issues. One is the different strategies of privatization and their consequences. Voszka shows that the model implemented by the former Czechoslovakia, which was relatively centralized by the state and based on market methods of allocation (vouchers), was more effective than the one followed by Poland, which was less centralized and more oriented toward nonmarket mechanisms for the distribution of assets. Hungary occupies an intermediate position. The resulting property structure is different in the three countries. And Frenkel and Rozenwurcel point out that privatizations in Argentina were financed in part by greater foreign indebtedness and resulted in the formation of private monopolies. These traits have obvious alternatives, which would be more desirable from the standpoints of economic efficiency and contribution to the consolidation of democracy.

Another crucial issue is the nature of the outcome of the transitions underway in both regions. Whether the intended institutional end point—that is, an open market economy and a stable liberal democracy—will be reached remains an open question. The revolutions from above in Eastern Europe are producing societies in which bourgeoisies are forming, but the institutions of the market are only partially developed. Frenkel and Rozenwurcel point out that it is questionable whether the kind of privatization experienced by Argentina, whose focus was on the nontradables sector of the economy, will result in an increase in the overall level of competitiveness and thus in more efficient participation in the world economy. They also argue that privatization is concentrating the control of the economy and impairing the regulatory capacity of the state, a formula that does not bode well for democracy in the substantive sense. Nevertheless, and in spite of all the shortcomings pointed out by our authors, economic and political liberalization is taking place—with varying degrees of effectiveness—in the two regions (except for the war-torn republics of the former Yugoslavia). Clearly, we need a better conceptualization of the range of outcomes of the processes of transition, in particular of the different types of capitalism and liberal democracy that are being constructed in these and other regions of the world.

Finally, the chapters in Part Three stress the fact that the course of privatization, and of economic liberalization in general, is strongly affected by institutional legacies. Voszka's central proposition is counterintuitive: She claims that the extent to which the institutions of central planning were dismantled before the onset of privatization is negatively correlated with the effectiveness of privatization strategies. In the case of Brazil, Lopes shows how the institutional structure inherited from the import-substitution period has enabled firms and regions negatively affected by stabilization and liberalization policies to thwart their implementation. The record of world development since World War II, in particular the experience of nations in southern Europe and East Asia, however, indicates that different kinds of institutional (and also cultural) legacies have been compatible with effective capitalist economies. This issue—one of the classical ones in the sociology of development—is still with us, and it requires further analysis. □

EXPLANATIONS

In explaining the pattern of economic liberalization in the countries under analysis, Voszka explicitly resorts to structural causation. Neither Lopes nor Frenkel and Rozenwurcel address the issue explicitly, but their analyses are more compatible with explanations based on agency. This is, by itself, an interesting difference between the chapters on the two regions.

Voszka argues that the extent to which the state controls the economy at the outset of the privatization process determines the state's capacity to relinquish that control in an effective manner.

Frenkel and Rozenwurcel, as well as Lopes, stress elite rationality as a main cause of the course of economic liberalization in Argentina and Brazil. In the former country, large-scale privatization was used at first by the Menem administration as a device to maintain the support of business circles in the face of a dismal economic situation. Later, privatization was fashioned in such a way that it allowed the government to balance its fiscal accounts and pay the public debt. This argument is compatible with an explanation focused on government officials' interests. Lopes, for his part, emphasizes the role of knowledge in shaping policy preferences. Until very recently, "developmental capitalism" appeared viable to Brazilian elites because of the fact that their experience was very different from those of the Argentine or Chilean elites. In Brazil, performance under import substitution thus far had been very good in terms of growth rates, pattern of diversification of the economy, and ability to export manufacturing goods. Further, developmental capitalism in Brazil had not had the chaotic political consequences it produced in Argentina and Chile. In these countries in the 1970s and 1980s, the catastrophic economic and political consequences of autarkic industrialization had convinced elites that existing economic institutions were simply not viable and that the only solution was a transition to open market capitalism.

It makes sense to think of structural and actional approaches as complementary rather than mutually exclusive. The argument about the long-term lack of viability of the economic institutions of state socialism (and much the same could be said about autarkic industrial capitalism) is compatible with an actor-centered framework. The dismal economic and political performance of the ancien régime (plus, it makes sense to hypothesize, international demonstration effects) was what convinced established elites in these societies that existing institutions had to be changed. But this realization itself did not determine the direction of change. We could only explain why these elites selected economic and political liberalization from a repertoire of possible responses to the crisis by taking into account their interests, as understood by them, and their knowledge about the situation and about the likely consequences of alternative courses of action.

In contrast with the chapters in Part Three, the message that comes through clearly in all of the analyses in Parts One and Two is that political self-interest, that of both politicians and their parties, is the dominant motivation behind the choice of institutional designs. And these politicians are not just self-interested thinkers but also short-term thinkers. A further extension is the proposition that since all of the parties in negotiations try to maximize their own self-interest, the institutions that are adopted are mainly expedient bargains. This is the consistent leitmotiv Geddes establishes in her chapter and for which she marshals impressive evidence.

Our other authors provide numerous additional examples that bear out Geddes's point. Gebethner shows that PR was easily adopted in Poland because all parties had strong, selfish reasons to push for PR. The adoption of the 5 percent threshold—entailing a more moderate, less proportional form of PR—for the 1993 election can also be explained in terms of partisan self-interest: Parties that won more than 5 percent of the vote in the 1991 election together controlled 88.7 percent of the seats in the Sejm. Another striking example from the Polish case is, as Wiatr explains, the establishment of the Senate. This was done as part of a political bargain between the Communists and Solidarity—in spite of the absence of any tradition of bicameralism or any strong feeling about the desirability of a bicameral legislature per se.

As we note in our postscript to Nino's chapter, the constitutional amendment adopted in Argentina in 1994 moved, albeit only a short distance, in the direction of semipresidentialism and the limitation of presidential power. This development, too, had little to do with the objective merits of the reform: It was a bargain between the ruling Peronists and the opposition Radicals—the Peronists winning the right for incumbent President Carlos Menem to be reelected for a second term, and the Radicals receiving the satisfaction of a slightly weaker presidency that they did not control and were not expected to win in the next election. The military reformers in Chile, who did not have to bargain and compromise much, could simply dictate an electoral law that assured the overrepresentation of the political Right. The pursuit of partisan self-interest does not invariably mean parties will always try to maximize their own representation. In the Mexican case, as Molinar explains, it was in the self-interest of the PRI to dominate but not to dominate too much: The aim, therefore, became to safeguard not only the ruling party's majority control but, simultaneously, to guard against the complete exclusion of the opposition.

Of course, Molinar's analysis also shows the logical limitation of explaining institutional design exclusively in terms of politicians' and parties' self-interest. If the PRI in Mexico had tried to establish a pure one-party system without even a weak opposition, this goal could have been explained just as plausibly in terms of partisan self-interest!

In addition, our authors also provide a number of examples of constraints on self-interested behavior. One such constraint that is explicitly acknowledged by rational-choice theory is incorrect or incomplete information. In Eastern Europe, a prominent factor of this kind was the overestimation of popular support for the Communist Party and an underestimation of that of the non-Communist parties. Important constraints that are beyond the scope of rational-choice explanations are institutional conservatism—what Geddes calls the "stickiness" of established institutions—and the strength of political traditions. One of Szoboszlai's explanations of the emergence of a pure form of parliamentary government in Hungary is that country's strong tradition of parliamentarism going back as far as 1848. And Nino argues that the tradition of presidentialism in Latin America makes it virtually impossible to institute any system that does not entail a directly elected chief executive—which means semipresidentialism and Nino's semiparliamentary proposal for a directly elected prime minister belong to the realm of the politically feasible, but pure parliamentarism does not.

There are even a few examples of motivations based on the "common good." Ironically, the clearest case is that of the most reluctant democratic reformers—the Chilean military. Their electoral law was based in part on calculations of narrow self-interest but, according to Siavelis and Valenzuela, also in part on the notion that a two-party system would serve to make Chilean democracy stable and effective (a notion with which Siavelis and Valenzuela strongly disagree, but this does not mean the motivation behind it was not based at least in part on general-interest considerations). Another example, given by Gebethner, was the reluctance of the Polish electoral engineers to institute election rules that involved a second or runoff ballot: Their fear was that too frequent elections would depress even further the already low voter turnouts and hence undermine the democratic legitimacy of the elections.

The preference for PR systems also cannot be explained entirely in terms of partisan self-interest. In any legislature elected by PR, the larger parties with a legislative majority can conspire to help each other at the expense of the weaker parties by adopting a higher threshold, lower district magnitudes, or both for the next election. After the new election, the same incentive to adopt further obstacles for the relatively smaller parties would be present again. The likely end point would be something like the two-member–district system in Chile or even a single-member–district plurality system. The fact that this is not the normal outcome, and that PR in various forms remains the world's most common type of electoral system, shows that parties may be self-interested but not to the exclusion of any sense of democratic fairness. On the whole, however, we do not dispute that the evidence in this volume clearly points to the preponderance of self-interested motivations rather than common-good concerns in the design of democratic institutions. ☐

CROSS-REGIONAL DIFFERENCES

With regard to the design of democratic institutions, the evidence contained in this volume justifies the view that common motivations like partisan self-interest predominate over geographical-cultural differences. We believe this is the case, but we also want to emphasize three exceptions.

One exception is the greater variation in institutional design in Eastern Europe. Electoral systems in Latin America tend to cluster more around the moderate PR type compared with the wider range from relatively pure PR to mixed PR-majoritarian systems in Eastern Europe. Moreover, most Latin American political systems tend to be of the straightforward presidential type, whereas East European systems of government range from semipresidentialism to pure parliamentarism.

A second exception foreshadowed in the previous paragraph is that the "central tendencies" in the two regions are slightly different. East European electoral systems tend to be slightly more majoritarian than the Latin American ones, and Latin American systems of executive-legislative relations tend to be considerably more presidential than East European ones.

The first exception—the greater variation in Eastern Europe—is largely explained by a third exception. In Latin America, the forces of political tradition and institutional conservatism are considerably stronger than is the case in Eastern Europe. These Latin American forces form constraints predisposed toward presidentialism and PR. In Eastern Europe, the Leninist legacy is mainly a negative one: The long period of Communist rule severely weakened preexisting traditions in most cases, and Communist institutions and traditions were swept away by a wave of popular disapproval. As a result, new institutions had to be established in something like an institutional vacuum. In all probability, however, institutional conservatism will soon become a strong force in Eastern Europe, too.

Many of our authors are not just analysts; they also aim to formulate proposals for further reforms and improvements. In sharp contrast with the self-interested behavior of the politicians they describe, their own recommendations are based squarely on the common interest. Regardless of the countries or regions on which they concentrate, however, they are all realists who take both the self-interested orientation of the politicians and existing traditions and institutions into consideration. As a result, the recommendations for democratic institutional reform—especially those made by Gebethner, Nohlen, Siavelis and Valenzuela, Szoboszlai, and Nino—clearly represent strong convictions, but, very wisely, they are also modest and incremental reform proposals.

The scope of the economic transformation is obviously greater in Eastern Europe than in Latin America. In the former, the actors and institutions of the market economy existed at best as secondary mechanisms in the centrally planned, state-owned economy. The agrarian sector was private in Poland, and the second economy had made major inroads in Hungary, but in general a class of private capitalists and a full-fledged labor market had to be created in all of these societies. As Voszka makes clear, producing the legal framework for the functioning of markets and making those markets work effectively are as complex as creating the actors themselves.

The actors did exist in the Latin American societies under discussion, and so did much of the legal framework, but these were capitalist societies with major restrictions on the functioning of markets. In the ideal-typical autarkic capitalist case, bourgeoisies were shielded from foreign competition by very high tariff and nontariff protection, and they were dependent on the state for financing, contracts, and export and other subsidies. At the same time, the operation of labor markets was hampered by corporatist mechanisms and paternalistic regulation. In these societies, the challenge is to transform a rentistic and state-dependent bourgeoisie into a genuine capitalist class and to liberalize labor markets so a strong civil society can come into being.

The danger in the former state-socialist societies is the prospect for their "latinamericanization"—that is, for the creation of private property without the effective institutional and legal infrastructure of an open market economy. It would be paradoxical if such regimes were to form in some East European countries just as Latin American nations are shedding them. Prospects for this scenario seem to be stronger in countries further east and south in Europe than in the ones under discussion in this volume, but an awareness of the possibility of this outcome as one of the instances of failure is essential for understanding of the logic the transition to capitalism.

As stated in Chapter 1, our basic assumption and point of departure for this volume was that in spite of the obvious structural, institutional, cultural, and geographical differences between and within our two regions, the process of designing markets and democracies was sufficiently similar to be compared fruitfully. Hence, we argued, the most-different-systems design, rather than the most-similar-systems design, is the most appropriate comparative method to be applied. The empirical results reported in

Chapters 2 through 12 and highlighted in this concluding chapter clearly validate our assumptions. Differences exist, to be sure, but these are mainly differences of degree rather than of kind, and they are overwhelmed by the similarities. As far as the design of markets and democracies is concerned, and in spite of geographical distance, Eastern Europe and Latin America are conceptual and theoretical neighbors rather than distant strangers. The joint study of both regions contributes to our understanding of the transitions each is undergoing, as well as of institutional change in general.

NOTES

1. For the case of Argentina, see Carlos H. Waisman, "Argentina's Revolution from Above," in Edward C. Epstein, ed., *The New Democracy in Argentina* (New York: Praeger, 1993).

About the Book

Countries throughout Latin America and Eastern Europe are moving from authoritarian to democratic political systems and from semi-closed to open economies. Despite important differences between the regions, these transitions involve similar tasks: the establishment of governmental institutions and electoral systems conducive to legitimation of the new and fragile democracies and expansion of the institutional infrastructure of a market economy.

This volume looks at both regions, focusing on the relationship between the tasks of institutional design and the outcomes of the process of political and economic liberalization. In particular, the contributors emphasize the design of electoral laws, of executive-legislative relations, and of institutions to serve a market economy. Each chapter discusses the legacy of the preexisting authoritarian regime, the range of preferences among various strategic actors (the government, state bureaucracies, opposition parties, and interest groups) with regard to the pace and mix of reforms, and the consequences of final choices for the institutionalization of effective economies and the process of democratization.

About the Editors and Contributors

Roberto Frenkel is professor of economics at the University of Buenos Aires and director of the Economics Department at the Centro de Estudios de Estado y Sociedad (CEDES). He specializes in Latin American macroeconomics and has published widely in Spanish and English on economics issues. Recent publications in English include *Economic Development in the 1990s* (1992), *The Rocky Road to Reform* (L. Taylor, ed., 1993), and United Nations Conference on Trade and Development, *International Monetary and Financial Issues for the 1990s*, Volume 1 (1992) and Volume 2 (1993).

Stanislaw Gebethner is professor of political science at the University of Warsaw. He is the author of *Rzad i opozycja JKM w systemie politycznym Wielkiej Brytanii* (1967), *System Organow Panstwowych w Polskiej Rzeczypospolitej Ludowej* (1968), *Systemy polityczne wybranych panstw kapitalistycznych: Francja i Wielka Brytania* (1968), and *Dlaczego tak glosowano Wybory Prezydenckie '90: analiza polityczna i socjologiczna* (1993).

Barbara Geddes is associate professor of political science at UCLA, where she teaches courses on Latin American politics, revolution, and research design and methodology. Her publications include *Politician's Dilemma: Building State Capacity in Latin America* (1994) and articles on civil service reform, support for authoritarian regimes, corruption, and comparative methodology.

Arend Lijphart is research professor of political science, University of California, San Diego. He is the author of *Democracy in Plural Societies: A Comparative Exploration* (1977), *Democracies: Patterns of Majoritarian and Consensus Government in Twenty-One Countries* (1984), *Las Democracias contemporáneas: Un estudio comparativo* (with T. Bruneau et al., 1987), and *Electoral Systems and Party Systems: A Study of Twenty-Seven Democracies* (1994). Lijphart is a member of the editorial boards of the *Journal of Democracy* and the *Journal of Theoretical Politics*.

Juarez Brandão Lopes is professor of political science, State University of Campinas (Brazil), and president of the Brazilian National Association of Graduate Studies and Research in the Social Sciences. He is the author of *Crise do brasil arcaico (1967), Do latifundio a empresa: Unidade e diversidade do capitalismo no campo* (1976), and *Desenvolvimento e mudanca social: Formacao da sociedade urbano-industrial no Brazil* (5th ed., 1980), as well as of numerous journal articles and chapters in edited volumes. He has served on the boards of the National Council of Technological and Scientific Development, the International Federation of Social Sciences Organizations, and the Institute for Economic and Social Planning, among others.

Juan Molinar Horcasitas is research professor at the Center for Sociological Studies, El Colegio de México in Mexico City. He is the author of *El tiempo de la legitimidad. Elecciones, autoritarismo y democracia en México* (1990).

Carlos Santiago Nino was professor of law at the Universidad de Buenos Aires and director of the Center for Institutional Studies until his death in August 1993. Nino chaired the Council for the Consolidation of Democracy, a position to which he was appointed by the then-president of Argentina, Raúl Alfonsín. His publications include *Introducción a la filosofía de la acción humana* (1987), *The Ethics of Human Rights* (1991), *Rights* (1992), *Fundamentos de derecho constitucional: análisis filosofico, jurídico y polítologico de la práctica constitucional* (1992), and *Un país al margen de la ley: Estudio de la anomia como componente del subdesarrollo argentino* (1992).

Dieter Nohlen is a professor of political science at the University of Heidelberg, Germany. He specializes in comparative politics, with an emphasis on elections and electoral systems in Southern Europe and Latin America. His publications include works of general interest like *Handbuch der Dritten Welt* and *Lexicon der Politik* (1974), as well as studies on electoral systems like *Wahesysteme der Welt* (1978) and *Wahlrecht und Parteiensystem* (1990) and, in his field of specialization, *Parlamentarismus in Spanien* (1971), *Chile—Das sozialistische Experiment* (1973), *Presidencialismo versus Parlamentarismo, América Latina* (1990), *Decentralización Política y consolidación democrática* (1991), *Spanien* (1992), *Enciclopedia electoral latinoamericana y del Caribe* (1993), *and Sistema electorales en América Latina y el debate sobre reforma electoral* (1993).

Guillermo Rozenwurcel is senior researcher at CEDES in Buenos Aires, Argentina, and he teaches economics at the Universidad de Buenos Aires. He specializes in Latin American macroeconomics. His most recent works include chapters in *The Market and the State in Economic Development in the 1990s* (Alvaro Zini Jr., ed., 1992) and *Latin American Political Economy in the Age of Neoliberal Reform* (William C. Smith, Carlos H. Acuña, and Eduardo Gamarra, ed., 1994).

Peter Siavelis is a Ph.D. candidate in the Government Department at Georgetown University, currently undertaking his dissertation research on the Chilean Congress. His scholarly interests include political parties, legislative politics, and electoral systems. He is the author of several articles on Chilean electoral politics. He has been a visiting professor and visiting researcher at the Catholic University of Chile and a Fulbright-Hays scholar.

György Szoboszlai is a senior research fellow at the Institute for Political Science of the Hungarian Academy of Sciences. A lawyer by training, he specializes in constitutional models and electoral systems. As the general secretary of the Hungarian Political Science Association, he was the editor of the yearbook of the Association between 1983 and 1992. His publications also include *Statehood and the Political System* (*Allamisag es politikai rendszer*, 1987]). *Democracy and Political Transformation: Theories and East-Central European Realities* (editor, 1991), and *Flying Blind: Emerging Democracies in East-Central Europe* (editor, 1992).

Arturo Valenzuela is professor of government and director, Center for Latin American Studies, Georgetown University. His research interests include the origins, consolidation, and breakdown of democratic regimes; authoritarianism; political parties; and the nature and functioning of democratic regimes. He is the author of *Political Brokers in Chile: Local Government in a Centralized Polity* (1977) and *The Breakdown of Democratic Regimes: Chile* (1978). He is coauthor and coeditor of *Chile: Politics and Society* (with J. Samuel Valenzuela, 1976), *Military Rule in Chile* (with J. Samuel Valenzuela, 1986), *Hacia una democracia moderna: La opción parlamentaria para América Latina* (with Juan J. Linz, 1990), and *A Nation of Enemies: Chile Under Pinochet* (with Pamela Constable, 1991).

Éva Voszka is associate professor of economics at the University of Budapest, Hungary. She is also a senior researcher for Financial Research Ltd. and the economic adviser to the president of Hungary. She specializes in government-enterprise relations, change in organizational and ownership structures, and economic and sociological aspects of privatization. She is the author of three books in Hungarian—*Interest and Mutual Dependence* (*Erdek es kolcsonos fuggoseg: atszervezesi tapasztalatok*, 1984), *Reform and Organizational Changes in the 80s* (*Reform as atszervezes a nylocvanas evekben*, 1986), and *The Triple Way* (*Harmasut: kormanyzati felfogasok a gazdasagpolitikaroles as iranytasr*, 1990)—and she has contributed to numerous edited volumes.

Carlos H. Waisman is professor of sociology, University of California, San Diego. His fields are comparative political sociology and the comparative study of development. He is the author of *Modernization and the Working Class: The Politics of Legitimacy* (1982), *Reversal of Development in Argentina: Postwar Counterrevolutionary Policies and Their Structural Consequences* (1987), and *From Military Rule to Liberal Democracy in Argentina* (with M. Peralta-Ramos, 1987), as well as of articles and book chapters.

Jerzy J. Wiatr is professor of sociology at the University of Warsaw. He is the author of *Local Politics, Development, and Participation: A Cross-National Study of Interrelationships* (with F. C. Bruhns and F. Cazzola, 1974), *Polish Essays in the Methodology of the Social Sciences* (1979), and *The Politics of Democratic Transformation: Poland After 1989* (1993), as well as of numerous books and articles in Polish.

Index